THE ART OF DIVINITY

THE ART OF DIVINITY

Finding Beauty Within and Without

TEACHINGS OF THE MASTER PAUL THE VENETIAN

VOLUME ONE

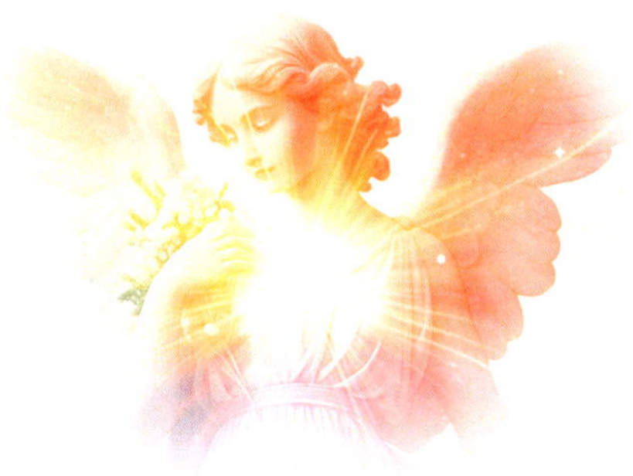

MARK L. PROPHET
ELIZABETH CLARE PROPHET

SUMMIT UNIVERSITY PRESS®
Gardiner, Montana

THE ART OF DIVINITY Volume 1
Finding Beauty Within and Without
Teachings of the Master Paul the Venetian
by Mark L. Prophet and Elizabeth Clare Prophet

For information, contact The Summit Lighthouse,
63 Summit Way, Gardiner, MT 59030 USA
Tel: 1-800-245-5445 or 1 406-848-9500
info@SummitUniversityPress.com
SummitLighthouse.org

Library of Congress Control Number: 2026930493
ISBN: 978-1-60988-453-6 (softbound)
ISBN: 978-1-60988-454-3 (eBook)

SUMMIT UNIVERSITY PRESS®

29 28 27 26 1 2 3 4

Contents

Foreword

You are the art of God. Though you might discern that God's artwork in you is not yet perfected, you are invited to participate in that gradual perfecting—by your own free will.

In this beautiful process of becoming the creation of your True Self as God intended, who would you choose as your mentor? As an evolving work of art, you have the opportunity to discover the true symmetry and design of your being. In order to find the David amidst the stone, as Michelangelo did, you may want the advice and encouragement of a master artist who has been where you are.

What if you could invite such a being into your life and ongoing creation? What if you could learn from him to maintain contact with divine beings who selflessly convey the essence of their holy life to you? What if you could learn directly through heart-to-heart contact with an artist who was not only a true master of the physical arts but the spiritual ones as well—one who truly became a mirror of the love of God?

This master artist and the author of these volumes is known as Paul the Venetian, now an immortal being, and yet very accessible to you as you become the artist of your own life. As you create and re-create your being in the image of your own Higher Self and bring artistic creations into the physical, you can deepen your understanding of yourself and God's loving universe. The moment you ask him to, this ascended master will tutor your soul in the ways of art and creation.

These two volumes provide a biography of Paul the Venetian as the ascended master through his dictations and his biography as a mortal being, and through the many examples of his famous art. His final physical embodiment was as the leading Italian Renaissance artist, Paolo Veronese (1528–1588). Among his many lifetimes of service to humanity, this life was exemplary as an innovator of paints whose vibrancy never faded—brilliant colors whose depths had never been seen before in the arts, in design and technique, in the sacred geometry and realism in his characters' anatomy and emotional expressions.

Paolo taught the souls of the people of his time—who were mostly illiterate—through visual wisdom and beauty. Through his art, Paolo demonstrated deep reverence for the holiness of his religious subjects and good-humored irreverence for the stasis and stifling conformity of the clerical Inquisition.

Church officials accused him of heresy and blasphemy and tried to imprison him multiple times, but on each occasion Paolo gently outsmarted them. He repeatedly stood against the Inquisition's threats to freedom of expression on behalf of all artists. Through it all he never ceased to be intelligent, witty, and courageous.

After his life as Paolo Veronese, which was the culmination of numerous such lives, his soul joined his permanent atom of being through the ascension, as shown to us by Christ Jesus.

The grace of God flowed through his soul in the process of this ascension—a rare occurrence then, as it is rare now. As an immortal like Jesus, he became an ongoing expression of God's grace, continuing to teach humanity at the soul level rather than in the physical. He is a part of a celestial brotherhood of men and women who have ascended into immortal light, but like the bodhisattvas of old, they tarry with us—reaching out their hand to help us up the mountain.

As you read the master's own words of wisdom and understanding, you can sense his grace, generosity, and kindness. He is ready to hear your questions even before you can frame them in prayer. Yet he encourages you to ask, to take your communion to higher and higher levels of attunement as your Higher Self continually reveals God's vision for your own soul's perfection, seeking the beauty of divine expression.

At each level you will feel the challenge, radiating between and through his words, to purify your motives, to set aside self-aggrandizement, and to pursue art for the benefit of all humanity.

Within these two volumes are the intangible, unfolding stages of the universal consciousness of oneness. You too can be the mirror of God as love for humanity, for you are the living art of God.

The Editors

Paul the Venetian's Embodiment as the Sixteenth-Century Artist Paolo Veronese

The Magician of Light

In 1528, Paolo Caliari was born in Verona, Italy, and later became known as Paolo Veronese after his birthplace. The Caliari ancestors were artists, and Paolo's father determined that his son should become a sculptor. Paolo was first apprenticed as a stonecutter, his father's trade. With unusual dexterity for one so young, Paolo changed mere clay into remarkable statuettes.

At the age of fourteen, Paulo showed such a marked interest in painting that he was apprenticed to a painter named Antonio Badile, whose daughter Elena he later married. From Badile, Veronese derived a sound basic painting technique as well as a passion for paintings in which people and architecture were integrated. He had found his vocation in painting and devoted himself to mastering the techniques of Albrecht Dürer and other Renaissance artists.

His fellow artists soon recognized Paolo's skill. He was commissioned while a young lad to paint a Madonna for the church in San Bernardino. Cardinal Gonzaga was so impressed by the masterpiece that he asked Paolo to compete with the distinguished painters of Verona to decorate the cathedral at Mantua. His painting *Temptation of Saint Anthony* was so magnificent that he was established as a peer among the artists of Verona.

In 1553, at the age of twenty-five, Paolo Veronese went to Venice and launched on a long collaboration with the Venetian authorities

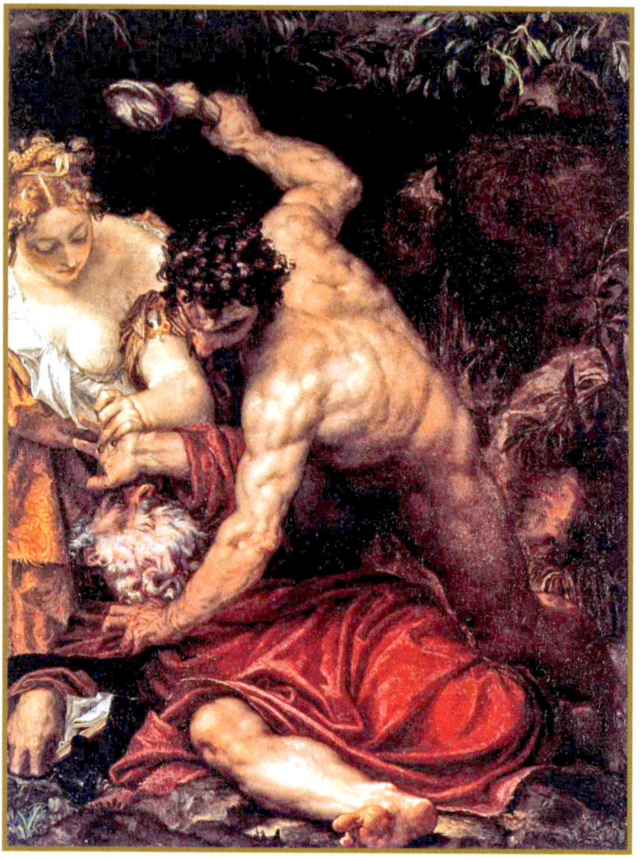

Temptation of St. Anthony, c. 1552–53

in connection with the decoration of different parts of the Palazzo Ducale. The walls of the imposing palaces in Venice were often adorned with murals and works of art by Venetian masters.

At that time, Venice, Queen of the Adriatic, was at the height of its cultural glory. It offered greater opportunity for artistic expression as the emphasis shifted from religion to the classical culture reflected in the painting, sculpture, and architecture of the period. The Polo brothers (father and uncle of Marco Polo) had returned from the East with a bountiful supply of extravagant goods—spices, fine silks, precious jewels, and oriental carpets. A lively trade had sprung up between the merchants of Venice and Cathay (modern day China).

One might suppose that in this atmosphere the sensitive Paolo

Veronese would naturally absorb and imitate the accomplishments of his contemporaries who had set the standard for the world. But not so! Veronese was a spiritual revolutionary who waged battle against the forces of anti-life in the arts. He did not conform to tradition but was an exponent of a beauty distinctively his own. It was a momentum gathered from many embodiments of the remote past.

In 1555, Veronese began the decoration of San Sebastiano, the church in Venice that was to become his burial place. His painting *Coronation of the Virgin* rated him second to none among Venetian artists. From this time on, successive masterpieces emanated from his brush without interruption. All of Venice was astounded by his genius. He became a painter of mythical and historical figures as well as religious scenes. His biblical characters were beautifully garbed and set against a background of Venetian grandeur.

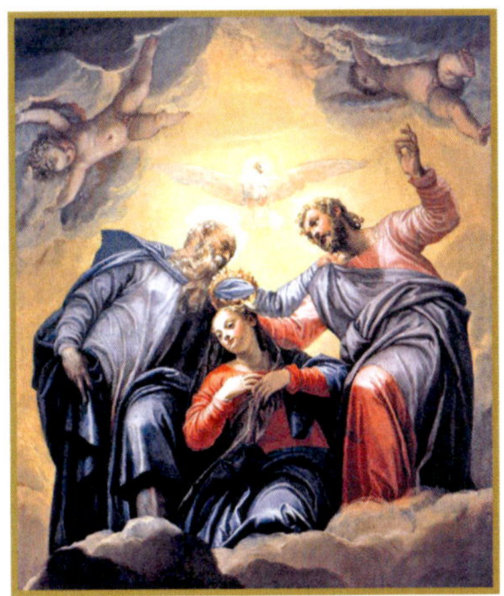

Coronation of the Virgin, 1555
(full-scale on p. 37)

The Pursuit of Pure Color

Veronese's ornamentations soon led to dramatic experiments with new colors. In his quest for beauty, he freed himself from the dull browns and grays of his predecessors by modeling in full light, making his already graceful figures iridescent and nearly transparent.

He developed glistening pastel hues of azure, coral, pearl, lilac, and lemon yellow, which startled and fascinated his patrons. He loved deep, bold contrasting colors, and he combined shades never used before—ruby and rich velvety green, pink and emerald, aquamarine and violet.

As if to stress that true beauty endures forever, Veronese searched for and discovered a technique of pigment preparation that is unsurpassed for preserving paint. His magnificent colors still radiate brilliantly today, compared with the fading ceiling of the Sistine Chapel and even Tiepolo's now-deteriorating frescoes painted two centuries later.

An adept of color, its creation and its preservation, Veronese earned from one biographer the title "The Magician of Light."

Heaven on Earth: Man's Domain

The striking use of color was not Veronese's only gift to Renaissance art. Paolo saw beauty as the most powerful catalyst for enlightenment, and he endowed the figures of Jesus, the apostles, and saints with lifelike expressions. By associating them with easily identifiable places and things, he put them within the reach of the common people.

With fresh perspective, he approached serious and sacred subjects with a simple familiarity that shattered the idolatry inherent in previous medieval and Renaissance painting—an idolatry that had separated the common people from God and his saints and had oppressed them with a sense of their own sin. Veronese opened the world of the holy to all, portraying it with a delight and a sense of mirth.

In his painting *Annunciation,* for example, the Virgin Mary is greeted by a beautiful, shimmering-robed Archangel Gabriel, while her dog trots out to investigate the heavenly being. His *Mystic Marriage of Saint Catherine* shows two angels in the lower left corner apparently disputing a book of scripture and thus vying with Catherine's mystical ceremony for the viewer's attention.

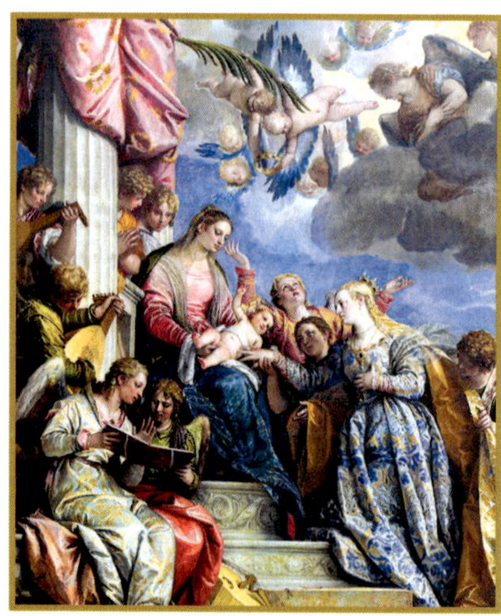

Mystic Marriage of Saint Catherine, c. 1565–70
(full-scale in Volume 2 on p. ix)

This seeming frivolity in Veronese's work does not indicate his mockery of religion. On the contrary, it brings religion from a stiff pomposity and fearful worship back into man's domain, imparting the experience of the sacred to all, including the common people.

The study of his paintings will reveal the love with which he painted the face and attitude of man in the garb of heaven. His conviction that heaven is man's destiny shines from his faces and figures and speaks of his hope for man's elevation.

But the approachability of his saints, their faces and their gestures, baffled and even infuriated some of his religious contemporaries, who accused Veronese of a lack of sanctity, a disrespect for God and the saints.

Defiance of the Inquisition

Inevitably, Veronese's controversial views drew the attention of the Inquisition. At the very height of the Renaissance, the inquisitors scanned the flourishing world of Italian art for heretical contents. They exacted conformity in religious scenes, banned nudity, and required ecclesiastical approval for the contents of major compositions.

Untempered zealots roamed Italy destroying paintings, decapitating statues, and threatening artists. Pope Pius V and the Spanish painter El Greco even advocated the destruction of Michelangelo's Sistine Chapel because of the nude figures upon its ceiling.

Veronese was summoned before the tribunal of the Inquisition under suspicion of heresy for the "irreverences" and "fantasy" in his painting of the Last Supper, which included in it a dwarf, a parrot, guards in German armour, dogs, and a jester.

Veronese staunchly defended the artists' right to freedom of imagination. He was wholly innocent that there was any disrespect for the Deity expressed in his externalization of beauty. "Others," he pleaded, "expressed what to them seemed beautiful without sanction of the orthodox." The tribunal acquiesced and resolved the question by suggesting that the name be changed to *The Feast in the House of Levi.*

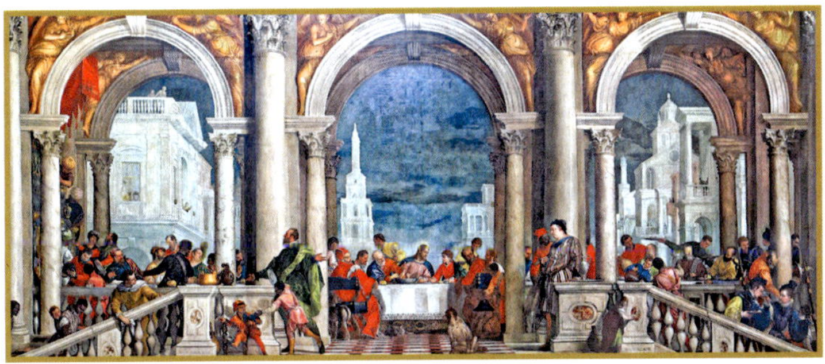

The Feast in the House of Levi, c. 1573 (full-scale and detail on p. 132)

Veronese inscribed on the painting the new title and a fitting Bible quote directed to his persecutors: "But their scribes and Pharisees murmured against his disciples, saying, 'Why do ye eat and drink with publicans and sinners?'[1] And Jesus answering said unto them, 'They that are whole need not a physician, but they that are sick.'"[2]

By disregarding the Inquisition's demands, Veronese embodied the spirit of the Renaissance in his determination to create without Church controls. In this, he effectively demonstrated the power of creative genius over the confines of blind dogma.

Art for Enlightenment

Public attention on Veronese's trial caused a great increase in his popularity, and his commissions rapidly multiplied. Yet fame and wealth did little to affect his simple and affectionate nature. He was once contracted by the Pisani family to paint *Family of Darius.* It is said that Paolo hid the painting from the Pisani family so that he might escape from the premises before his host discovered it, and in so doing the latter would feel no obligations to thank the donor with either words or coin. The painting *The Family of Darius before Alexander* now hangs in the National Gallery of London.

In private life, Paolo was a man of economical and well-regulated habits. He rejected commissions from royalty, choosing rather to stay in Venice with his family and enthusiastic students. That Veronese was an excellent teacher known for his "indescribable care" establishes

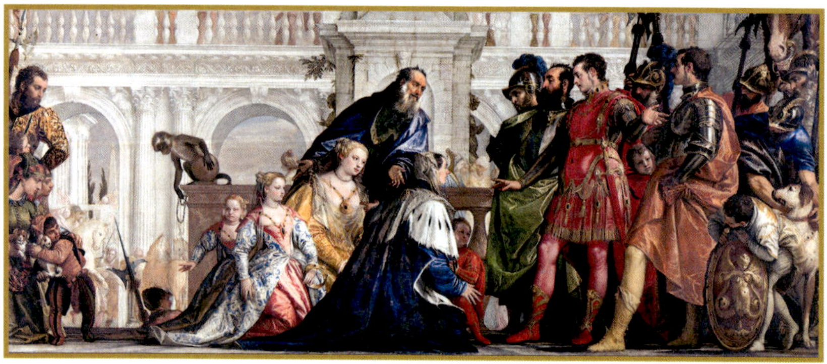

The Family of Darius before Alexander, c. 1565–67
(full-scale detail in Volume 2 on p. 102)

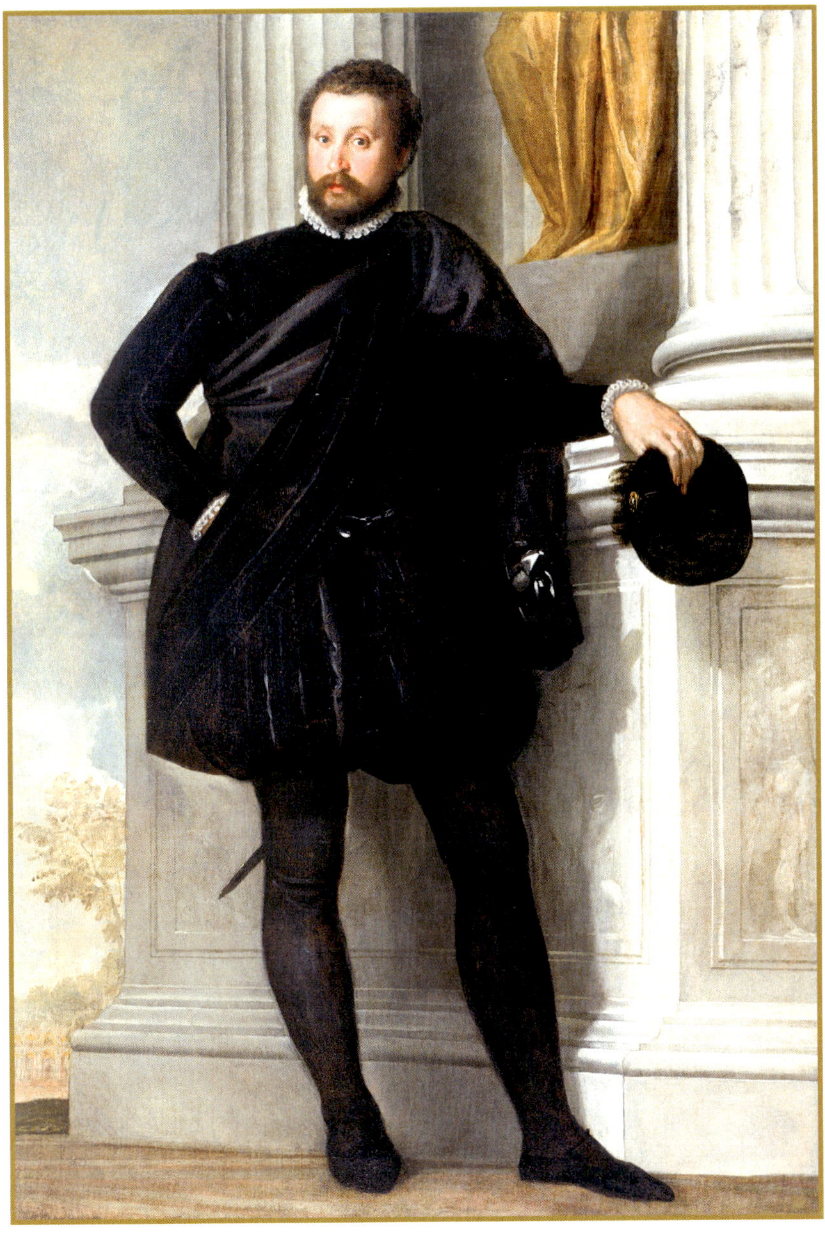

Portrait of a Man, 1578—thought by some to be a self-portrait

his concern for communication and education and the purity of his motive as an artist. He was also profoundly interested in his two sons, to whom he entrusted the brush as soon as they were old enough to hold one.

A Legacy of Beauty

Paolo became one of the major artists of the sixteenth-century Venetian school. Today, his masterpieces grace the galleries of many of the nations of Europe as well as the National Gallery of Art in Washington, D.C.

As an observer, we might look upon each magnificent canvas and say, "What a genius!" Yet we may not realize how many times Paolo struggled and erased, struggled and erased, and experimented with various media to capture on canvas a particular angelic form that existed in the etheric realm of heaven. For eighteen years he persisted with one particular painting until one day he stood before the canvas and knew that at last, to the best of his ability, he had executed below that which was Above.

Yes, as onlookers we often do not take into account that each one of us is also an artist in some particular field of human endeavor. Every man has his own heritage, an equal potential of genius. If it has not been externalized, it is because we have not exercised the quality of application.

To Paolo, his work was his way of expressing gratitude to the Deity for his heritage of Sonship from the Father. Labor was an obligation, an opportunity to fulfill his contract with life. To him, labor was worship.

Veronese, though little celebrated today, was a pivotal artistic genius in sixteenth-century Renaissance Italy. His creative talents yielded innovative and astonishing uses of light, color, form, and composition. He was the first to capture on canvas the graceful movement of an angel in flight, the purity of pastel coloring, and the joy and delight of the divine kingdom that had formerly been cloaked in somber awe.

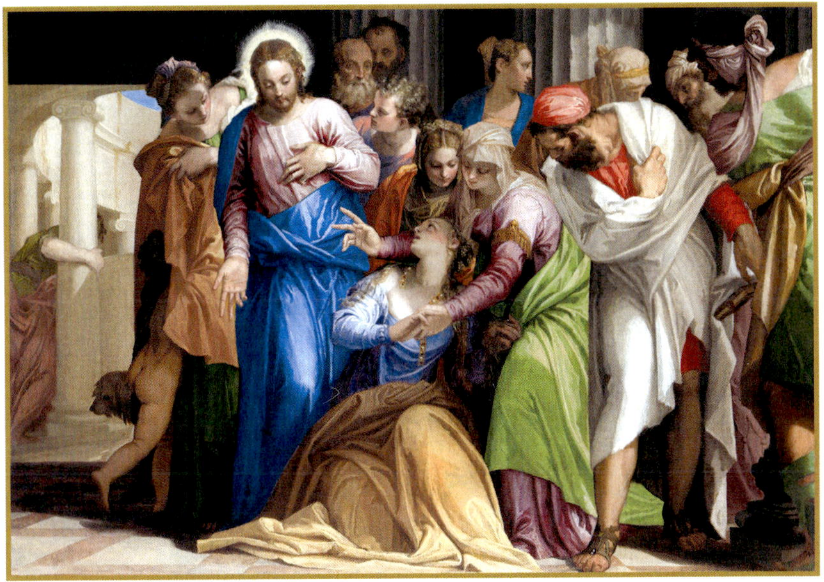

The Conversion of Mary Magdalene, c. 1548 (full-scale detail on p. 22)

Veronese's transcendent sense of beauty distinguishes him from other Renaissance artists. Rome produced Michelangelo, whose studies of human anatomy led to outstanding sculptural masterpieces but whose brooding frescoes were filled with a weighty sense of sin. Florence's da Vinci, with his scientific and philosophical genius, launched a new era for man, yet his painting retains a pensive and enigmatic tone. Venice produced Titian, whose attempt to make the divine world human steered his art into the sensual, away from the exceptional and the saintly.

But Veronese—in his expression of refined innocence, of joy and the sweeping grandeur of the celestial—reached an apex of artistic and spiritual insight that helped catapult Western art beyond the heights of the Renaissance.

Near the close of his earthly life as the Venetian artist, Paolo Veronese was advised by his guru that he, Paolo, had earned his release from the schoolroom of earth and was ready to enter the realms of immortality. In 1588, Paolo contracted a fever, and after a few days of illness he died on April 9. His brother and sons buried him in San Sebastiano, where a bust of himself was placed above his grave.

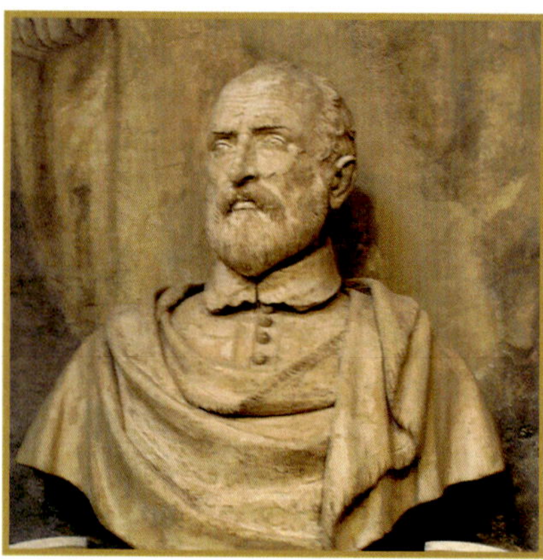

Bust of Paolo Veronese above his tomb

The Ascension of Paul the Venetian

Paul the Venetian's embodiment as Paolo Veronese culminated in his reunion with God in the ritual known as the ascension. From the ascended state he has described the process of the ascension so that one day we may follow in his footsteps.

> If you are victorious on this path, the day and the hour of your ascension will come when the sacred fire shall rise on your spinal altar with an intensity so great as to almost overwhelm you. Your I AM Presence and Holy Christ Self shall then draw you up into the arms of everlasting love, and you shall make the transition from mortality to immortality.
>
> And you shall hear the words of the Father: "Well done, thou good and faithful servant: thou hast been faithful over a few things, I will make thee ruler over many things."[3] Rise to the levels of the kingdom of God and let others follow in your wake!

This is precisely what Paul did at the conclusion of his embodiment as Paolo Veronese. He accelerated consciousness and reunited with his God Source, ascending from the Château de Liberté in the heaven world over southern France on April 19, 1588.[4]

The consensus of human appraisal in the mid-sixteenth century considered that Veronese's *Triumph of Venice* was the acme of his expression in painting. But this was not to be. Within the majesty of his being, greater majesty was pulsating for expression from within.

After Paolo's passing and yet prior to his ascension, Paul began the most important of his works, *The Holy Trinity.* The canvas has the unprecedented distinction of conveying the vibrations of both dimensions of activity—the earthly and the heavenly—for the canvas was completed after his ascension. Beneath the painting of *The Holy Trinity,* beloved Paul has inscribed in gold letters: "Perfect Love Casteth Out Fear."

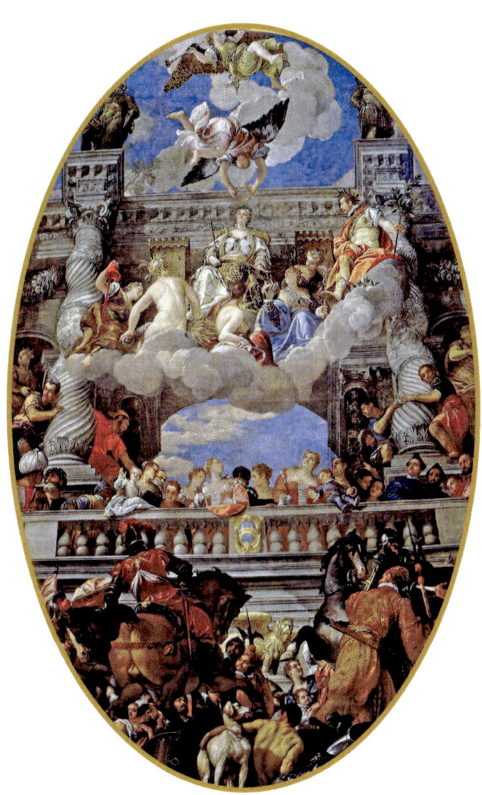

The Triumph of Venice, c. 1585
(full-scale in Volume 2 on p. 226)

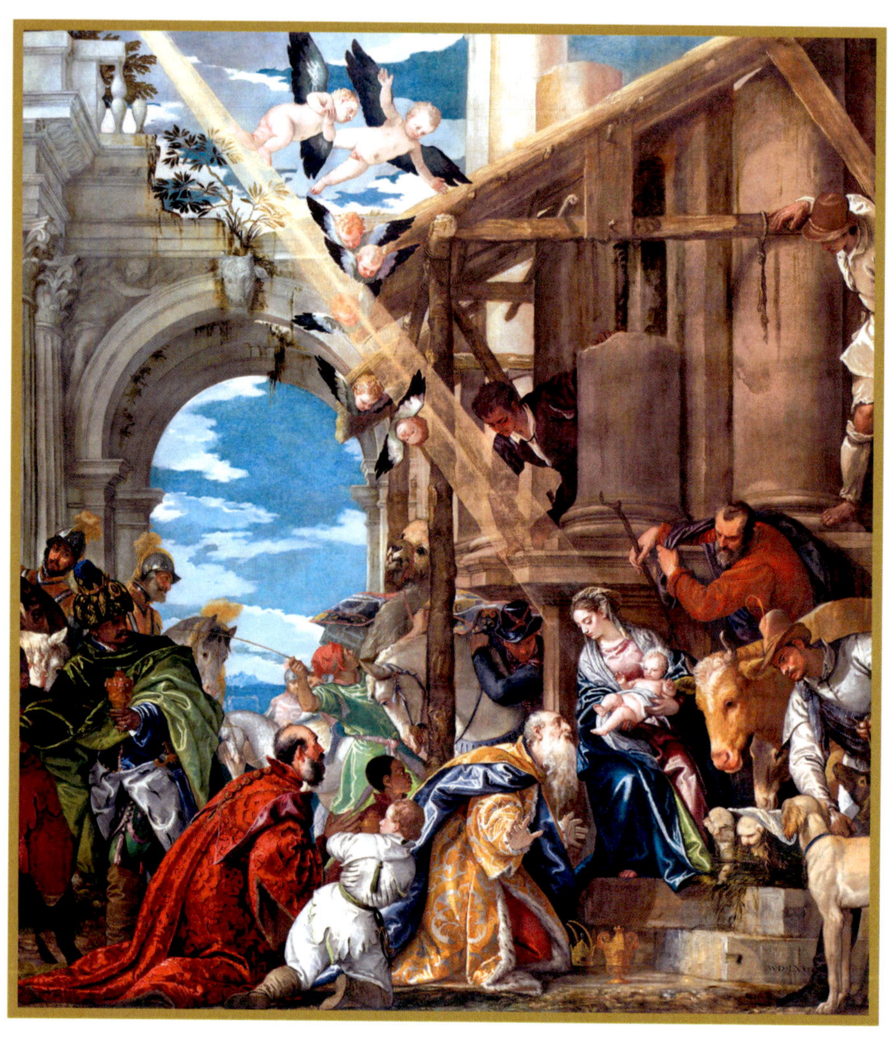

Adoration of the Magi, 1573

Those of you who are accustomed to appreciating the greatness of art will understand that it is the greatness of the thought within the heart of the artist or sculptor that is expressed and that lends nobility and enchantment to the creation of that individual.

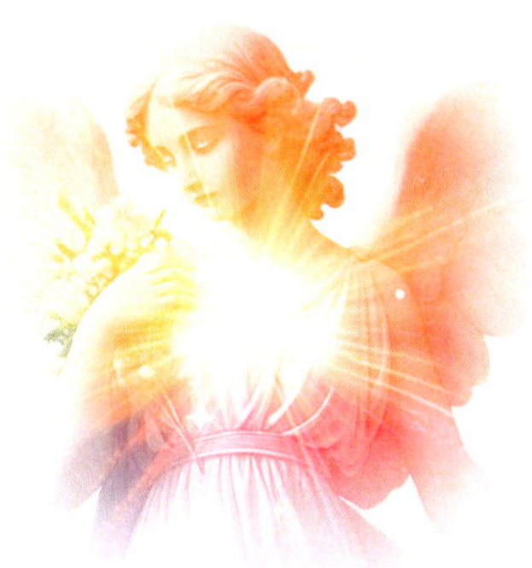

CHAPTER 1

THE LIGHT WITHIN

Profound is the wonder of the Presence of God! I would this day, as upon a magic carpet from the *Tale of the Arabian Nights,* exalt your consciousness to bear with me upon the wings of the wind and to travel over a planet of shining perfection endowed with the beauties of immortal life.

Beloved ones, as you gaze downward upon this earth, with its alternate patterns of green, brown, and the white of the snow-covered hills, you may recognize that below are human hearts like unto your own, endowed with the same thoughts and feelings, the same hopes, and, unfortunately at times, permitting the same despairs to occupy their mind.

I am this day speaking unto the students so that they may understand the need to express the power of love as a radiance, as a sun shining in its splendor, that all who are below in consciousness may be endowed with the best that is within you.

Have you stopped, beloved ones, to pause and reflect upon your own individual manifestation of the light of God? You are as a magic lantern, as a motion picture projector. The light of God is within you, and your consciousness is as the film or negative through which the light passes, blazing upon the screen of manifestation that specific quality that the film itself outpictures.

Beloved ones, the light of God that does not fail continues to emanate from the center of your being and floods forth a splendid ray of crystal-white purity. The colors, beloved ones, are within this radiance of purity, but the film, the negative, the individualized expression, is your own. It represents the externalization of your own thoughts and feelings, the action and reaction of the play of energy upon the forcefield of your being. It represents at times, as it were, a haphazard manifestation that mankind have not attempted to control. And then again, it represents a perfected manifestation from the ascended masters' octave of consciousness.

The Shining Light of the Great Divine Self Within

Beloved ones, if you will pause again now and reflect upon yourself and the use of energy that you use daily, you will recognize that you have the power within you—the light of God as shone within the splendid consciousness of the Christ, the light of God as it shines within the consciousness of every ascended master and cosmic being—and that this light that emanates from you can be released in the full intensity of your Great God Self, unqualified by the imperfections upon the temporary film of your conscious being.

Beloved ones, as you use the violet transmuting flame, you are washing the imperfections and streaks from the film of life, from the lens, and you are purifying that lens. And that film is being washed and altered by master artisans so that it can reflect the purity of the light rays that pass through it. And thus, you are no longer an individual expressing temporal manifestations of imperfection, but you are a son or daughter of the Most High God, as you drink into the consciousness of the eternal light that is within you.

Now then, as you take this journey around the earth upon the magic carpet of your mighty I AM Presence, as you gaze down upon those below, would you, beloved ones, offer them the weeds from the garden of your consciousness? Would you qualify the imperfection of your world and pass it down upon them? I think not. Beloved ones, you would offer them the light of God that is within you, charging forth its radiance through your consciousness and blessing them, for only the light can bless mankind.

Precious ones of the light, human personality, created by the misuse of consciousness even when individuals have noble aims, is no substitute for the shining light of the great Divine Self within. This light within is the selfsame Source that is within all, and there is no difference in the qualification of this light. Therefore individuals expressing it do not think in terms of lesser or greater, but only in terms of the greater light itself as it represents the purity of the allness of God.

Therefore, precious ones of the light, as you pass over the earth you offer the best part of yourself to mankind, and the best part of yourself is the best part of ourselves. It is the best part of all life, and thus the raising action that you shed upon the earth, like a sunbeam of shining perfection, elevates in consciousness those whose consciousness is below.

The Glamour of the Outer World

Precious ones, the squalor and the misery, the imperfection, the disharmony and disunity, all that which shines upon the screen of life as shadow and reflects there as imperfection, can be altered by the radiant light of God.

Now, some of you may have wondered why I said "shines." Beloved ones, imperfection has a sparkle because it is sustained by the power of misqualified energy. The light of God is misqualified by mankind, and therefore there is a sparkle of allurement, the maya and the glamour of the outer world. This does not substitute for the radiance of the shining perfection of God. It may seem to do so for a time, but it will be found to be merely a pall upon the senses that will not satisfy the soul that is hungering and thirsting after the righteousness of pure perfection, which can only come from the Source, the allness of God.

Beloved ones of the light, Jesus said unto mankind, "I AM the way, the truth, and the life."[1] It is the I AM of all that is the way, the truth, and the life. Mankind, seeking and seeking to find happiness, pursue the phantoms of vain imaginings and do not find in them the satisfaction after which their souls thirst.

The Greatness of the Thought within the Heart of the Artist

As I am come this day into the city of Washington, D.C., where a work of art is presently on display from my own homeland of France,* I come to you to charge into your world that supreme consciousness that exalts mankind and lifts his mind up to behold the sustained beauty of life that is unperverted by misused human intellect. I would like to make you aware of this life that is God so that you will always sustain its action within your world and so that you will be able to "kiss goodbye" those aspects of human consciousness that have produced misery and unhappiness in your world.

Now, beloved ones, some of you who may desire to see the *Mona Lisa* may also desire to see some of the works of my hands in my embodiment as Paolo Veronese.[2] But I would like to tell you (as I have said before) that today my services to life are to assist mankind to be artists and artisans of the Spirit, that mankind may make of themselves self-sustaining creators, as God intended—a work of art, a thing of beauty that is a joy forever to all with whom they associate.

The highest expression of art and music, the highest expression of culture, is always high only because it is charged with the divine radiance of the Spirit. Precious ones of the light, so long as the human ego and human consciousness are utilized by an artisan, that individual colors with his own ego the work that he produces, and he prevents the full manifestation of the inner aesthetic beauty that is inherent within a pure thoughtform.

Those of you who are accustomed to appreciating the greatness of art will understand that it is the greatness of the thought within the heart of the artist or sculptor that is expressed and that lends nobility and enchantment to the creation of that individual. It is not, beloved ones of the light, the mere fact that an individual is able to understand the laws of symmetry and motion, which can be learned.

*the painting of the *Mona Lisa*

Young Artists Today Have Forgotten to Express the Great Art That Is within Them

Many artists study at the feet of a very great teacher, and they memorize the forms and the various curvatures of line that blend the skillful attitudes of human anatomy and other forms into a creation of linear symmetry. And yet, beloved ones, there is lacking in their creation a soul—the breadth, the depth, and the height of nobility. Mankind, then, in their inner perceptions, stand before such a painting and do not give recognition to it. They recognize it not, because there is not a masterful production inherent within it. There is a production of mere line, of form and ego, and the desire to express greatness.

Young artists today, in their desire to find name and fame, have frequently forgotten to express the great art that is within them. And therefore as I am speaking to you today, I would like to draw a parallel thought to your own individual lives and to make you aware of the fact that you individually, as you change and transmute the film that is in the projector of your consciousness, will be altering the picture that is cast upon the screen of life. And thus you can become a manifestation of artistic perfection, designed in the form of a son or a daughter of God.

To accept the present standard—whatever it is that is expressing in your life as the acme of perfection—is of course an error of which even your finite self is instantly aware. But to understand that now is the hour when you can begin to change those unwanted conditions into the perfection of God and the allness thereof is an entirely different idea, which may require some assimilation by your inner consciousness.

I, therefore, urge upon you that you speedily understand and accept within your world the fact that you have been given the power by God to alter all circumstance according to a set of cosmic laws—those standards of perfection and those standards of cosmic law that are understood and manipulated by every ascended being.

The Voice of God Always Speaks of Truth and Beauty

You, then, are no exception to those laws, and neither is anyone else. None upon this broad planet is an exception, for all come under the same domain of cosmic law. Some think that they are above the Law or without the Law. This they cannot be, for life itself has an equity that is within it, and the equity of life is the equity of God expressed by the Goddess of Justice.[3] Her voice is heard. All of the divine beings must be heard, whether it be in a soundless sound, which is not captured by your ears, or whether it be in a sound that you can hear audibly.

Some of you have heard voices speaking to you. Well, beloved ones, the voice of God always speaks of truth and beauty. The voice of God always elevates the consciousness. The voice of God always elevates man's thought and raises it toward those heights that are absolutely pure and beautiful. When, then, individuals hear a voice that urges them to commit an act that is not compatible with the decency of an ascended being, let them instantly know that it is not the voice of God.

The voice of God is pure and peaceable and gentle, and yet it has the power of immortality and the power of the crashing worlds within it. For all the worlds that have been created in the past, in universes unknown to your present history, were all formulated by the voice of the "Word made flesh,"[4] made manifest in form by the power of the Great Cosmic Law.

Mankind will someday be able to understand how to go back and read the akashic records as they now read the histories of the world. Then those archivists of spiritual law will assist mankind as they unfold an understanding of how perfection can come about. Mankind have read history and have observed in history all of the imperfections of the past, but have they understood from those mistakes how to correct them and amend them?

You can behold for yourselves that this has not been, and therefore I would like to remind you today that the need is to look toward the future of the shining perfection of spiritual law—to that which is not embellished, for it needs not to be, but to that which *is* the radiance of all eternity, stainless and pure, manifesting in octaves of light and yet available to every son of heaven.

Precious ones, mankind strain every ounce of their energy. They strain their very souls to obtain some particular eminence among men, and yet how few upon this broad planet truly seek with their all to know the Father's will, the Father's beauty, the Father's greatness? How few are willing to offer their all? How few are willing to be a server of higher dimensions, to serve the great cause that will cut the earth free?

The Fetters That Bind Mankind

I would like to speak to you for a moment, beloved ones, about those fetters that mankind have installed so securely about themselves, as though they were afraid that if those fetters were cut, they themselves would float away and drift into an empty nothingness. I would like to tell you, beloved ones, that this is not true. This is not true! Mankind need have no fear that if they cut the fetters that bind them to the earthly consciousness, they will drift away. For the immortal consciousness of God is within the holy temple of their being, and as the psalmists of old said, "Whither shall I flee from thy presence?"[5]

Beloved ones, where can mankind go? Where can they flee from before the face of God, seeing that they dwell within him and are active in the principle of immortal life? Pause, then, again and recognize that as you cut those weights and sins of human omission and commission from your consciousness, you will be enabling that consciousness to rise. And as it rises and looks up toward God, it cannot escape entering into some measure of the eternal Mind. That measure at first may seem small because it will be limited by the finite.

It is as though a person stood before the window of a large shop covered with the accumulation and dust of centuries, and then they dipped a cloth into water and began to make a small hole in the dust of this window. At first a small ray of light would come in. If they pressed their eye against this tiny hole, they would be able to see far and wide. But if they stood back from the window, the hole would still seem small. And so it is with the window into eternal beauty.

Mankind, as they press their eye for a moment against the small hole—while they sit in heavenly places and are in our radiance in an exalted consciousness—are able to catch a glimpse of the wonders of our octave. When absent, then, and separated, as it were, in physical form from one another and from those heavenly places of consciousness, it is as though they backed away from the window. The hole fades into a limited nothingness, and the shadowed window itself seems once again to occupy their consciousness.

What is the remedy? It is so simple that I am certain that you have immediately deduced it. It is to clean the *entire* pane of consciousness, and then you will be able to see *all* of the purity of God at *all* times. You will not blame others. You will not blame organizations. You will not blame religious institutions. You will not blame individuals among mankind for your lack of vision and perception. You will immediately recognize that *you* have in the past neglected to clean the consciousness of the eyes of your soul and to gaze at the purity and beauty all around you.

You Ought to Become Godlike

And so today, as I have carried you in a spiritual sense upon the magic carpet of the world's greater and larger view of beauty, I would like to point out that to God the world is a shining planet of splendor and perfection. Its people are pure and noble and grand—sons and daughters of God radiant and shining with light.

Man finds it difficult to understand that God would not understand the existence of sin and inequity. Well, these are theological matters, which I shall not touch upon on this occasion at length. But those of you who are hungering and thirsting after righteousness will understand this one idea: It is impossible for the mind of God to be full of iniquity, and therefore the mind of God cannot contain *any* iniquity whatsoever. It is all purity, all perfection, and it is not, therefore, aware of human emotion.

I would like, then, to say unto you that you ought to become Godlike, and then all of the maya that is around you and surrounding you as tangible fetters to your consciousness, mark you well, will be found to be nothing. It will be found to be as bands of salt immersed in the sea. It will evaporate, dissipate, and be found to be nothing more than spray or foam spewed upon the human consciousness *in temporum.*

Beauty and Loveliness Are Born of Divine Love

I would like, then, to ask you now to think of a pink rose. And as you think of this pink rose, recognize that cherubic and loving beings have formed it under divine direction. Realize that those beings who have formed it cherish it. Recognize that those beings who have formed it give of themselves, as the bee gives of his being to make the honey. The nectar of the flowers, beloved ones, taken by the bee is charged with a specific quality from the bee himself, and this quality manifests in the honey. And so, the perfume of this rose is a saturation of the essence of love from the heart of those cherubs who have created this beautiful rose.

Mankind, in their love of the perfumer's art, are aware of the fact that floral fragrances stimulate spiritual understanding and assist mankind in recognizing and sensing inward beauty. Now then, as you gaze upon this rose, be aware of these factors and recognize that the love of God is ensouled within the pink radiance of this beautiful rose.

Recognize now, beloved ones, that the never-failing love of God is shining through the radiance of this rose out into the world of form and is not limited by time or space or dimension, that in every human consciousness this lovely rose—symbolizing the love of the Maha Chohan and beloved Mother Mary, of beloved Chamuel and Charity,[6] and of everyone who serves upon the third ray as well as the chohans of every ray and every son of heaven—is a symbol, then, to all of hope and loveliness.

So is divine love. Divine love is greater than the rose. Divine love is greater than every floral offering. Divine love is greater than all manifestation. Divine love is greater even than beauty. But remember well that beauty and loveliness in form and being are born of divine love.

I thank you.

January 13, 1963

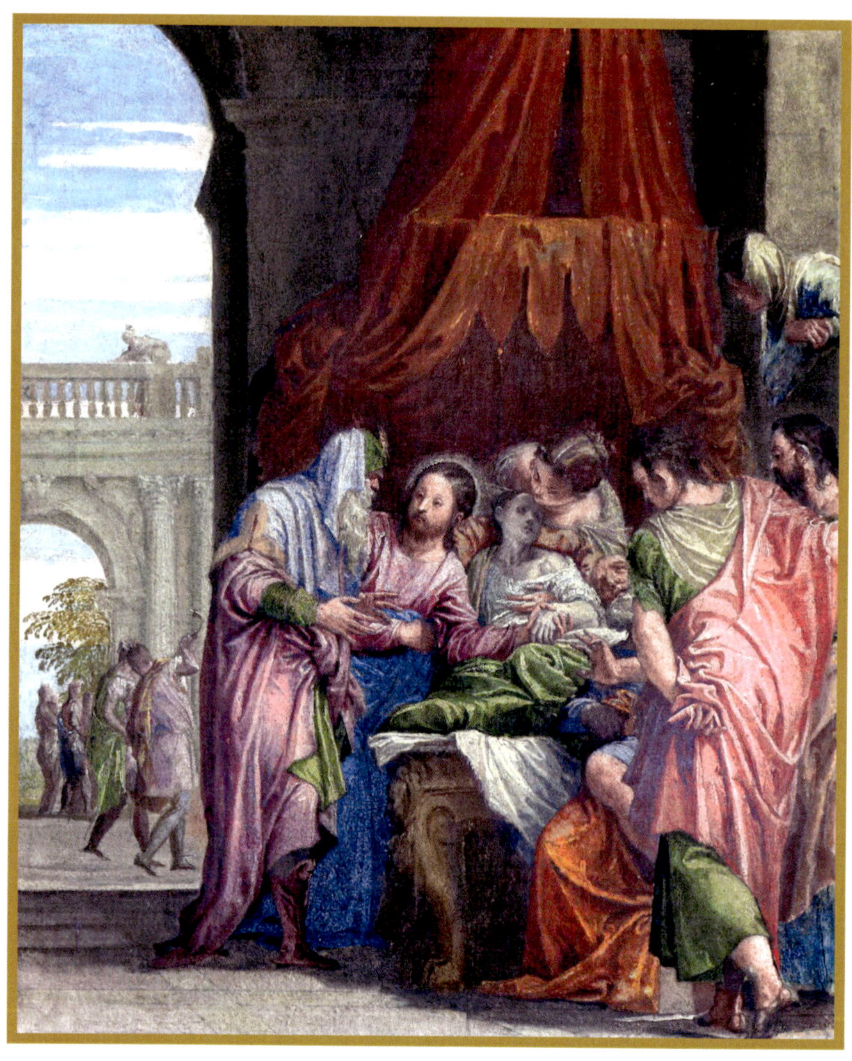

Resurrection of the Daughter of Jairus, c. 1546

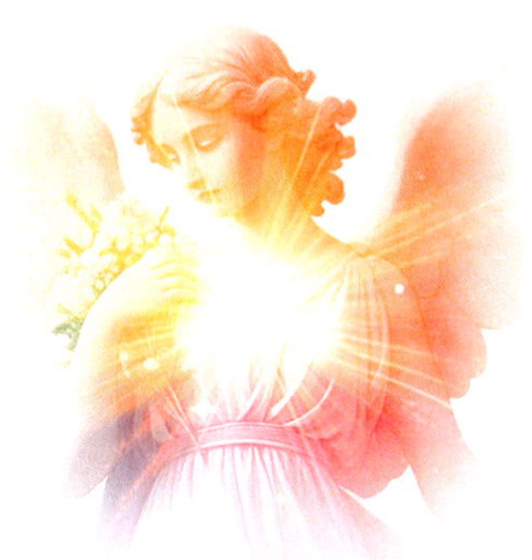

Culture is acquired within the heart and the feeling and thinking world of mankind as it applies itself to its Source and realizes the simple meaning of the word of, knowing that it came from God and is of God and therefore loves God.

CHAPTER 2

A Secret and High Calling of the Heart

Sons and daughters of Christ-liberty, earth has no sorrow that love cannot heal. The action of the healing flame is an action of divine love. The action of all the sacred flames of the sacred fire is a manifestation of divine love and of divine beauty.

In coming into your lovely temple this morning and beholding your hearts, so hallowed because they are so charged with the sacred fire, I first ask and request that twelve magnificent angel devas from the music temples come and abide here and pour their celestial harmonies and radiance through this physical temple and through your worlds while I speak to you. May their anthems and their radiance make a melody out of my words, which shall linger long in your memory and bring you a greater realization from day to day of the power of love.

Love is of Christ. It is of your Holy Christ Self. And if you stop and consider for a moment, many times when you are disturbed, that somewhere between your God Presence and your physical form there dwells a magnificent Christ-being* (with a robe of *righteousness* and the *right use* of God's divine powers), this will help you to hold to an immaculate concept of saying to yourself, "This which I do is that which

*See the Chart of Your Divine Self on p. 245.

my Christ Self would do, and therefore I AM a being of divine love. A being of divine love will act in a manner in keeping with that love."

All Things Have Their Center and Source in Love

I would give you this morning my understanding of a very simple word, and this too I pray that you shall not forget. The word is *of,* "o-f." Many of you do not know the full science of even the English language, and this is understandable.

Of can be spelled many ways—perhaps "o-f" or "o-v"—but it is the sound or pronunciation that is important. *Love* and *of* are truly synonymous, yet this has not been realized by many people. For example, when you say "the king *of* France," you are saying "the king *loves* France." And this is the proper understanding of the simple word *of.*

When you say "the Son of God," it is one thing. But when you say "the son of man," then you are saying "the son *loves* man." I am sure you see this. And you will realize that in the simple connecting words, oftentimes great manifestations are possible. You see, beloved hearts, all things do have their center and source in love. It is much more than just a word. It is a radiance. And it has been well said that God is love.

The Meaning of the Great White Brotherhood

There are a few issues today that I would clarify for the sons and daughters of freedom. Much misunderstanding has existed down through the centuries concerning the Great White Brotherhood. The name, like so many other words, has become somewhat bandied about. And in that disciplinarian sense, I would give you your God-liberty this day by speaking some words concerning the Great White Brotherhood.

The Great White Brotherhood, as you know (that is, as most of you know), has no connection with any race. It is a term that is sacred and comes from the sacred, white fire. The word "Great" refers to the fact that the Great White Brotherhood is a magnificent cosmic action. "White" refers to the fact that the Great White Brotherhood manifests all the colors and radiance of Almighty God—if you will, the full rainbow that the Master Painter uses to actually create his beauty on the canvas of eternity. Therefore, "White" is symbolic of God-purity, of God-unity, of wholeness, of oneness.

(Micah, the Angel of Unity,[1] has joined me here as I speak to you, because of the very fact that I mentioned the word "unity." Therefore, I think you will find it somewhat interesting to see how magnificent our cooperation is.)

Beloved ones, the Great White Brotherhood is also a "brotherhood." Now, a brotherhood does indeed have this sense and feeling of one for all and all for one. It is somewhat impossible for a brother of the fire of God to have feelings generated within one's consciousness that do not come to a state of concord and unity. Therefore, those who would manifest the *Spirit* of the Great White Brotherhood cannot do otherwise than to love—remembering their Source, that they are *of* God, which means that they therefore *love* God. Do you see? This is most simple, and yet in simplicity the greatest profundities of the universe are made manifest.

The First Secret to Abundance Is Love

It would be a very simple thing for most of us of the ascended realm, having a great vocabulary and command of thought and feeling, to speak words so far over your head, shall we say, in many cases, that individuals in the audience would not even be able to understand or cognize just what we are talking about. Therefore, it is quite our manner and is usual that we speak somewhat in simplicity and clothe our thoughts, which are often profound, with simple expressions so that you may remember them and therefore derive benefit and value from them.

Many people enjoy going to hear a good speech or sermon, and this is also quite natural for mankind. What we say to you today and at every one of these meetings is spoken for your soul's good and for the healing of all the hurt of mankind. Limitation, regardless of what type of limitation it is, is not the intention of the Infinite Father, who holds within his hand a cornucopia of cosmic abundance.

The first secret to abundance is love. Realizing that you are of the Source, you are logically and rightly entitled to the glory of your Father. When you do not manifest or express the glory of your Father in any way, this ought not to become a reason for distress. But I can well understand why it does bring distress in your own particular world. However, I wish to give you this encouragement today—that the power of infinite love and brotherhood and light is all within the name "the Great White Brotherhood." This is not something that can be appropriated by any outer exoteric organization.

The Muddied Waters of Our Past Endeavors

Down through the centuries we have, in the name of the Infinite Father, created and sustained various endeavors that were created and sustained entirely for the sake of the release of divine illumination to mankind. The reason why we released illumination and love to mankind was to bring them back to a knowledge of their Source and, simply put, to remove the spheres of limitation and the consciousness of limitation from their worlds and consciousness.

However, through distortion, through commercialization, through greed, which is focused in the individual worlds of mankind, often some of our endeavors fell into disrepute—not because of any lack of love or compassion on our part, but because the consciousness of mankind became like a muddied river and someone poured the silt from the bank into the clear, crystal waters of our outpouring.

I am sure that most of you will realize that this was certainly not the intention of the Infinite Father, neither was it the intention of the Great White Brotherhood nor the hierarchy of heaven. However, unfortunately it seems that many among mankind, once they revolve their consciousness in mud and discord, are unable to wash themselves clean and free from it. It is as though it becomes caked upon their hands and enters into their pores.

However, today I would like to speak words of healing and to remove from the consciousness of our chelas, at least, any sense of immersion, as it were, in human discord. I would like to remove the effect of this muddied water, which has been poured forth to all who are athirst, that they might drink and find their eternal freedom.

Therefore I say that no exoteric organization has ever had the right to make the statement that *they* are the official channel of the Great White Brotherhood. It is true that the Great White Brotherhood does sponsor various organizations for the purposes of divine love and eternal salvation to mankind and the raising of this sweet earth, but no one has ever been empowered to declare that they are the only channel of our light. How could this be, seeing that the hearts of mankind are ever contrite throughout the world?

The Painting of *The Angelus*

Many of you are familiar with the beautiful painting of *The Angelus.*[2] You perhaps have stood at times and observed the peasants as they bow their heads when the hour of prayer comes. You have perhaps felt and sensed this great awe and this reverence. I, of course, admire paintings because in my embodiment as Paolo Veronese I was able to draw forth from the heart of God much of the beauty and capture it upon canvas for mankind.

Therefore I say to you today that in this painting of *The Angelus* there is a very great beauty. Some may term it a "peasant" beauty. This is because it is simple. Its thought is simple but it reaches the heart, and love reaches the heart. Therefore in the contemplation of this painting of *The Angelus,* you are able to almost hear the tolling of the bell as it calls mankind to a solemn hour of prayer.

This occurs across the vast expanse of the world. For example, over in Europe—a great center of culture and light in times past, and even to the present time there is still a great residue remaining—many of the people of Europe have a different understanding than the people of America, yet they are children of God. And therefore they bow their heads in prayer. They bow their consciousness to the light. They may not have the same degree of intellectual comprehension of the teachings that many of you have, or the same opportunities even to partake of the same bread that you break. This does not matter. They are grateful to an Infinite Father for his divine capacities and outpourings to their particular lifestreams, and they express that gratitude.

Think you, then, that these two peasants in the painting of *The Angelus* are less than the masters of the Great White Brotherhood because they stand on the fields of earth and take a simple instrument, perhaps, and till the ground? Think you that those who still use the oxcart are less the children of God than those who use a McCormick-Deering reaper?

The Simplicity and God-Beauty of Life

I tell you, children of God, that the wonders of this century, the mechanization of America, the spread of the light across America from the east to the west, the great caravans sweeping across the nation—these have been very wonderful and they have brought a wealth of abundance and happiness to your land, because it is our land.

But today throughout the world there still exist many cultures that are quite primitive beside that of America. There is no need for the rest of the world to be jealous of America, neither is there any need for America to raise her head in a false sense of pride.

Those who loved America when she was founded in the early days of the history of this great nation loved her with the love of the simple peasant. They were not immersed in many things that today distract the attention of mankind and take them away from the simplicity and God-beauty of life. This is a misfortune—a misfortune we would speedily correct.

Culture is not something that mankind can communicate and purchase with money. You cannot buy culture with dollars. You cannot acquire culture merely by attending a church of your choice. You do not acquire culture by merely reading a book. Culture is acquired within the heart and the feeling and thinking world of mankind as it applies itself to its Source and realizes the simple meaning of the word *of,* knowing that it came from God and is *of* God and therefore *loves* God.

True Culture Is That Which Is Drawn Forth through the Sacred Fires of the Heart

The Great White Brotherhood—forthright, honorable, divine, inspired, and inspiring—is an organization that any man or woman or child might enjoy being a member of. There are no dues or fees or assessments against those who serve the Great White Brotherhood, except the type of assessment that is freely given to God as Christ Jesus gave his great light in Gethsemane and poured out his heart with folded hands, saying, "Father, not my will."[3]

Therefore, I say to you that in this day and age it is proper and fitting that mankind should have an understanding of the Great White Brotherhood, that they should understand that its members are often found in every walk of life. These members do not go around and prate and declare that they are members of the Great White Brotherhood. This is a secret and high calling of the heart. Its members recognize each other not by outer symbols but by the inner light that is within the heart of every God-being who will petition for entrance to that sacred and august body.

From the Château de Liberté today, as I am speaking to you to clarify in part some of these issues, I trust that further meditation by you individually will disclose to you in the privacy of your own rooms and sanctuaries a greater understanding of the meaning of the Great White Brotherhood. I trust that you will realize that our solemn and silent assemblies, to which many of you have been invited and have partaken of during the hours of sleep, will become more sacred to you and that you will cease to be annoyed by trifles in consciousness.

We perhaps may demonstrate to you some impatience with mankind's foibles, and this is true, but it is explained quite simply. Most of us who have made our ascension were perhaps a bit more diligent than some who have not made their ascension. We were more dedicated, and this is fact, not fiction.

Because of our greater dedication, we made our ascension somewhat earlier. We do not say this with a sense of pride. It is a fact. And therefore because of this, you see, we perhaps have not acquired the same patience that some of you have, who have dallied a little longer in human consciousness.

This is not, however, an excuse, and I shall not say that I condone it. I only charge you with the love of heaven to love your God Self more, to forget your puny, physical accomplishments, and to try to remember that a true culture is that which is drawn forth through the sacred fires of the heart and magnetized by divine love.

True culture is not something that you yourselves desire to have so that you might express egotistically your own outer accomplishments, but it is something that you might draw forth and magnetize through the sacred fires of your heart so that you might cut yourself free forever from the ego and its desire to exalt itself above its fellowmen, that you might instead consider and ponder this sacred gift and use it wisely and well.

This day, if there were anything that I could give to you in the name of divine love, it would be to free you from your ego—which, I am sorry to say, has often been like a great and heavy weight upon the shoulders, bending the backs of mankind and causing them to stoop toward the earth when their heads should have been lifted up to the heavens, from whence they came.

Those who came from Venus (and there are some in this audience) are perhaps able to get a little better sense of the supreme radiance of God because of the great love that comes from the planet Venus and from beloved Sanat Kumara,[4] its magnificent friend of light who so long served this planet.

You Too, with Christ Jesus, Are a Son and Daughter of God

There is one other subject in particular that I wish to touch upon before I take my leave of you, and that subject concerns the Second Coming of the beloved master Jesus the Christ. This is another subject that the mankind of earth do not fully understand or comprehend. It is true that some among mankind do, and it has something to also do with climaxes.

Most of you, if you stop and think of it, will also see in the word *climax* a very great, a very magnificent idea embodied there. *Climax* comes from the word, in a sense, "to climb" or "to rise," and it denotes that one has risen to a certain point of accomplishment where a great action is completed.

When that action is completed, it does not mean that all life ceases because that action has been completed. Many individuals have felt that life is actually built up from a beginning and moves toward a final climax. They do not realize its eternal values, and therefore these individuals look for an outer expression or manifestation of the ascended master Jesus—that he shall come in clouds, with a great climactic situation developing where some individuals will be raised up and actually float up in the air (somewhat as a balloon) to rise to meet the Christ upon this cloud, and then they shall go to some vague and vapory heaven, which unfortunately they are not able to tell us where this particular sphere is.

Beloved ones, in clarification thereof, I want to point out one thing. I do not intend to completely describe this situation to you. I merely give you a hint so that you might be able, through your own God Presence, to develop still further the ideas that I am trying by radiation to convey to you.

Are you not all Christs in the sense that God has planted within you a dependence on him, the Father? If you are dependent upon God the Father for your Source, for your life, for your being, then, beloved hearts, you must continue to depend upon this Great God and you must recognize that you too, with Christ Jesus, are a son and daughter of God.

When the light manifests in you as it did in him, then remember that the same Christ-manifestation has occurred and he, too, then manifests through you in the same manner. This is done often in the twinkling of an eye, in a moment, and you are often caught up thereby in clouds of glory.[5]

We try to illustrate some of these facts in our magnificent paintings at inner levels. Those who are able to actually leave their physical forms and arise to our level are able to behold this magnificence in our sacred temples.

The Meaning of Love Is That You Are *of* God

This day, this Independence Day in the year 1960, I, Paul the Venetian, have desired and striven to give you of my love, to give you the love of God, and to tell you that the meaning of love is that you are *of* God. The use you make of my energy that I have released, the use you make of our God radiance that we have given you this day, is dependent on you, *but you are dependent on God.*

Honor your country. Honor its purity. Honor the will of God as it manifests through this blue field, symbolic of the canopy of heaven. Honor the stars, symbolic of the Christ radiance that shines in every heart. Honor every flag of every nation that is constructive, for all are one in one great unity of action. And the time has certainly arrived and is somewhat overdue when the Great White Brotherhood should be able to draw the hearts of men to a focus where those men might be able to work together as friends, placing shoulders to the wheel of Almighty God in the great scheme of world dharma until we can manifest that Brotherhood in action here, which exists so beautifully, so lovely, so magnificently in our octave.

Angel devas from the music temples, pour now the celestial chorus of heaven through the inner consciousness and feeling worlds of these precious souls, and let its radiance flood the city of New York.

As we cleared the atmosphere of this city by this tremendous outpouring of activity last night in the down-pouring rain, so may the latter rain of heaven pour upon the hearts of men and flood them with love, removing from them the desire and the consciousness of mere bohemianism. But may they learn the meaning of true culture, true art, true progress, to be true Americans, true ever to the I AM Race, true ever to the Great White Brotherhood, true chelas of the ascended masters, and in the due process of time, ascended God-free beings, even as I, Paul, AM!*

May God, the Infinite Father, seal you in his heart of light and love. May his eternal love and the love of the angelic hosts bless you and keep you confident in the arms of the eternal Father, until the Great Master Artist of all eternity produces on the individualized canvases of your consciousness the beauty magnificent and the eternal love and light that he, the Father, is and was from the beginning of time.

Thank you. Bless you. Good afternoon.

July 4, 1960

**bohemianism:* a lifestyle of wandering about, sometimes adopting an eccentric way of living

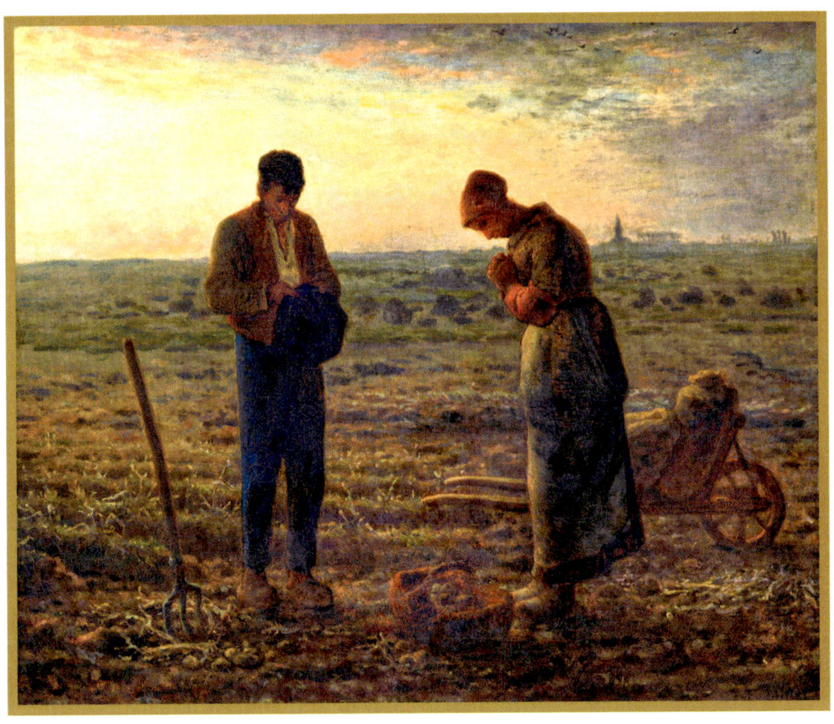

The Angelus, c. 1857–59 by Jean-François Millet

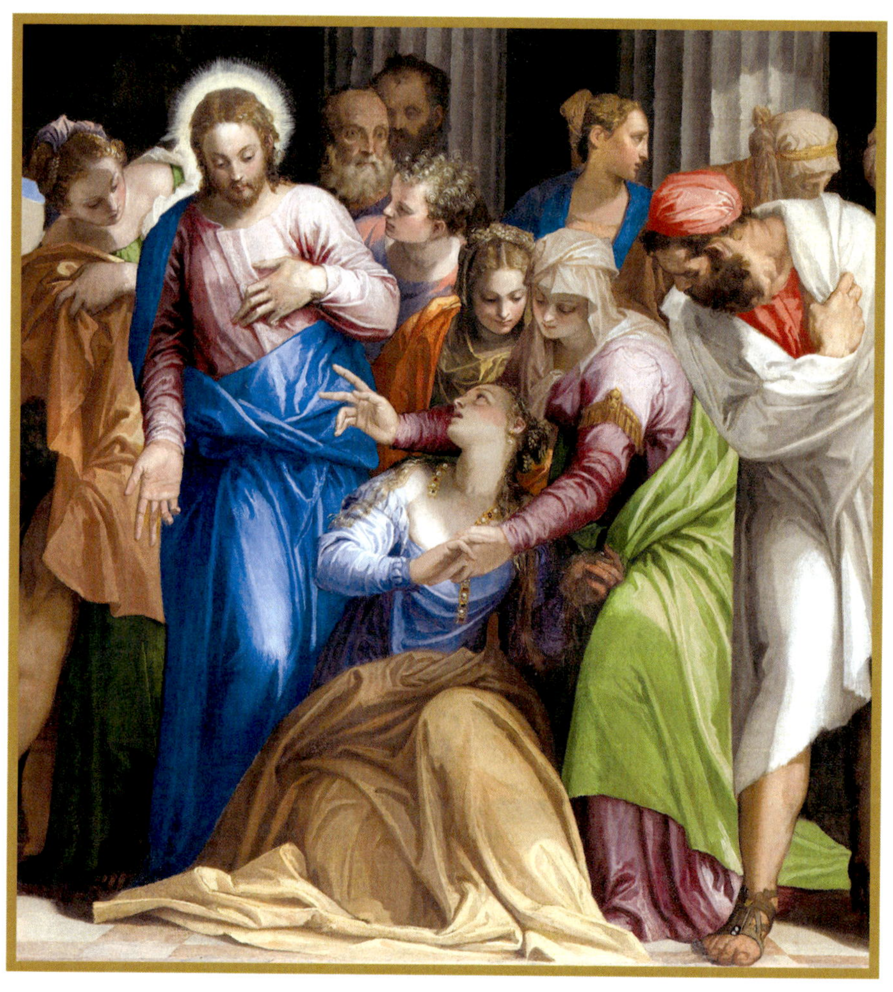

The Conversion of Mary Magdalene (detail), c. 1548

Love is the power that moves the world! Love is the power that frames the world! Love is the power that sustains the Brotherhood! Love is the power that is the cohesive force throughout the universe by which stars are born and through which is extended into the finite the grace of the infinite capacities of God!

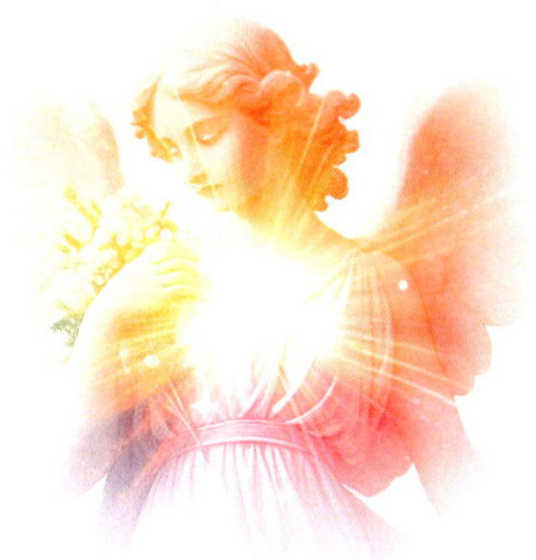

CHAPTER 3

Eternal Beauty Moves the Spirit of Man to Exclaim:

"O God, You Are So Magnificent!"

Magnificent souls, children of the infinite love of the Father, I come to you this night from the Château de Liberté to bring to your sense-consciousness the reality of God's beauty and the infinite fire of his love.

I AM infired with divine compassion this night as I extend the greetings of the Great White Brotherhood out into the world of form. I do so that mankind may not only conceive of the infinite meaning of beauty but that they may swiftly become breathing examples of the living God-beauty that is spread abroad everywhere because it is the intent of the All-Father. This is the vision held within the All-Seeing Eye of God, whose eternal destiny is the progression of the universal consciousness in all worlds everywhere.

As I look out upon the universal vision of the infinite cosmos, I behold in those flaming orbs a sense of divine majesty that moves me to exclaim in your midst: "Behold the wonders of God!"[1] I urge that each and every one of you will begin, now, to externalize the meaning of newness of life.

How many of you arise from your beds in the morning with a sense of lethargy, of fatigue, and with a feeling that this day is a day that will be difficult? I ask you to throw out of your consciousness this sense of difficulty.

Ladies and gentlemen, if you begin your day with a sense of the difficult, I do not see how you can end it with any other sense. But if you will begin each day with a sense of infinite beauty and will look out upon life with the thought that this day is God's, and with a feeling that this is a day when you shall sense the beauty of God in life, then you will see—as we who are artists and architects of the Spirit—a sense of the eternal beauty that moves the spirit of man to exclaim, "O God, you are so magnificent!"

Ladies and gentlemen, I address you thus. For thus you are eternal beauty in the eyes of Saint Germain[2] and in the eyes of those of that august fraternity known as the Great White Brotherhood.

You have perhaps pondered the mystical idea of the Great White Brotherhood as some conception of the finite mind. Let me here and now remove from your consciousness such a misconception and hasten to assure you that the infinite power of this august fraternity of spiritual beings—the spirits of just men made perfect[3]—is to assist the great divine plan in being called forth from the heart of God and externalized among mankind.

Out of the Flame of Divine Love Is Born Divine Beauty

I have served in the past and I serve today with gratitude for the opportunity and privilege to love. To love is a privilege, never a duty. To love *God* is a privilege beyond all privileges. And to love mankind, made in his image, is the second commandment made like unto the first.[4]

Oh, I enfold you now with a sense of love, of divine love that reaches out to embrace the eternal concept and to know that out of the flame of divine love is born divine beauty. The sense of divine beauty is the ever-newness of each day, of each hour, of each moment—fresh, perennial, and lovely beyond compare.

Blessed ones, why is it that with the first blush upon beholding a friend, man is able to sense the majesty and beauty of this friend;

but then as time goes on and the friend becomes more known unto that one's consciousness, this friend becomes less magnificent rather than becoming more magnificent?

This is because the attention that is now placed upon the friend is not upon the Great God Self of that individual, but it is placed upon the ephemeral, the transitory, the human. The attention is placed upon that side of the friend that is but a child in the hands of its Cosmic Mother, extending those tiny hands upward, looking hopefully to that Cosmic Mother to guide, to guard, to protect, to direct the footsteps of that tiny babe until, growing up in Christ consciousness, the babe shall become the Manchild, with all of the beauty of Christ-accomplishment.

Ladies and gentlemen, *love* is the power that moves the world! *Love* is the power that frames the world! *Love* is the power that sustains the Brotherhood! *Love* is the power that is the cohesive force throughout the universe by which stars are born and through which is extended into the finite the grace of the infinite capacities of God!

Is not love, then, to be adored? How many of you have thought of adoring love? Adoring love is to love *love,* and it is the very selfsame nature of God to adore himself. This is not a divine narcissism. It is a case of God being the great giver, and no receiver at all. For God has given life to all, and he has given beauty to all. He gives to all mankind his eternal compassion in order to guide them and to guard their footsteps until they come to that place in life where they are masters of force, masters of energy, masters of divine power. And there is no power whatsoever in the world that can move them, aside from following and pursuing the spiritual path all the way to their eternal Victory.

When You Enter a State of Divine and Cosmic Achievement, You Will Want No Other Vision

I would like to address you at this time with a word concerning the purity of your aura. As a divine artist now, although a well-known earthly artist in the past, I am ever so interested in utilizing those spiritual chemicalizations wherewith we are able to paint upon the canvas of eternal life a more beautiful soul.

While I was embodied as Paolo Veronese, it was my passion and desire to externalize on canvas all of the fire of life. I desired to express the sunlight as though it were actually shining through the canvas. I desired to express in color and form that rhythm of the eternal movement of the Spirit, which I perceived as the inner culture of man. But these seem, now, as I look upon them, but pitiful executions in charcoal or traceries upon the sand. For I now behold the beauty of God face-to-face, and beholding, I am now completely and all-powerfully enamored with the vision which I see, and I want no other.

When you enter a state of divine and cosmic achievement like unto my own, you will want no other vision. You will no longer *want.* You will know the meaning of that great passage uttered by David, "The LORD is my shepherd; I shall not want."[5]

You will understand how to contemplate the mysteries of God and how to extract therefrom their full meaning. And your mentors will not be removed into a corner. They will abide with you, by your side, and you will have the "open sesame"* that brings to your consciousness the answer to every problem whatsoever.

At the present time it is necessary, because of the cosmic moment, for me to speak through this instrument whose consciousness and lips I use in order to reach your hearts. The day will come, indeed, when this epoch shall pass. But when it passes, I pray God that man will have that same direct apprehension that this instrument has—the capacity to reach into the great cosmic light and to draw therefrom the consciousness of those of us who have won our victory, who have attained through the pain and the suffering of human consciousness and have bypassed it and mounted up into the God consciousness and the victory of immortality.

Peace Be unto You at Every Hour with a Sense of God's Beauty

Peace be unto you in this cosmic hour and moment. Peace be unto you during the wakeful hours of the night, when your soul seems to be troubled by human thoughts. Peace be unto you at every hour

**open sesame* [fr. French *sésame, ouvre-toi*]: something that unfailingly brings about a desired end (*Merriam-Webster's Collegiate Dictionary,* 11th ed.); the magical command used by Ali Baba in *Ali Baba and the Forty Thieves* to open the door of the robbers' den

with a sense of God's beauty. If this sense of God's beauty shall become strong enough, it shall be because nothing can resist the onrush of its cosmic perfection. And so you will have, by the enfolding softness of divine love, a cushion to assuage all human grief, a balm to wipe out all human fear.

O beloved ones, the Great White Brotherhood, beholding the perilous hours facing the mankind of earth, now urge that as never before there shall be a unity of spirit among all those who profess to serve the cause of the great Brotherhood—a unity of hearts, a unity of your being with your own Great God Presence. This is so needed if you are to accomplish the fiat of the moment.

God has sent forth the call to man. Will man answer it and raise his brother? Will he raise the fallen among mankind? Will he assist the Brotherhood in doing the necessary and averting from the earth the pain of war and the discord that is now threatening the planetary body? I am so hopeful.

The Maha Chohan[6] has raised his head and has invoked this cosmic hope anew. We invoke it in your hearts tonight. We invoke it in the hearts of all mankind. It is not within our power to respond for you. This you must do for yourself.

As I leave you now, I leave you not comfortless but I leave you with a great Cosmic Christ blessing from our sphere and octave. This blessing is our light, our sense of the Divine, and the peace which passeth all human understanding.[7]

Peace, Cosmic Christ peace, be unto you from all at the Château de Liberté, from all who work with the sacred fire, from all who serve the cause of freedom from the heart of Saint Germain, from beloved Jesus, from Ascended Master Morya El.[8]

To those of you in Boston who have faithfully served this cause, we extend our personal hands in greeting. We thank those who have sponsored this place.[9]

Sometimes in moments of loneliness you may think that your thoughts go unperceived by us. May I assure you that you are never alone. We are as near and as close as your hands and feet and as your incoming and outgoing breath.

The Golden Age Will Be a Reality from Sea to Shining Sea

We hope that you will hold this focus steadfast until, pushing out beyond these walls, you may expand this activity in a limitless way in order to assist the earth and its people in finding that freedom which God intends. It is a freedom that, up to this point, all of the blessed religions of the world and the sincere people have not been successful in prosecuting* for God. But today, pinning our hopes on the hearts of the few, we are certain that you shall perform a mighty work for the freeing of the earth, its environs, its people, and every deva and builder of form until the perfect archetype shall be manifest among mankind.

The new civilization that shall be born in South America[10] shall become a reality fostered and nurtured by the Great White Brotherhood until those sacred temples brought forth there, as in days of yore, [3-second break in audio recording] to bring to the heart of every incoming child.

The golden age that shall come will be a reality from sea to shining sea. And America's heart, together with India's head,[11] shall rejoice evermore in the great mantram of the Brotherhood, *Om Mani Padme Hum,*[12] that the great shining jewel within the heart of the lotus may come into full manifestation.

The Spirit, which was never born and which shall never cease to be, shall manifest in form those capacities intended in that divine blueprint—that great Reality held in God's own heart and consciousness. And then every tear shall be wiped away from every human eye, and they shall know peace without limit.[13]

I thank you and bid you good evening.

c. August, 1960

**prosecuting:* following to the end, pursuing until finished; to engage in, take advantage of

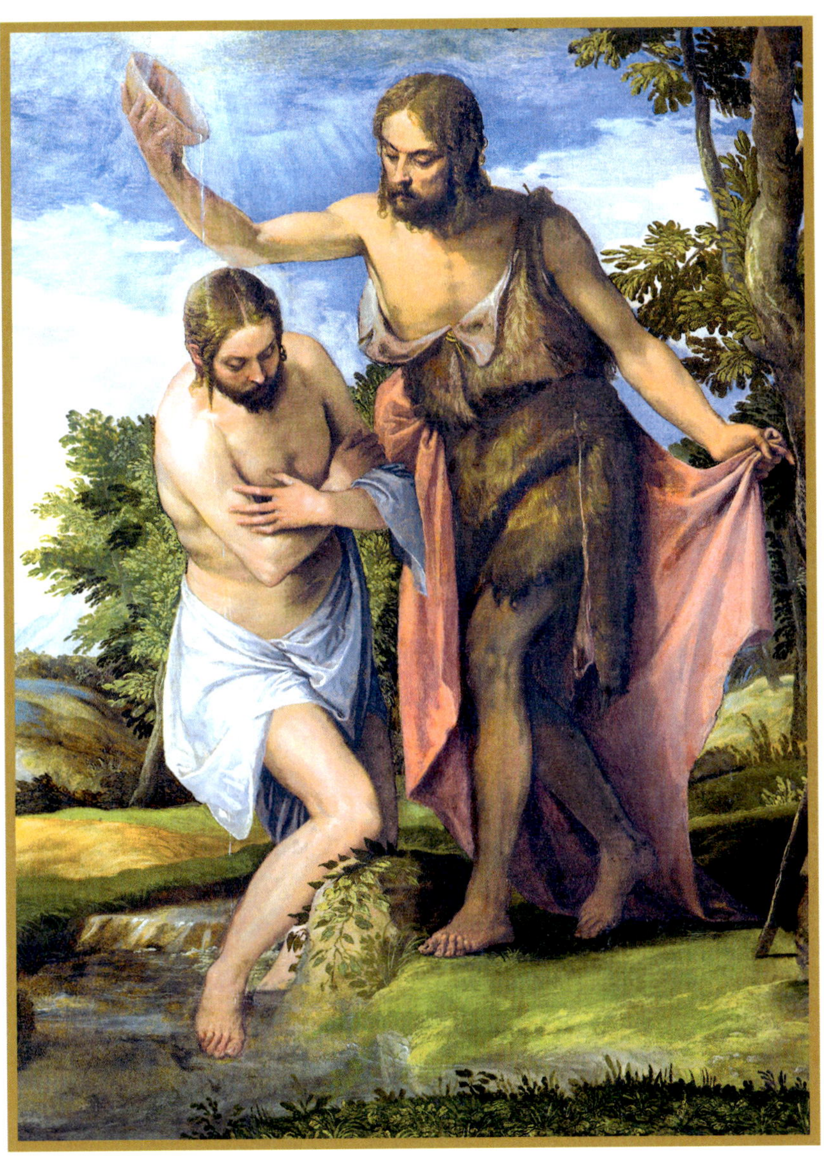

The Baptism of Christ (detail), c. 1550–60

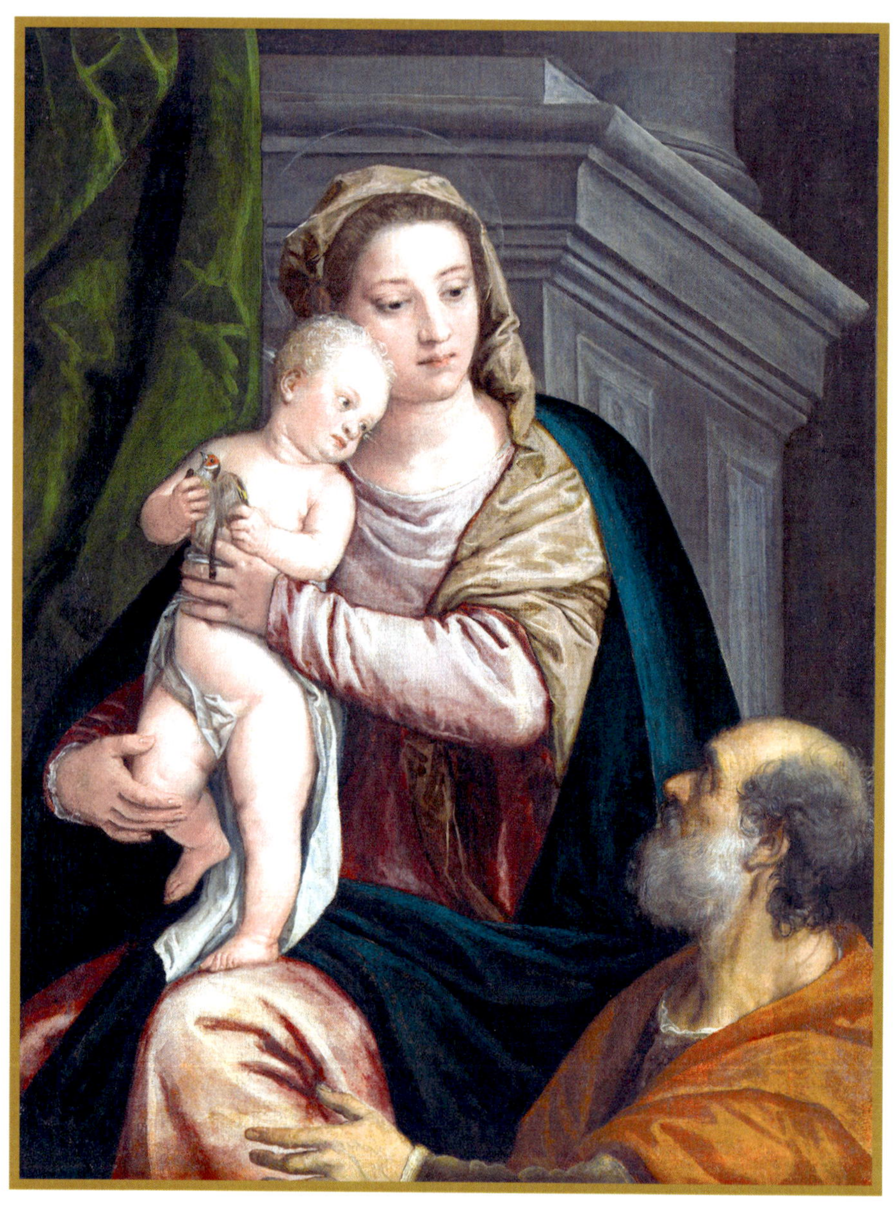

The Holy Family, c. 1550–55

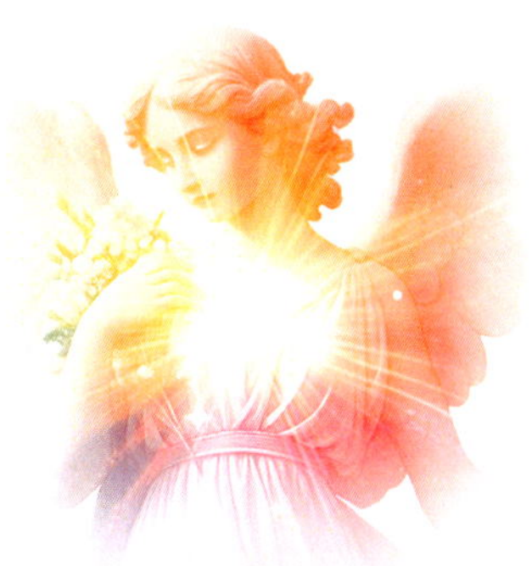

The divine beauties are yours for the taking. They are yours for the asking. Beloved Jesus declared, "Seek, and ye shall find; ask, and ye shall receive; knock, and it shall be opened unto you."

CHAPTER 4

"O God, Help Me!" The Call Compels the Answer

Every good gift and every perfect gift is from above, and cometh down from the Father of lights . . .

Beloved heart friends, children of the Infinite God whose capacities to appreciate the eternal beauty are expanded in accordance with your adoration to your own God Presence, I greet you one and all with the infinite love of the eternal Father.

I ask that the pulsations of the liberty flame be expanded throughout your nation and throughout this hemisphere. I ask that you, making yourselves a committee of one, will attune wherever possible with me daily in the adoration to your Presence and in the humble gratitude for all of the blessings that life has bestowed upon you and will bestow upon you as you make the necessary attunement to bring forth in your personal world all of the victory that God intends you to have and to share.

I am privileged, indeed, to address you tonight. I am privileged, indeed, to bring to you by the power of divine radiation a sense of the divine majesty.

Most individuals today, until they develop a sense of beauty, may stand before the old masterpieces in the cultural centers of the world and perhaps wonder just what sort of old fogies we were. And they perhaps think, in their first glances upon some of our works, that these works are not quite as wonderful as some of the other more perceptive individuals from among mankind say they are. And this is most understandable even to us who possess in retrospect now the power of looking back upon our own work.

As we behold the radiance of heaven, we must express to you that indeed these are poor works of art from the standpoint of the divine realities. But nevertheless they do convey the innovative disciplines of our school by the guiding hand of our own God Presence and Holy Christ Self, as it then functioned in accordance with our capacities at that hour, to bring forth the best that we could offer.

And this is what we ask that you shall do. Ladies and gentlemen, you cannot reach for the moon and draw the moon down to earth, but you can take the luminosity of that august body and bring that luminosity and power down into your feeling world and then produce balance in your feeling world.

All of the gifts and graces of God are yours for sharing with one another. Unfortunately, somewhere along the line in the history of this earth and its evolutions, some from among mankind decided that they wanted to be exclusive possessors of all the glory of God and especially the material treasures of earth. They have divided the parcels of ground. They have fought and argued and deprived one another of liberty, all for a paltry trifle. And yet as free as the air they breathe are the greatest blessings of life—the understanding of beauty, the joy in the face of a receiver of a gift. Have you ever observed the happiness in the face of a child when a gift for which that child has longed for is bestowed upon him or her?

The Judgment of Another Lifestream Ought Not to Be Undertaken

I know that some among mankind are prone to think that this generation is hardened, but I examine their feeling worlds from inner levels and I realize that people today are almost the same in their feeling worlds as they were in the days when I was Paul Veronese and in other previous embodiments. I realize, also, that there has come about in the feeling worlds of mankind a great shift and emphasis.

Nevertheless, I would like to point out that while many of the souls presently upon this planet now are those who were here back in the days of the French Revolution and other eras, there are some on this planet at present who are very highly evolved beings, having been brought in for the seventh root race.

You must understand, blessed ones, that all lifestreams are not the same, that the energies, temptations, and problems of individuals often differ. And therefore, for mankind in their outer consciousness to make a proper judgment and assessment of another lifestream is exceedingly difficult and ought not to be undertaken by the uninitiated or by those who are not especially trained and skillful in the manipulation of those energies and perceptions. Such an assessment ought to be brought about only by God-guidance, by ascended master instruction, and by the power of one's own Holy Christ Self when one is placed in a capacity of a psychiatrist or someone especially trained to analyze others.

Emancipation Comes through Simply Making a Call

I am sure that when the average individual today who will contritely fall upon their knees privately beside their bedside and—looking up toward heaven to their own God Presence as they did when they were but a child—shall say the simple words "O God, help me," the Deity will respond to them just as effectively as though they were to make a long and arduous prayer, which in itself might be very flowery and very sincere but nevertheless oftentimes unnecessary.

For the Deity does not expect mankind to be confined to a prison cell or a monk's cubicle in order to achieve emancipation. Emancipation often comes through simply making a call, knowing that that call will be answered.[1] For through this faith and knowing, the cable to the higher heights of heaven is woven and the energies of a man's or a woman's or a child's lifestream pour over that cable and magnetize the glory and attention of heaven and the love of the great Father of lights for the prodigal child.[2]

Therefore, ladies and gentlemen of God's own heart, the divine beauties are yours for the taking. They are yours for the asking. Beloved Jesus declared, "Seek, and ye shall find; ask, and ye shall receive; knock, and it shall be opened unto you."[3] These truths are just as effective today as they were two thousand years ago when wandering the Judean hillsides he uttered them. And you have only to prove to yourself their effectiveness by making the call.

There Are No Unanswered Calls

I am aware that there are those even among you who say, "But I have called and I have called sincerely, beloved Paul, for this or that to manifest, and yet it has not manifested."

Beloved ones, God tempers the wind to the shorn lamb,[4] and therefore I am sure that there is some special reason why your particular request was not granted. Perhaps it was not wise on the part of your own God Presence to bring to you the particular request that you asked for, and perhaps the greatest thing that ever happened in your world was that the Presence withheld that particular manifestation from you. And then again, perhaps it was only a trial to test your faith. There are many reasons why a call goes seemingly unanswered.

For truly the call does compel the answer. And in God's own way, the great Karmic Board,[5] your own God Presence, and your Holy Christ Self do truly answer every call. And none of your calls are ignored where sincerity, application, devotion, love, and strength are put into them as the energy of God returning by the great law of the circle to its Source.

This is the flame sent forth to manifest as life, which loving its own Source seeks greater identification with its Source, with the eternal fire—the sacred fire of the Presence before the great throne. And this call going forth asks for more of the Father's love and essence, and therefore there is always a response. If the response does not manifest in your outer world, it is always securely deposited within your causal body. For truly there are no unanswered calls.

Ladies and gentlemen, sometimes it is necessary that in addition to making the call to God, you should, after all, call to your Holy Christ Self for the extraction of this great answer from your own causal body, for it is deposited there in "the bank" and you must make the withdrawal.

I hope you understand the point that I am making. Sometimes you ask for a certain thing to be done and it is done at the moment, however it does not manifest in your world. It manifests in the causal world, in the etheric world, but it must be drawn down and magnetized by you.

Blessed ones, I know, for I recall one particular angelic figure that I worked on in my artwork for eighteen years. And I looked into the etheric realm in my memory and I saw this cherubic face, and I struggled first to execute it in charcoal. And then I tried later to put it into oils. And there was a great difficulty in putting it into charcoal.

I struggled and I erased, and I struggled and I erased, and I used medium after medium. And yet I could not capture on canvas that face that hauntingly stood before me in the etheric. And yet for eighteen years I persisted, until at last I stood before it and knew that to the best of my ability that which was Above was executed below.

Give First to Others

Patience, blessed ones, is a great virtue. And yet in this hour of peril I do not expect that you shall have patience in the world order of things. I expect that you shall have patience in your personal worlds, for your personal worlds ought to be subservient to the cause of the world good. For this has always been the fiat of our Brotherhood—to give first to others and then to ourselves.

Knowing the Great Law, we sought to magnetize for the world, for mankind, for others, the blessings of God, and we placed ourselves second in all cases. This is truly a precept of the Brotherhood and one that is often overlooked by the beginning chela upon the Path, who enters into a communion with the ascended masters almost solely for that which he or she expects to receive.

But when the blessed chela comes to realize that in kneeling before his own Presence he ought to invoke for others the precious gifts of God as treasures of heaven brought to the earth for the relief and the release of the suffering of mankind, then there is a manifestation in his countenance of true beauty, and we who perceive the soul of man blooming in mankind's countenance are then able to behold the true face of a man or woman.

And this is art divine. This is art that we appreciate. This is art that the angels magnify. This is art that the blessed Christ himself epitomized as he lay in the manger when the angelic hosts and the shepherds came in loving adoration, when Mary[6] herself kneeled within her heart and said, "This is a Christ, the Son of God."

This is the light that we desire to see manifest in every one of your faces and in the faces of all mankind, because it means a sublimation of a man's individual identity for the good of the whole. And the whole, by a divine recompense, returns in glorious magnification the beauty of the entire cosmos to that individual until there emerges from the stiffness and the hardness of the marble the eternal perfection of life immortal.

I thank you, and in the name of your own God Presence, bid you good night.

September 3, 1961

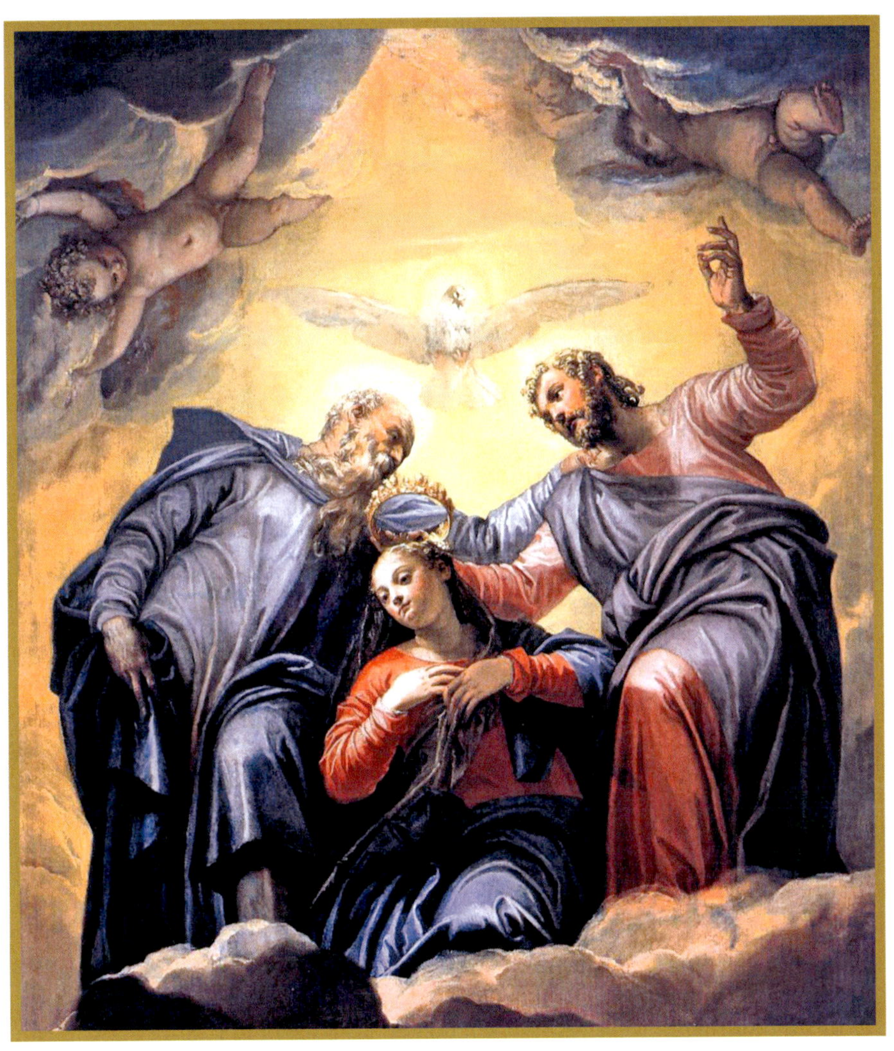

Coronation of the Virgin, 1555

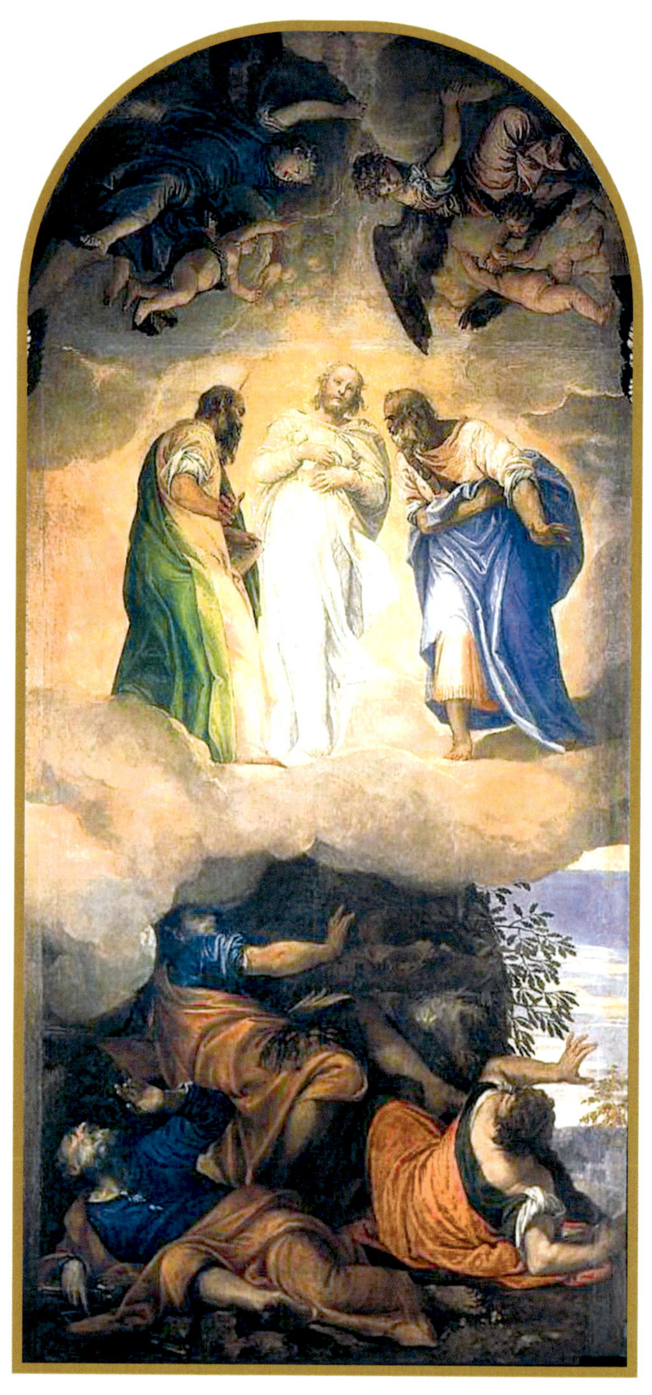

Transfiguration of Christ, c. 1555–56

*"Mighty God Presence of me, reveal the beauty,
the perfection, the light, and the glory of my
Christ image to me, and reveal it now!
And reveal to me the perfect outpicturing of light
for everyone whom I meet."*

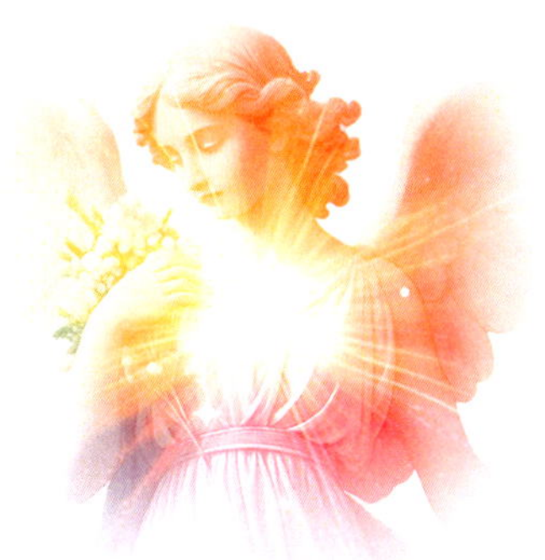

CHAPTER 5

The Manifestation of Divine Perfection

Where Harmony Abides, Beauty Abides

Most gracious ones, I am come tonight in a reverent sense of divine unity, which is beauteous in itself. For wherever a spirit of unity dwells and abides, by the law of infinite harmony individuals are able to sense their own divinity.

With the appearance of discord it is as though someone were to take a paintbrush and dab it across the canvas of life and remove that painting upon the easel, which was placed there by the Master Painter, and substitute chaos for beauty.

Each one of you is aware, I am sure, of the full meaning of harmony if you will separate yourselves in thought from your own human and mundane form, from your outer ideas, the weight of your body, the sense of your human personality, your idea of placement in time and space, and the idea that you are not now a divine personage but a person relegated to a place of lesser perfection.

If you will separate yourselves from this idea and will consider yourselves now as you are, as sons of God splendidly shining and radiant, I am certain that it will enable you to hold a vision comparable to the vision that God holds for each and every one of you. And if you hold, blessed ones, an image that is akin to the Divine One so that within your consciousness there is invoked a spirit of light's perfection, then I am certain that by cosmic law your outer self shall outpicture that which is within.

When there is an intrusion between the inner perfection of the inner spheres and the outer, there is a mist that forms between the consciousness of the light and the projected image. And therefore upon the screen of life there appears a dim shadow of the beauty that could be.

When mankind cease to stand in the way of their own light and they remove the impediments to their progress and their perfection in life, they will all manifest the same Spirit of Christ-obedience, Christ-reverence, Christ-dedication, and Christ-victory.

Mankind Must Learn to Draw Forth the Original Conception of Light's Perfection

One of the particularly impressive images that comes to my mind now is my first experience in attending an ascended master function after my ascension. Ladies and gentlemen, I realize that the mankind of earth have the wrong conception of our way of life. They seem to feel that because we are ascended beings we are bereft of beauty and dwell in some sort of a misty world of unreality. I hasten to assure them that this couldn't be further from the truth, for we dwell in a realm of exquisite perfection.

If there were a cameo image of a beautiful Greek child or a Grecian woman placed upon a table here on earth, I hasten to assure you that that same image in our sphere would have none of the human distortions but it would reflect in the pure light of God the image as it was held in the etheric mind of the artist at the time it was executed, as the rays of divine, transcendent light poured forth from that artist's own God Presence and gave him the original conception of light's perfection.

This type of perfection is that which mankind must learn to draw forth if they are to express it. In other words, beloved ones, rather than pay heed to the outer distortions and ideas, the whisperings of the carnal mind, and the thoughts and vain imaginings of men's hearts, if they will turn to their own great Divine Source and, looking there with a constant gaze, call to their mighty I AM God Presence and say,

> *Mighty God Presence of me, reveal the beauty, the perfection, the light, and the glory of my Christ image to me, and reveal it now! And reveal to me the perfect outpicturing of light for everyone whom I meet, and enable me to hold for them an immaculate concept of divine perfection.*

Then I am certain, ladies and gentlemen, that the Presence will reply and that that reply will have all of the dignity of heaven's love, all of the compassion of the Christ, all of the perfection of God in redundant manifestation, and none of you shall feel that you are lacking in any good and gracious gift.

There Is a Perfection Shining behind the Veil of Mortality That Can Be Contacted

I, therefore, recall that upon my first occasion when I attended an ascended master function, I was quite amazed at the beauty of the antechamber where this entertainment was taking place. For I wish to specifically state to you that it was an entertaining occasion when the ascended masters of the great karmic councils came together to discuss spiritual matters concerning the welfare of this planet. And if marble halls and presidential palaces and palaces of kings on earth can be said to reflect divine beauty—and I am certain that they do—then I tell you that that beauty was paltry and would pall into insignificance beside the glory of that antechamber.

I recall my thoughts. For as I walked into this great hall, I said to my own beloved God Presence, "O thou magnificent God Presence, I am so grateful for the opportunity to behold thy eternal perfection mirrored in living light substance and to no longer be subject to the carnal mind or the imperfection of mortality."

And as I looked upon this great hall, my gratitude mounted to my Presence for the thought that I should forevermore behold that love and that perfection. And as I have the soul of an artist, I am sure that those of you who have a soul responsive to the divine art will realize that in absolute cosmic hope the Father himself—the greatest artist of all, the great divine mighty I AM Presence in the Great Central Sun—conceived all of his creation to be a thing of beauty and a joy forever.

Therefore in that divine sense I urge upon all of you a seeking of the eternal treasures of heaven by trying to realize with your own God-given minds, even while yet unascended, that there is a perfection shining behind the veil of mortality and that this perfection can be contacted.

The Mighty Elohim Arcturus Is Blazing Light Rays throughout America and This Entire Continent

Ladies and gentlemen, how many of you are aware that while I am speaking to you the mighty Elohim Arcturus[1] himself has descended in the midst of this city?

How many of you are aware that he is blazing light rays throughout the land of America and throughout this entire continent tonight to preserve this continent from a wave of destruction that was launched against it, unknown to mankind in the outer world except for a few individuals?

How many realize that Arcturus has descended with a light of a thousand suns and tonight stands as a guardian presence of America's heart?

O blessed and beloved ones, you ought to give eternal gratitude to Saint Germain for his constant watchfulness over America and over America's heart. You ought to give constant gratitude to Saint Germain for his love of freedom for the earth and the love and devotion that he pours out to each and every one of the students of this activity and all the constructive activities of light, which in God's eyes are always one.

Stand Guard and Protect the Beauteous Sanctuary That Is within Your Being

Immortality—O beauteous and wondrous idea—I would sing an ode in my heart to thee, to the idea of forever adoring God, forever beholding Good, and forever knowing that I AM the perfect outpicturing of that eternal Good.

O ladies and gentlemen, do not let any outer condition prevent you from entering into the freedom of your Divine Presence! Do not let fear or doubt or jealousy or outer disturbing conditions enter your world! Stand guard and protect the beauteous sanctuary that is within your being!

Magnificent Cuzco,[2] the magnificent cosmic being, recently released through the *Pearls of Wisdom** an instruction for protecting mankind against the riptides of life,[3] and I am certain that the response of the student body has been most gratifying. I am particularly concerned with the students' use of that particular decree† because it helps to maintain a spirit of harmony within their hearts. And if harmony abides there, beauty abides there, for they are synonymous. God, harmony, beauty, love, light, strength, health—all are synonymous with one unity, the unity and perfection of your Presence.

Perfection, ladies and gentlemen, contains all the qualities of God, because all the qualities of God are perfect. And because they are perfect, you see, they are all alike because they are manifestations of divine perfection. Although mankind have named them and given them different names, yet actually they are one unity. And yet they are a variegated manifestation of that unity here upon this planet and in the hearts and minds of mankind.

Ladies and gentlemen, as I take my leave of you tonight, I wish to urge each and every one of you to let nothing hinder you from accepting the full beauty and perfection of your world. (Will you please be seated.)

I am most grateful, gracious ones, for those of you who stood, but it is best that either all of you stand or all of you remain seated in order to prevent a breaking of the cosmic pattern established during the time when these dictations are rendered. And so I trust that you will understand and will feel in no sense a rebuke of your individual lifestreams, for you are magnificent children of the light and I love each and every one of you.

**Pearls of Wisdom* are weekly letters of instruction dictated by the ascended masters to their messengers Mark L. Prophet and Elizabeth Clare Prophet for students of the sacred mysteries. For more information, see SummitLighthouse.org/Pearls-Of-Wisdom-Morya.

†Paul the Venetian is referring to "the Count-to-Nine Decree" by Cuzco, which can be found on p. 242. See pp. 236 and 273–75 under "Spoken Word" for an explanation of decrees.

Shed All That Is Not Good from Your Worlds and You Shall Enter into a Spirit of Beauty and Perfection

Dear ones, when the sun shines in its strength at noonday, who could capture that blazing light and put it upon canvas? And yet the memory of man is able to realize the meaning of "noonday."

When the full dawn of the cosmic light comes, it will flood the earth with a golden radiance of God's golden age. And then this blessed earth shall once again take on the true art of divine knowledge and all else shall pass away and fade into a pile of discard, there to be transmuted, released from manifestation in the outer world, and returned to the Great Central Sun for repolarization and released as life's energy to bless this planet and other portions of the great solar system and universes without end.

The cosmic scheme goes on and on and on, for the universe is vast and infinite. But we of the ascended masters' octave continue to sing our ode to immortality, for immortality itself is endless and the hope of an endless Good is ever present with us.

Therefore, shed all that is not good from your worlds and you shall enter into a spirit of beauty and perfection, which will enable you to reach the crest-tide of life that leads to your own individualized ascension.

The Unfinished Painting of Mother Mary's Ascension

I recall many years ago, after my ascension, how I had the opportunity of examining some of the etheric records of the minds of great artists through the centuries.

One of these artists—and I do not choose for personal reasons to reveal his name—dwelled for many years upon the idea of beloved Mother Mary's ascension. And he was able to create at inner levels a painting of her ascension, which so closely resembled the real thing that according to the etheric records there was very little difference between this painting that he created in mind and the actual event itself. It was an almost perfect picture of reality.

But there is one particular thing I would like to tell you about this. That painting was never completed! For the artist passed from the screen of life without finishing that grand conception that he had. It remains unfinished to the present day. And I hope that someone who reads these words in print or hears this statement or hears it upon tape, or in some way is made aware of this fact (which I am releasing tonight to you), will undertake to capture upon canvas the true picture that yet remains in the etheric realms of the ascension of Mother Mary. This would be a source of great inspiration to the world and would exalt in the coming age the idea of the Mother of the World.

May divine love seal you forever close to the heart of God, your own beloved mighty I AM Presence.

I, Paolo Veronese, Paul the Venetian, bless you all in God's name, I AM, and bid you good evening.

February 1, 1962

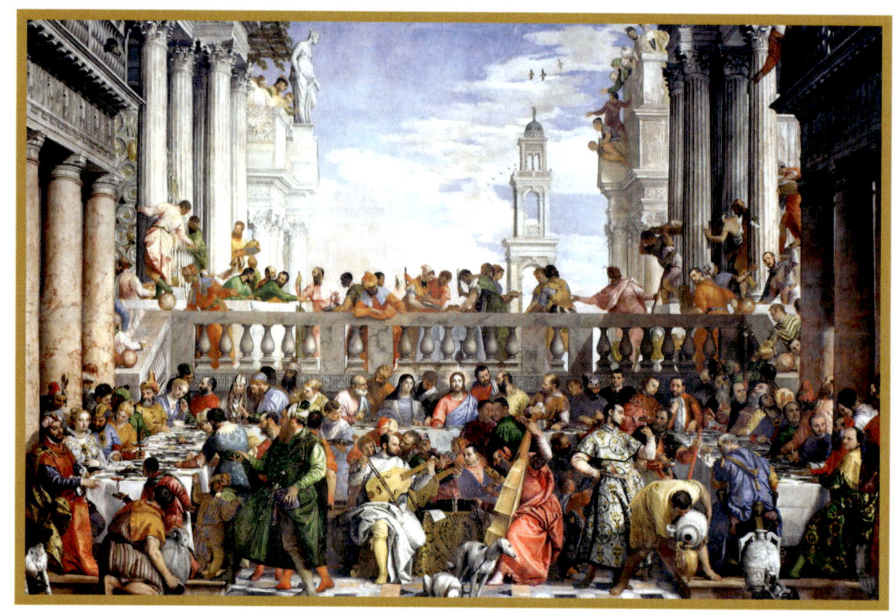

The Wedding Feast at Cana, 1563

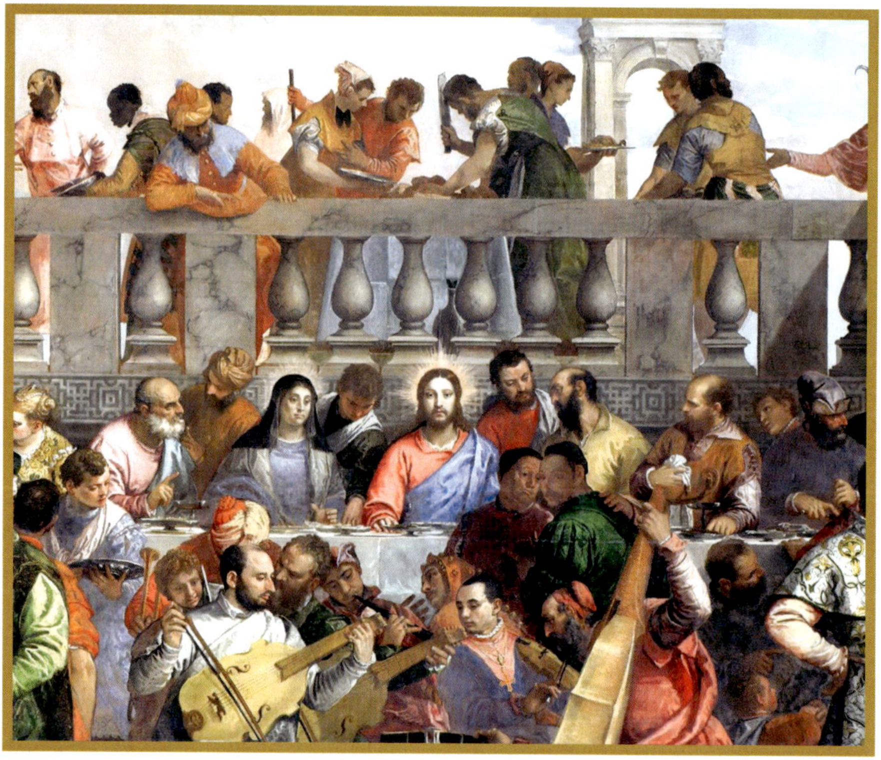

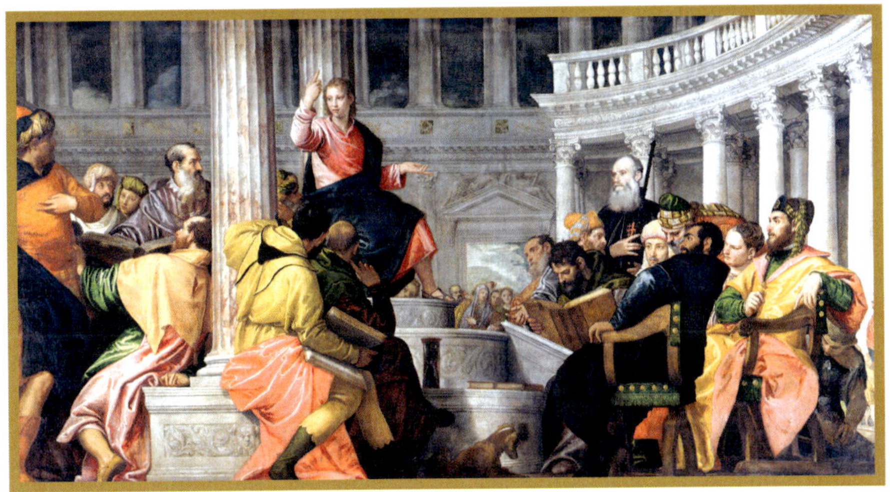

Christ among the Doctors in the Temple, c. 1550–56

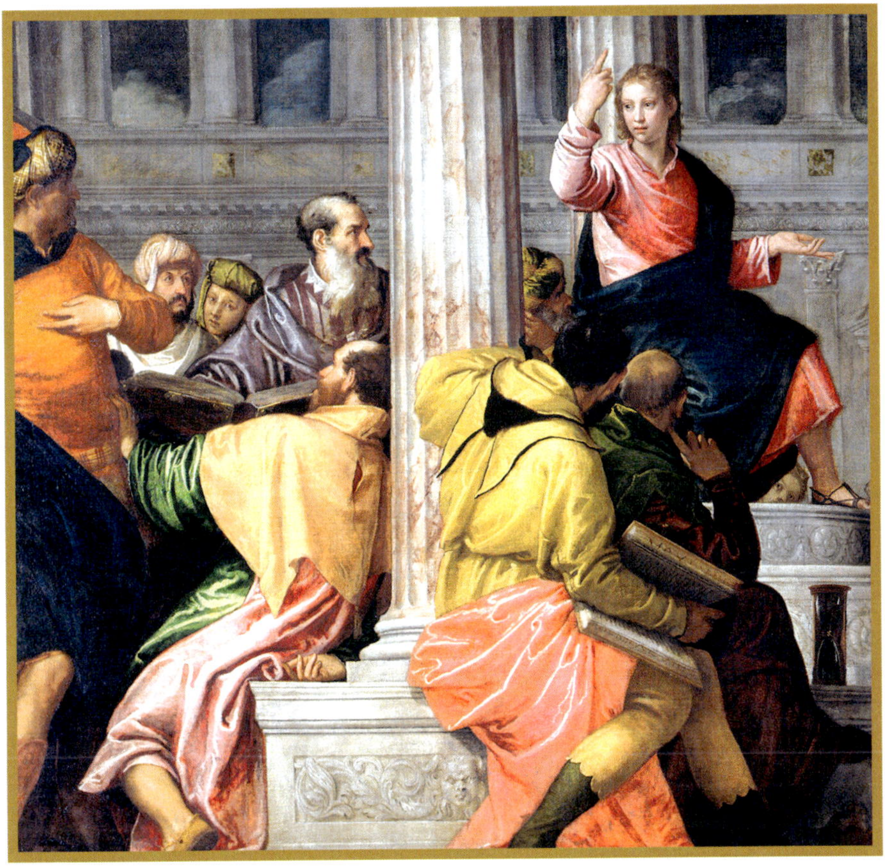

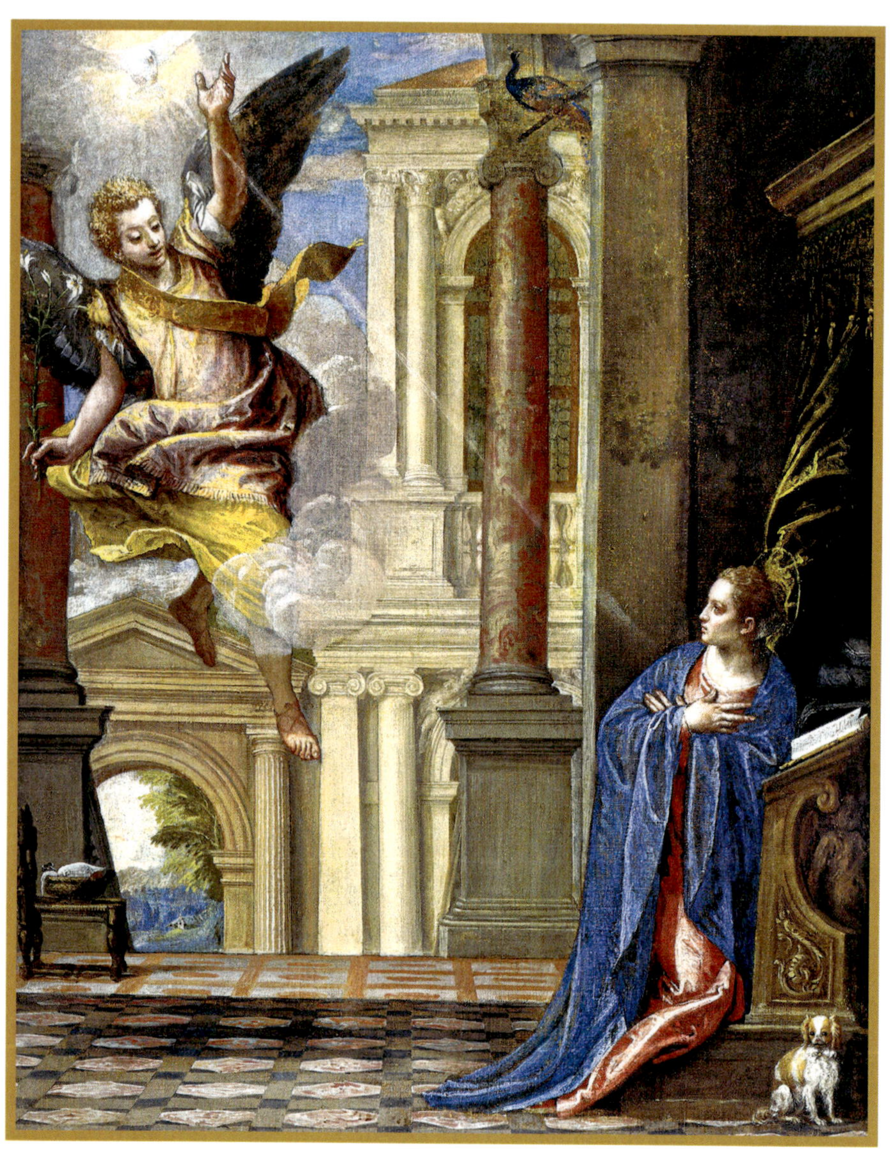

The Annunciation, c. 1560

Although individuals may seek on land and sea, in husband, in wife, or in home, in brother or in sister, in name and fame or fortune or place, wherever they will go they will never find any place so wonderful, so magnificent and so comforting as their own heart.

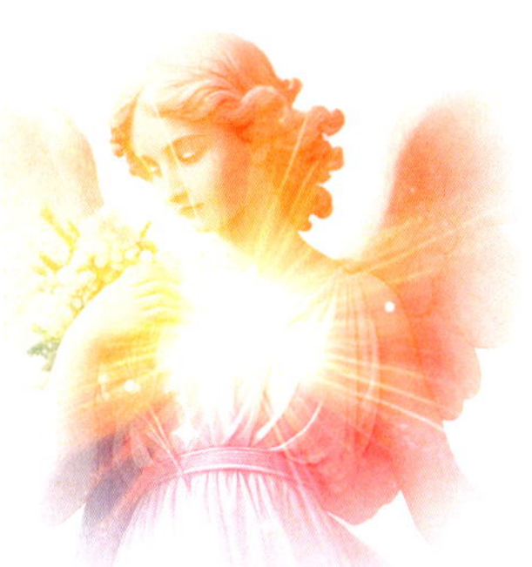

CHAPTER 6

A Chalice of Light

Act as God Acts; Ennoble Creation

I will lift up mine eyes this morning unto the eternal hills of light and behold there, in the radiant concepts of divine beauty, the splendid liberty of God, which he has consecrated to the creation of those objects and manifestations that are eternally true and perfect.

As co-creators with God and as agents of his eternal perfection, man was given the stewardship of life, light, and love. Everyone on earth was endowed with the immortal threefold flame, fashioned by the Deity within their heart. Everyone was given the co-equal opportunity of life, light, and love, enabling all to fashion and create perfectly.

As I behold this morning the beauty of God and, by contrast, realize the squalor of human creation, I am not bowed down by an impoverished sense on behalf of Almighty God, but I am somewhat concerned with mankind's need to learn how to create directly from the image and manifestation of God abiding eternally in the heavens.

Many of you are aware of the fact that in my embodiment recorded in history as Paolo Veronese, I was a painter of some renown, and some of you have seen my paintings on display in the National Gallery of Art in the city of Washington, D.C.[1] But although given worldly recognition by mankind today, those works of my hands seem somewhat pitiful by contrast to the actual beauty that I beheld even then. I feel that the technique that I possessed—for which I am eternally grateful—was perhaps limited in comparison to that which I am now endowed.

Therefore, this morning I have taken the "brush" of my words in my hand to frame in your minds through the use of these symbols—inadequate though they may be—the glorious inheritance and ability that has been conferred upon each of you by the threefold flame within your hearts. For I am somewhat concerned, as I said before, that mankind should understand the difference between the destiny to which they were directed by God and the detours and pitfalls of human creation into which they have strayed. And, as a result of which, they are outpicturing something far less than the loveliness with which they were originally and immortally endowed by God.

I do not come here this day to charge forth condemnation. But, rather, I would spur you on by the majesty of the eternal Presence to realize the need to gird up your minds and your beings for an eternal purpose.

The Transcendent and Infinite Glory of God

"Action," it has been said, beloved ones, "speaks louder than words." Therefore, when mankind shall begin to act as God acts, their actions shall so ennoble the creation and so exalt themselves that those so engaged will stand among their fellows as peers and yet as Christs, as God's man brought into manifestation. And think ye not that this is blasphemy. For the only blasphemy that mankind can perform, which is blasphemy directly against the Holy Spirit, is that which denies the design of God and the plan of God and the beauty and perfection implanted by the eternal One within the hearts of all men.

To deny the action of the perfect plan of God is to deny God. And such a denial is ever a sin, which is unpardonable so long as it endures. The moment this sin ceases to be committed, it is no longer the unpardonable sin. And since there is no vacuum in the creation, when man is not in a state of sin he must be expressing perfection. Man then becomes in action a co-creator with God, and he manifests in part the beauty of which he is capable. I have added the words "in part" because none of us in our octaves would ever begin to think that we could manifest, even here at this particular time, all of the infinite glories of God.

There is no ultimate, as we have told you before. The transcendent and infinite glory of God ever moves onward in ascending spirals of perfection. But we can behold face-to-face that perfection of God, which our eyes can see because they are illumined and touched by the fire of heaven, enabling us to see and perceive in the so-called invisible octaves.

Blessed ones, if your eyes were "opened" this morning, you would be able to see into our octaves as easily as I do. This expanded vision requires a special gift from heaven to be conferred upon mankind—the gift of seeing into the octaves invisible. In some cases it would prove to be disconcerting and somewhat uncomfortable for those who do not have the full protection, or perfection, of light and the full understanding of all that light can mean to them.

Let Your Gaze Be upon the Perfection of God

I am here this morning to prepare your consciousness for a descent of the great angelic power and the radiance of Saint Germain, which shall descend during the forthcoming Freedom conference, July 1962. Although I shall not be speaking at that time, I shall attend with other great ascended beings to lend the radiance of my presence to those auspicious gatherings and to bless each meeting with the God flame of eternal liberty.

You have heard it said over and over again that eternal vigilance is the price of liberty. And so I urge you not to succumb to the world of appearances. Remember, beloved ones, that the appearance world is the outpicturing of those among mankind who are neither artists nor sculptors of the divine perfection of God. They are men and women who are still apprentices at learning how to be Gods—and by that I mean how to become Godlike, how to sense that they belong to God. Therefore, they are lesser men and women only insofar as they have not yet attained the technique of using the brush or scalpel in a divine way, charged with divine love, so that they can outline upon the screen of their existence the perfection of God. Such as these are not worthy of imitation.

Therefore, you ought to imitate your own great Divine Presence, your Holy Christ Self, and the immaculate pattern of God held in the mind and consciousness of the Great Silent Watcher.[2] You ought to imitate the ascended hosts, the perfect Christ pattern of your perfection, and not some lesser image.

Countless times down through history, great hosts of ascended masters have empowered a lifestream to carry the torch for us and to go forth in the arena of life to represent us. Individuals, in their wrongdoings and in their desire to do despite to the great and noble cause of God, have sought to tear down the image of our representatives and to rake them into the mud of human creation.

Beloved ones, do not gaze upon mankind, no matter what their station, and expect to find perfection there. Then you will not be disappointed. Let your gaze be upon the perfection of God as it is manifested through the great ascended masters—through your beloved Saint Germain and those who have already made their ascension.

I do not say that you ought not to love one another, to charge understanding and compassion and gratitude to one another for the blessings you receive from the hands of friends. But I also counsel you to realize that those blessings—although sometimes wrought imperfectly—are performed by the power of light through their lifestreams, and it is the light of God in all men that must be revered and loved.

Remove the Results of Wrong Thinking and Feeling and All Human Creation

I am speaking now of individuals who are artists or musicians or who have some superior performance and culture to bring to you. If a great musician, for example, were to strike ten thousand perfect notes, men would crucify him for the performance of one imperfect note, all the while expecting mercy for themselves if they were to strike a dozen imperfect notes. This is human nature in its present state of development. It is not the divine character, which forgives and assists and renders a service to the light to assist each lifestream to become more noble, more elevated, and more a part of the great perfection of God.

Progress, beloved ones, is made both individually and collectively. There are those among you who lose sight of this fact and who sometimes feel they struggle alone amidst the turmoil and confusion of life. You do not struggle alone. Just as the hairs of your head are numbered, so you are observed in your struggles, and the assistance of heaven is given, especially at the hour of greatest need!

And yet there are times when the gloom of human thought so discourages individuals that they, as it were, take a paintbrush dipped in black oils and smear it across the canvas of their consciousness and then search for the original picture that the fingers of God previously traced upon the canvas. A real artist would wipe his canvas clean before attempting to rework his initial drawing. Likewise, the students of light must first remove the results of wrong thinking and feeling and all human creation from consciousness with the violet transmuting flame, and then they shall perceive that the fingers of God have traced their perfection and that this perfection was worth waiting for.

I know something about patience. I have spent hours and hours laboring to produce a perfect image upon canvas. Once before my ascension I actually produced an image that I thought to be perfect, and in a moment of frenzy I destroyed it because it appeared to me not to be the exact replica of the ideal I held in thought. The world will never see that painting because I felt it was not perfect enough. Yet, earlier in this address I said that the work that I performed while upon earth was—by contrast with that which I am now capable—most inferior.

Look upon the Pure Image of Your Own Divinity

O beloved ones, the liberty that God has, the liberty that your souls have to express the perfection of God, is so glorious, so wonderful, such a benign opportunity, that I cannot but comment upon the fact that individuals, in the narrowness of human concepts, become bored with divine ideas. Boredom results from a lack of understanding of the divine ideas, which are ever present in infinite versatility. This state persists because mankind have not yet removed the veil that hides from their view the beautiful God-creation—a veil that they themselves have placed across the canvas of life.

Smearing paint across a beautiful canvas is an act of vandalism, beloved ones, and yet so many upon earth are guilty of this act. Because the law of karma is inexorable and cannot be broken, individuals must make recompense to the Great Law for each act that they either do ignorantly or in the full possession of their faculties of discrimination. Therefore, mankind can be said to be that which they are because it is that which they have perceived and envisioned.

How many times have you walked the streets and gazed upon some misshapen body, some twisted limb, some human deformity, and you felt your heart go out in pity to that individual? Beloved ones, I daresay that the more sympathetic among you have often responded to these appeals with the comfort of their hearts and hands extended in brotherly love to these unfortunates.

Do you think heaven turns a deaf ear to these appeals? We do not! But we turn first to the great Karmic Board and we read the record of these individuals' lifestreams. And when we perceive the reason behind it and that which is being produced because of the great karmic law, we understand why sometimes these souls cannot be delivered on an instant. In other cases, individuals can be healed instantaneously by a touch of the hand, by a prayer, by a glance, by a ray of light poured out from heaven. "Be thou made whole"[3] can be spoken to them, and they will respond to the great call and ever thereafter lift their eyes adoringly to their own Great God Self, desiring to outpicture it among men.

Oh, that man would learn to look upon the pure image of their own divinity and then attempt, if but feebly, the portrayal of that image among men! How often, how often do individuals declare, "I will not attend church services. I will not go here or I will not go there because I do not wish to be a part of human strife and human misery. I do not particularly desire to mingle with people, for I feel that people are discordant."

These people are misanthropes and do not realize it. They hate mankind only because they hate the creation that they themselves are expressing. And because of personal shame, they do not wish to fellowship with others so that the thorns of another's branches may not become caught in their own!

Beloved ones, feel free at all times to mingle with those of spiritual tendencies—those who desire to exalt life. Be happy and joyous that you can come together and assemble yourselves among mankind for the purpose of worshiping Almighty God and the great ascended masters.[4] This is a divine spirit of liberty, which sweeps across the world and cuts people free from the briars of delusions that they have imposed upon themselves.

Many people in the world are full of myriad excuses, which they give as to why they will take no interest in God. None of them are valid. None of them are real. They are all rationalizations of the human intellect and error. But you, blessed ones, have the opportunity to make calls for those lifestreams, that they may be delivered from the evil of human creation and that the paint that is smeared upon the canvas of their lives—no matter by whose hand it has been done—will be removed by the infinite power of the Holy Spirit and there will be revealed in their lives the proud perfection of God.

You may wonder as to why I use the words "the proud perfection of God." It is because the Spirit of God takes delight in the work of his own hands. He is joyous because of the perfection and the quality of perfection that manifests in that which he has created. This beautiful manifestation of God's perfection is a chalice of light forever!

The Chalice of Comfort Given to the Maha Chohan

Speaking of chalices, I want to tell you that for a period of seventeen years I have been at work at inner levels in constructing a beautiful chalice to present to the Maha Chohan, and this very day it has been taken to him in his home in Ceylon. There it stands in his retreat.[5]

The base of this magnificent chalice—which, incidentally, is snow-white in color—is set with three rings of precious stones, all resembling diamonds. One band, beloved ones, is pink, another is pale yellow, and the other is a radiant blue. These three concentric rings around the base of the chalice are charged with the wisdom of God, the will of God, and the love of God.

The symbol therein is this: The will of God can be a great comfort to those who understand it, for when the will of God is understood, men will say, "God is good." When the wisdom of God is understood, the "why" God has permitted this and the "why" God has permitted that will be answered in a manifestation of the great divine Law, flooding forth into the consciousness of men. And that too will be a chalice of comfort to them, for they will drink the comfort of divine wisdom.

Could divine wisdom be uncomfortable? I challenge you, beloved ones. Could it be? Then last but not least, the radiance of divine love itself will be partaken of as a feeling—a feeling of infinite care, a care for each of the creatures of God regardless of the size or dimension of that creature.

The Father, in giving life, has given himself to all. And because he has given himself, he gives the infinite possibility of expansion to all, and the leaven of the Christ light poured out into the heart's chalice of each individual is the greatest comfort they shall ever have.[6]

The Comforting Place of One's Own Heart

Although individuals may seek on land and sea, in husband, in wife, or in home, in brother or in sister, in name and fame or fortune or place, wherever they will go they will never find any place so wonderful, so magnificent and so comforting as their own heart. There, the life that God has created and sustained is flooding over the brim, hoping to express the perfection of which it is capable. It gives into the keeping of the stewardship of individual man the power to choose for himself, to walk through the narrow gate that leads to the fullness of his own God-identity, and the outpicturing upon the screen of life of the verdured perfection of God, which manifests then for all time as a *man* of God, a *man*ifestation of Liberty's flame—the fleur-de-lis of love, wisdom, and power—a *man*ifestation of eternal comfort.

You will then be a being of beauty and a joy forever, for you will then have become an ascended being, a Christ—a Cosmic Christ—infinite in conscious action. You will rise in the arms of infinite love until you, as the Maha Chohan does, will be able to render a service to a portion of life everywhere.

In the great perfection of life that swells through this galaxy, flooding out through the grateful cosmos, you will be a part of the flame of omnipresent life. That flame, like music and perfume and light, weaves upon the screen of cosmic law all of the unfolding mysteries of God made known to you from within and from without forever, by the charge of divine love.

God Shall Direct Your Journey unto the Temple of Comfort

Now, my beloved ones, this beautiful cup, which I have worked on for so many years, has been given into the keeping of the Maha Chohan. I shall not further describe it to you today for a very special reason. The reason is that I ask those of you who are spiritually perceptive and love the Father to call unto God with fervor and determination until, while you sleep at night, God himself shall direct your journey unto the Temple of Comfort in Ceylon, and your own eye shall behold the work of my hand. And then I think that you will be grateful that I did not try to describe it for you in words. For you will see an ascended master jewel of perfection resting there. The Great Divine Director[7] and the members of the Karmic Board, who have all witnessed it, have said that it is indeed a splendid thing.

I hope now that you too shall realize this day that you are a splendid thing, a *man*ifestation of God—not a puny personality, not a human creation full of faults and flaws, but a child of light, splendid in all your dimensions, the work of God's hands, the work of your own Divine Presence manifesting now and always joy forever, forever, and forever!

May the blessings and the pulsations of Liberty's flame blaze through you now to bring peace in God's name, which places within the chalice of your being the fleur-de-lis of eternal comfort, the presence of light there within you, beating your immortal heart.

Thank you and good morning.

June 24, 1962

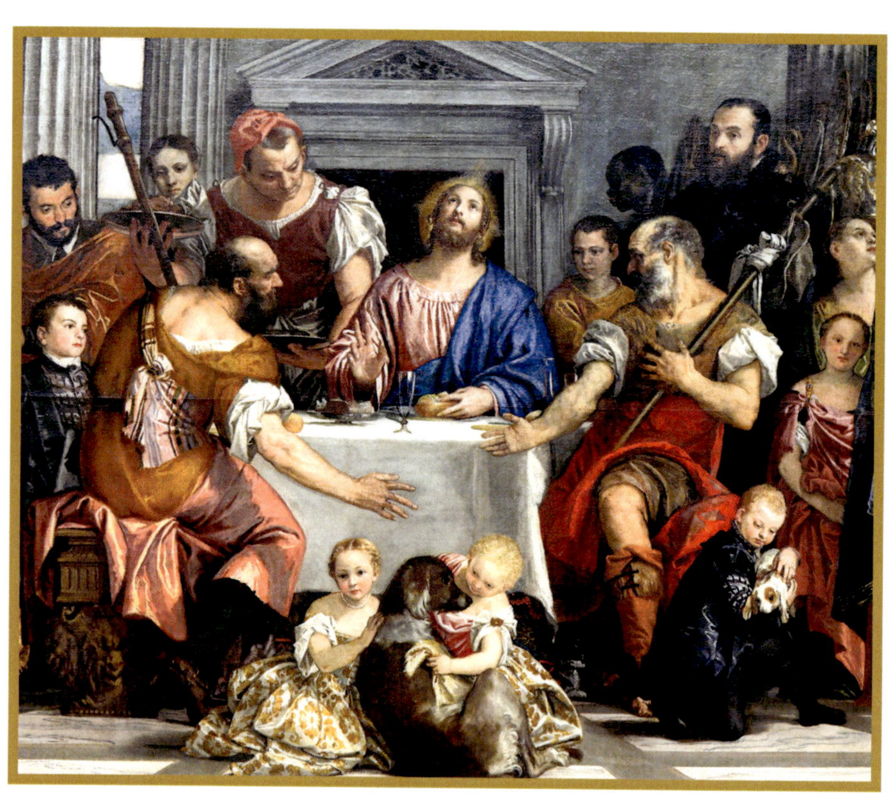

Supper at Emmaus (detail), c. 1559–60

When you too arrive in the octaves of light, as I did, you will be ever grateful for each rosebud of love and truth that you have garnered and nourished upon earth.

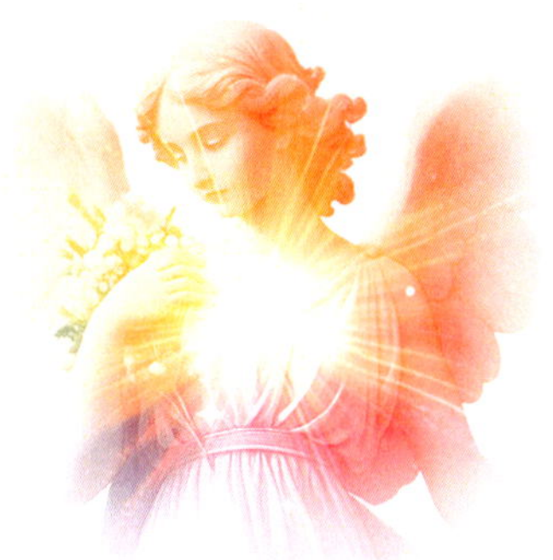

CHAPTER 7

Gratitude for All That Life Can Bring

O wondrous dawn of beauty and peace spreading o'er the world from the fountain of the Infinite! How roseate is thy majesty, the magnificence of love touching from the greater world, the higher Reality, the aureole of light within each heart!

Let the floodgates of heaven's mighty tide be opened! Let the dams of human constructions of man's hardened hearts break before the mounting pressures of life calling for a harvest of souls!

How long, blessed people, do you think Almighty God has waited to see the arrogance of proud spirits bow down to acknowledge his wonder within themselves? They do not concede or know his nature, and it is frequently as though they resent the helpfulness of his hands. And yet he continues to minister to as much of their needs as they will receive!

Years ago, when entertaining the blessed being known as the Goddess of Liberty,[1] who dedicated my humble château for God, she said to me when taking her leave:

> One day the service we do will be appreciated by many more than at present among mankind. It is like the worth of your paintings, beloved brother Paul, when you were embodied as

> Paolo Veronese. They had little value by comparison to their worth today. It is as though a man's true worth is perceived after his passing from the screen of life, and yet—because we do not pass from the screen of life—we must continually serve the needs of mankind and can never accept or be conditioned by their thoughts.
>
> One day mankind will all be happy to be conditioned by the greatness of their own spiritual nature and will seek it with renewed ardor. We can never enjoy nirvana and the full peace of heaven until our brothers of the lost sheep are safely nestled within the mighty protection of the Father's heart. Our service to the earth must continue, and we must prepare many to follow in our footsteps so that when the great law of initiation speaks unto us "Come higher," others will be ready to take our place in raising their brothers. You will find no difficulty, my brother, in having people appreciate your service of love. But to find one whose heart's chalice can compare with your own is yet another thing.

These intimate words have stirred and inspired me in those quiet times when, not showing loving souls through my retreat, I have contemplated the richness of universal love that has freed me from a body prison and has kept within me the immortal blessing of a living consciousness, of a breathing awareness of the transcendence of spiritual life.

When you too arrive in the octaves of light, as I did, you will be ever grateful for each rosebud of love and truth that you have garnered and nourished upon earth. You will know that the miracle of seeing God in man and nature is a wonderful preparation for expanding your spiritual light as you rise to our treasured octave.

Mankind have thought of the ascension as the attainment of all, and surely it is the brave beginning of victory, the reward of faithful service, and the fullness of God's gift to man. But wondrous though it may be, it is but a step on the infinite ladder of cosmic love and opportunity for service.

The Glory of Life

I want to nurture within you, beloved ones of the eternal Path, the need to fulfill your simple day-to-day destiny, and that well! "How can any good thing come out of Nazareth?" Well, dear ones, I will tell you. It is simply because a very wonderful gift was first put into Nazareth!

If mankind do not get out of life what they want, it is truly because they did not put into it what they wanted. It is never too late. As long as there is life, there is hope. The fairest flower—whether in bud or the fullness of bloom—bears the perfumed essence of immortality. Within the scattered seed is a perennial satisfaction, creation rising from creation in crescendos of loveliness.

To be any part of this glory of life is wonderful. Each year thousands upon your planet exit from life by opening themselves to the despondent vibrations of the suicide entity. Opportunity to aid these people may be forthcoming ere long, and wonderful ways of binding up the wounds of the world are being promulgated in our councils.

Let us all together now express our gratitude for all that life can bring—for satisfactions hidden and revealed, for harvest and season, for flower and fruit, for hope and fulfillment. And above all, let us keep saturated with the essence of that light that never fails in seed time, harvest time, winter or summer, to meet the many needs of all in our octave and yours, and as ladder-steps rise here and there, revealing a glimpse of that priceless glory and beauty that shall yet be!

Your brother's keeper—

Paul the Venetian

September 14, 1962

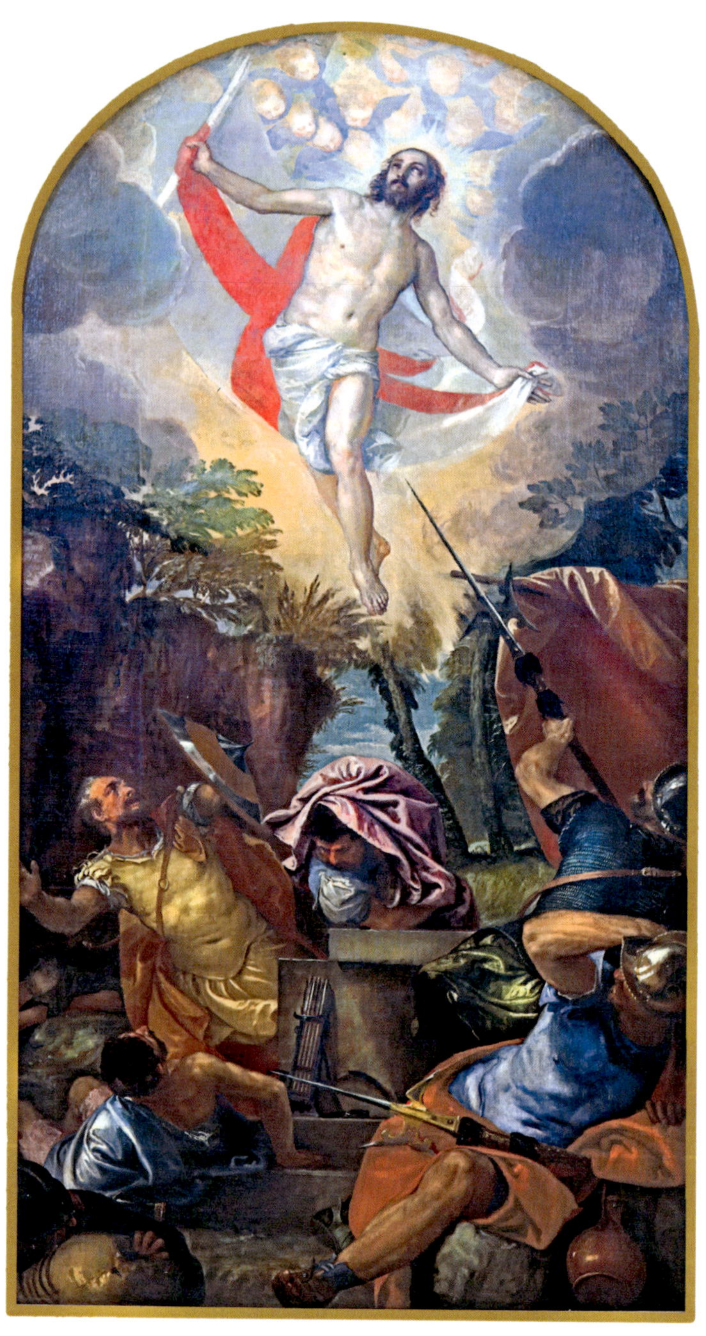

The Resurrection of Christ, c. 1560

When you begin to express gratitude to God for making the design of perfection for your own life, you, there at that moment, begin the release of the fullness of that perfection into your world! And beloved ones, that is the beginning of your ascension!

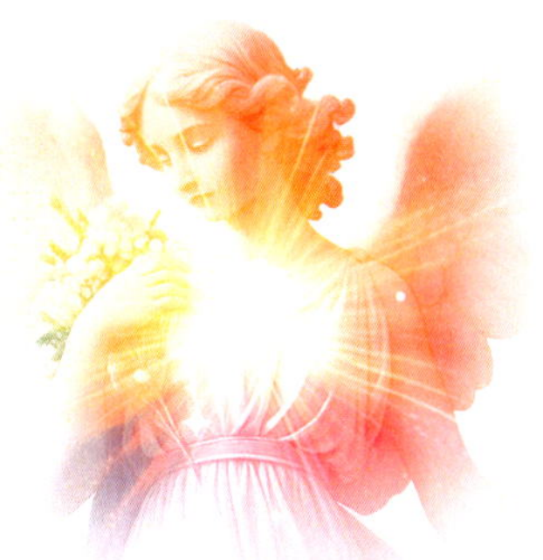

CHAPTER 8

DIVINE GRATITUDE

Rejoice in the Divine Abundance

O beauteous and wonderful door to the temple of the heart of every man, of every angel, of every cosmic being, open now. Open now to the consciousness of the light of gratitude as the catalytic power to release more abundant life into manifestation everywhere, in every beating heart.

I am come this night in the radiance of the consciousness of immortality to flood forth and charge that immortality into waiting hearts anxious to receive every good gift from the Father of lights,[1] whose God-design is the immortal birthright of every man, chiseled not with a sculptor's tool but by the power, the love, and the wisdom of Almighty God to work* in living flesh a new heart, to renew the spirit of man, and to exalt him into the wonders of eternity.

Beloved ones, pause for a moment now and reflect only for a moment upon the hardship that has been in existence upon this planet through the annals of history, and ask yourself if you believe that this hardship was the plan, the idea, or the concept of Almighty God.

I am certain that the answer will swiftly come from your heart of hearts that God could not design any condition or set of circumstances

*to fashion, create

that were not perfect. Rest, then, in his perfection, with gratitude for his heart. His heart is your own heart, a haven of refuge to all who will cast themselves upon the mercy of God, knowing that the mercy of God does not fail.

"I am my brother's keeper."[2] You have heard these words and expressed them often. But how many, beloved ones, are able to express them perpetually and under any condition with which they may be confronted. This is so frequently the initiatic experience that individuals fail, and therefore they are not able to express the fullness of divine gratitude. For there is lacking in them the completion of that God-design, which impersonally loves all life and desires that the God-design of every individual shall manifest in that individual the fullness of the divine plan.

Open your hearts, then, all upon earth, to receive the fullness of divine gratitude. Let gratitude, like an army, march into your heart. Let it become amplified by the power of ten thousand times ten thousand. Let paeans of praise rise from your immortal being as from the angelic hosts, the cosmic beings, and the ascended masters.

"My Burden Is Light"

Beloved ones, do you think that in our octave we no longer express gratitude? I tell you, there is not a moment in existence in the eternal realms that we do not pour out our gratitude to God, and the wonders of our gratitude are far beyond the gratitude that we expressed before our ascension in the light. This is simple and easily rationalized by even an ordinary individual. For the wonders of heaven are progressive wonders, and the unfoldment of the consciousness of immortality is a divine revelation that begins after man's ascension to express in a wondrous manner that which could not have occurred before, simply because of the calcination within man's four lower bodies.

You see, beloved ones, as soon as enough of the calcination and karmic conditions are removed, individuals do not long remain upon this planet in a physical form but rise on wings of light and love into the higher octaves, where dwell the cosmic beings and the ascended masters.

And, beloved ones, in our octave the reality there is far more transcendent than those realities experienced here, and the wonders are easier in their manifestation. For the law of the fire—the law of the sacred fire—pours forth and immediately produces the perfection that we desire.

You, beloved ones, continue to struggle at times for your existence, for even the breath of life at times, because of the enclosure of the atom, because of the density of human creation, and because of that externalized ugliness that has been a burden upon mankind's back until en masse there have been times when the human race has resembled at inner levels a hunchback walking with a tremendous weight and burden upon its shoulders.

The presence of the Holy Christ manifested so that mankind might recognize the weight of light. You have heard the words of the Christ, "My burden is light."[3] Well, beloved ones, the Christ, when he uttered those words, spake truly. For the light of God that never fails is the only responsibility and burden that rests upon cosmic shoulders.

Stop and think about this, beloved ones. It is true that the Father serveth and the Son serveth and the ascended masters continue to serve mankind. But it is effortless compared to human creation. For we but speak and the Word becomes flesh. That is to say, we but *desire* it, we but *will* it, and God wills it through us. And with the speed of light, instantly there manifests in our octave the perfection of God and the wonders of God.

Yes, beloved ones, in our octave we continue to create and to expand the mighty consciousness of individual duality.[4] For we are a *part* of God but we drink in the *all* of God from day to day, and there is never any "ultimate" anywhere in the universe but an ever-expanding, transcendental experience whereby those of us so counted worthy expand our light in cosmic initiations beyond compare.

Be Your Brother's Keeper

Beloved Gautama, the Lord of the World, had a series of experiences, even recently, that he will not discuss even with those of us who are his personal friends. This is because he cherishes these experiences so dearly that he desires to hold them between his own divine consciousness and the consciousness of God within the Great Central Sun.

There are certain experiences that come to individuals, beloved ones, that are so sacred that these individuals ought not to discuss them with one another but they ought to hold these experiences and to recognize that in doing so they will draw to themselves more and more of the wonders of heaven.

When these experiences are dissipated through idle conversation, there is a certain casting forth of the pearls before swine.[5] For, beloved ones, even though an individual may be discussing these personal and private matters of their inner being with one who is on the Path, that one who is on the Path may not yet have developed spiritually to the point where he or she can thoroughly understand the wonders that the other individual may have experienced. And in ignorance of the Great Law, [though that one who was told of the experience] may desire to do right, he or she may mock the one who related the experience, and consequently a karmic condition is established, which that beloved one must at some time pay for.

So, it is much better, in being your brother's keeper, to hold inviolate within your heart certain of the wondrous experiences that are afforded you at various times as sacred and thus secret.

This that I have expressed here is not a desire on the part of heaven to isolate you. But it is, rather, a desire on the part of heaven to bring you closer together in a great spiritual bond whereby as you draw closer to the sacred fire you will naturally gravitate closer to the sacred fire element within one another.

This work, beloved ones, is above and beyond personality. It is not desired, nor is it desirable for individuals in this work to merely seek to please the outer human self. It is far more desirous that they seek to please that mighty Divine Self, that mighty I AM Presence of all life, and thus win their eternal Victory.

Beloved ones, the mankind of earth, whose opinions are respected by so many (and this is understandable), can never grant you your ascension in the light. Even though the entire world should applaud your every act, this will not free you!

Beloved Jesus spoke long ago and said, "Friendship with the world is enmity with God."[6] He did not desire that the students or the Christians who followed him should feel an enmity with mankind, but rather a friendship. And thus the deeper meaning of his words must be sought and understood.

In expressing, then, divine gratitude, you need have no fear, because divine gratitude is an impersonal love poured forth through the heart of your mighty I AM Presence. And, beloved ones, when you meet one another in the fields, the forests, or the marketplace, you may praise the God within one another and expand that God Presence within one another whenever you expand the threefold flame by praising and blessing the threefold flame in that individual.

You may say, "Well, beloved Paul, I cannot expand the flame of God; only God can expand it." Well, beloved ones and dear hearts, let me say to you that you are now and forever a part of God. He destined you to be this, and only when you take command in his holy name to be your brother's keeper and to be the keeper of the sacred fire within him do you truly act the role of a God in manifestation.

And then the God in man is active in you, and you no longer are a "puny individual" seeking for praise and adulation from others by some exploit or some wondrous thing that you are able to externalize. But rather, you are great because the God in you is great! And then I think that "all these things shall be added unto you."[7]

Open the Door of Your Heart to the Power of Your Mighty I AM Presence

Name and fame, beloved ones, means nothing to God. For he can endow at a moment the smallest, the puniest, and the weakest individual with all of his power that the moment may require, and he can hallow individuals who may seem obscure and insignificant.

Beloved ones, remember that the angel appeared to the shepherds on the hillsides and filled their hearts with wonder and rejoicing at the birth of the Christ. So it is often, beloved ones, that the mighty I AM Presence chooses obscure and seemingly insignificant individuals for a mighty purpose. Often those individuals are not aware as to why they were chosen, and with incredulousness they turn to their fellowmen and say, "But I am not exactly fit for this. Why would God choose me? There are so many others more talented, having greater honor."

Well, beloved ones, the mighty I AM Presence makes no mistake and cannot fail. And although God has called all upon earth to a high and holy calling to externalize a beautiful and wonderful design that will make their hearts eternally grateful, it yet remains for individuals to accept the opportunities afforded them and to open up the doors of their own heart to the mighty power of their own mighty I AM Presence and to let that Presence flood through them the consciousness of the living Christ in manifestation. [10-second pause]

> *O angels of liberty, thou wondrous beings who pulsate in the liberty flame, who have for so long served the cause of liberty and the holiness of its meaning upon earth, come now and expand thyself through the consciousness of these individuals, who have journeyed here as wise men of old to behold the Christ within themselves. Let them feel now the wonderful liberty to perceive God without blasphemy, to perceive God within themselves, to perceive God within the hearts of all mankind.*

A Tribute to Saint Germain

Beloved Saint Germain, that wonderful friend of freedom known to many of you, deserves your support today as never before. He has never slackened nor has he been idle, but he has continued to serve the cause of freedom and the cause of liberty for the earth.

Let every elemental, every angel, every cosmic being pay him homage. And tonight, October 12, 1962, in commemoration of Columbus Day, I pay him homage in the holy name of God. [Congregation stands.]

[Paul the Venetian speaks to beloved Saint Germain:]

Holy Brother, blessed be thy name. At the Cosmic Council meetings, all mankind so fortunate as to be present in their finer bodies will behold the hosts of light arise and pay thee tribute. As Archangel Michael said this very week, "Thou ancient mariner who sailed the sea from Isabella's court and the land of the dons to the realm of

Massasoit, the sachem, to establish here in America a nation dedicated to liberty and freedom, may thy name be forever blessed."[8]

As a little boy long ago as the prophet Samuel, you said, "Speak, LORD; for thy servant heareth."[9] Today your radiance covers the earth with the power of freedom. Christopher Columbus, Francis Bacon, illustrious soul journeying through the living years,[10] thou livest still and forever, ascended and free—free not to serve mankind, if you would, but ever dedicated to this earth and the cause of freedom and the love of a people, who often do not know or appreciate all that thou doest for the light.

Hail, Saint Germain, thou friend of freedom eternal! May all honor thee, as thou so richly deservest. The Brotherhood saluteth thee and all who serve with thee in the cause of freedom.

Won't you please be seated.

Call Forth the Flames of Freedom over the Earth

As I began to speak this night, I advocated an opening of the door of your heart to God. I advocate now the sustaining of the open door. Beloved ones, the open door is sustained by cosmic unity—cosmic unity with all that lives, with the elementals, with the angels, with the ascended masters, and with your fellowmen.

I do not say that you should be brought under the power and dominion of mankind or that you should be obedient to mortal will against your own Holy Christ Self or God Presence. Nay! But I say, you should submit to the law of the sacred fire within all beings and recognize that there God walks.

It is true that individuals often choose or in ignorance walk in a manner wholly not in keeping with their own Presence and Holy Christ Self. These unfortunate individuals need your love even more, beloved ones, than those who are walking in the light.

I recognize, beloved ones, that some of these individuals are difficult to fellowship with. But, precious ones of the light, the mighty threefold flame within their heart is indistinguishable from your own! And you need not fear to fellowship with them at that level of consciousness where there is no distinction, and you ought to continue to call forth the flames of freedom over the earth so that the liberty that their heart and soul craves may come to them and that good may be multiplied and amplified.

Remember that upon the hillsides of Judea the Christ took the loaves and fishes from the small boy and brake them and fed them to the multitude.[11] He did not go to the kings or to the great and notable men among the audience, but he took them from the obscure child. And so a little child today shall lead them unto eternal life.[12]

The little child is the Christ Child within their own heart that has not been magnified by their own attention and therefore remains the infante.* And they remain undeveloped, spiritually retarded, not able to ascend as the Christ did nor to accept the breaking of the holy bread.

But this condition shall not always continue. A group the size of this one has the power according to the great law of the Karmic Board that was released a year ago in July[13]—the power of the ten thousand times ten thousand, in fulfillment of the ancient prophecies that one should put ten thousand to flight, and that one is a righteous one, armed with the power and might of the Holy Spirit.[14]

The Severing of the Veil

The Holy Spirit is the "Whole I AM Spirit" of God within you, your own mighty I AM Presence. This is God, your saviour. The magnifying of the Christ within you expands the light within the cells of your physical form. It expands the golden flame of illumination within your brain and mind. It expands the ancient spiritual memory of the very being of God within the etheric body of *you* so that you are able to remember the experiences of the immortal flame of God before you took individualization!

And when you come through the power of initiatic experience to that time—the *fullness* of that time when God shall sever the veil that separates the duality of man [from him] because every purpose in you is the purpose of God—that veil shall be rent in twain between the holy place and the outer world of form, and you shall emerge as did the Christ, a victor.

* *infante:* a younger son of a Spanish or Portuguese monarch

It does not matter from whence your outer origin. If your parents were farmers or Chinese or Caucasian, or whether they were pearl divers or painters of pictures, sculptors or musicians or laborers in the field, it does not matter because you all came forth from God. And in the great formless and form universe, you must be *in*formed that God is the author of the perfection of life. And the beauty of life—clearly delineated in the living Christ within you, made transparent in him whose aura in you will expand as the threefold flame in man—begins the process of creating a divine being out of that which for generations may have been a clod.

The soul of God is not a clod. And you, beloved ones, are a part of that soul, unseparated from it, as much as a drop of water taken from the ocean is still an unseparated part of the whole sea. And therefore, behold God in one another, and behold gratitude.

The God-Design Must Be Externalized in Divine Order

You may wonder why we stress gratitude. You may wonder why this evening I am speaking of divine gratitude so emphatically. Well, ladies and gentlemen, if you were able to see at inner levels, as I do, the mighty preparation that God has made for the creation and externalization of the God-design for one single lifestream, you would appreciate the individuality of yourself as a thing of wonder and beauty.

Precious ones, just as the Father designs the lacy textures and beautiful designs of a tiny snowflake, which exists for a moment and then melts in the heat to become water once again, so you, precious children of God, were called forth from the Great Formless Light to take embodiment upon this solar planet so that you might have those experiences that would exalt you, who were made lower than the angels,[15] to a place with the Christ, a Son and joint heir with God.

Religion, beloved ones, is manifesting upon earth because of the hunger within men's souls to search and to know the truth, because the truth does make men free.[16] But, beloved ones, the truth is not mastered in a moment. And if it were possible for us to convey all truth to you in one moment, we would do so because we know that at that moment you would be free. Do you see?

But, beloved ones, it is necessary, as a sower goes out to sow, that he put away his plow when the day ends and he begins again the next day and the next, until all of his fields are plowed and ready for cultivation, ready for planting.

Precious ones of the light, the God-design must be externalized in divine order, and you as children of the Most High God must in patience possess ye your souls.[17] In your eagerness to seek out the fullness of your divine victory, you sometimes unfortunately have trampled over one another, and with each trampling you have but trampled upon yourself.

I do not say these words to condemn you but to exalt you into the wonders of divine righteousness, for the laws of God are perfect and square and true. There is no angle to God except the triangle of perfection, the immortality of light. There is only one great circle of divine friendship between God and man, and none are excluded from it except they who exclude themselves.

I am here tonight to alert the chelas and the would-be chelas of the sacred fire to the need to express divine gratitude to its fullest measure in order that the seed-time may produce a fruitful harvest of divine abundance in their own individual worlds.

God has heard the calls and the prayers that you have made individually for perfection, for overcoming some particular and specific problem with which you have struggled. God has heard each such call. You may think that he has not answered you because you have not seen the manifestation of the answer.

Well, beloved ones, in your patience possess ye your souls! For often the answer has been forthcoming even before you were finished speaking, and it was God's ways and designs that were the answer and perhaps not your own. This was because you uttered these words according to the ancient mantrum, "Not my will by thine be done," knowing that the Father possessed the divine intelligence and capacity, beloved ones, to give you that right and proper gift that you *ought* to have and not that which you *think* you ought to have in human confusion!

Beloved ones, do you think Judas Iscariot would have betrayed the Christ if he had recognized the fullness of the great laws that were taught to him? Beloved ones, do you not realize that he subsequently and quickly recognized the error of his betrayal?

I wonder how many of you are aware of the fact that Iscariot has long since made his ascension, while some who walked closer to the Christ than he during the Palestinian embodiment of beloved Jesus yet remain in physical form.

This fulfills the sacred writings that state that many who are first shall be last, and the last shall be first.[18] Remember beloved ones, that "the zeal of thine house hath eaten me up"[19] is a proclamation of the intensity of the divine invocation whereby an individual may invoke in gratitude from God their spiritual needs and fulfillment.

Express Gratitude to God for Making the Design of Perfection for Your Own Life

Precious ones of the light, pause to consider for a moment that which you shall be. At this point, while you are now pondering upon divine gratitude, I would like each one of you now to enter into a spiritual artist's heart, one charged with the radiance of divine love. I would like you to forget your identity for a moment, and whatever pack of individual troubles you may have been carrying, and I would like you to enter into the Father's heart. I would like you to think of the Great King, your own mighty I AM Presence, the ruler of the kingdom of your own being, the ruler of the great macrocosmic world, the starry realms of the whole universe. I would like you to think of the great God-design that he has made for you, and I would like you to feel a sense of gratitude to him for making that design!

And beloved ones, do you know something? When you begin to express gratitude to God for making the design of perfection for your own life, you, there at that moment, begin the release of the fullness of that perfection into your world! And beloved ones, that is the beginning of your ascension!

For the light can penetrate between the atoms of your form and it can decrease the rate of human density and remove the cause and core of discord—and a divine man emerges. This is a thing of beauty and joy forever to the heart of God, and the great Godparents of this system of worlds, beloved Helios and Vesta in the very heart of this solar system, can rejoice.

May a Harvest of Abundance Unfold around the World

Now I would like to say a word to those of you to whom this system of dictation may prove new. Do not be weary, beloved ones, to hear my words, for there are not too many instruments upon this planet through whom the ascended hosts can manifest.

And beloved ones, I will tell you something else. The ascended hosts would long ago have stepped through the veil in many such meetings as these and would have manifested in a tangible form, except for the karmic responsibility connected with mankind, who would not recognize the greatness of that manifestation and would consider that it might be some human trick. And therefore, because they would think this—do you see, beloved ones?—and because they were dealing with a living, immortal manifestation of Christ victory, the karmic responsibility that would accrue to their lifestream would be much greater than that which would accrue to their lifestream were they to harm a lesser expression.

And so, beloved ones, we have deferred the stepping through the veil to most individuals until they have reached a place in consciousness where they are able to recognize us for that which we are, to recognize the humility of our being. For although there are those among you who consider us great, we consider ourselves only great servants and desire to be still greater servants of mankind.

Our hearts are charged with a love and a love-radiance that transcends the human imagination and concept. We want nothing from you except to share the love of God with you. We are not after either your purse or person. We are only after the externalization of the mighty Presence of God so that the Spirit of the Great White Brotherhood may expand throughout the earth and make of every government upon this planet a God-government of perfection, that a harvest of abundance may unfold the world around, which shall destroy all famine and want!

If I were, tonight, to open the spiritual channels of communication to you and carry you across the sea and even down into northeast Brazil and show you the squalor and the misery and the privation and the suffering of your fellowmen, some of you might be appalled. In fact, El Morya has commented that some of you might be so zealous that you would go out and start a mission to help those people and almost forget about the spiritual mission of life that has been assigned to many of you. Well, beloved ones, I am not about to do this, and yet I could take you, in this city itself, to places that would touch your very soul.

The All That You Give Is the All That You Live

As you ponder now the meaning of gratitude to God for all that you have—for your life, for your breath, for your intelligence, for the light of your eye, for the wonder within you that makes you seek for God, that makes you hunger and thirst after righteousness—remember the injunction of the living Christ: "Blessed are they which do hunger and thirst after righteousness: for they shall be filled."[20]

During this class it is our intention—and I refer now to beloved Saint Germain and myself, together with all of our beloved brothers of light—to pour out upon you the wonders of our octave, the love that we have and feel and are, that you may joy and rejoice in the divine abundance.

The outer symbols, which are here evidenced before you at inner levels, possess a radiance worthy of the attention of your being. I am sure that your outer consciousness may rejoice in this design. The fruits of the earth are yours, but the fruits of heaven are also. And we are more anxious to share these fruits with you than any others, for these fruits will remove from you every burden, will take away every necessity for struggle, and will produce in you and all mankind a peace that only God can give and only a godly one may know.

A godly one is one who seeks God with all of his heart, with all of his mind, with all of his being, who holds not back any part of the price. And this eternal vigilance is the price of liberty. For the all that you give is the all that you live. It is the life of God that manifests within you. And you can say with beloved Hilarion those words that he uttered as Saint Paul: "So then it is not I that live, but Christ that liveth in me."[21] And you will be God's man, beautiful, expanding, immortalized, worthy, cherished, abundant.

In God's name, I AM, may the eternal Christ peace of your eternal Presence abide with you now and always, guiding you through the day and through the shadowed nights until his light has turned you into the pure gold of his Being.

Then the high priest will have entered into the Holy of Holies and offered your life to God as a wave offering,[22] the sheaf of wheat, the grain of corn, which does not abide alone but falleth into the ground and dieth unto itself and its outer physical, materialistic manifestations, that it may expand and become many, many, many manifestations to the glory of the eternal Presence, to the unity of life, to the oneness of the divine plan fulfilled.

I thank you. Good evening.

October 12, 1962

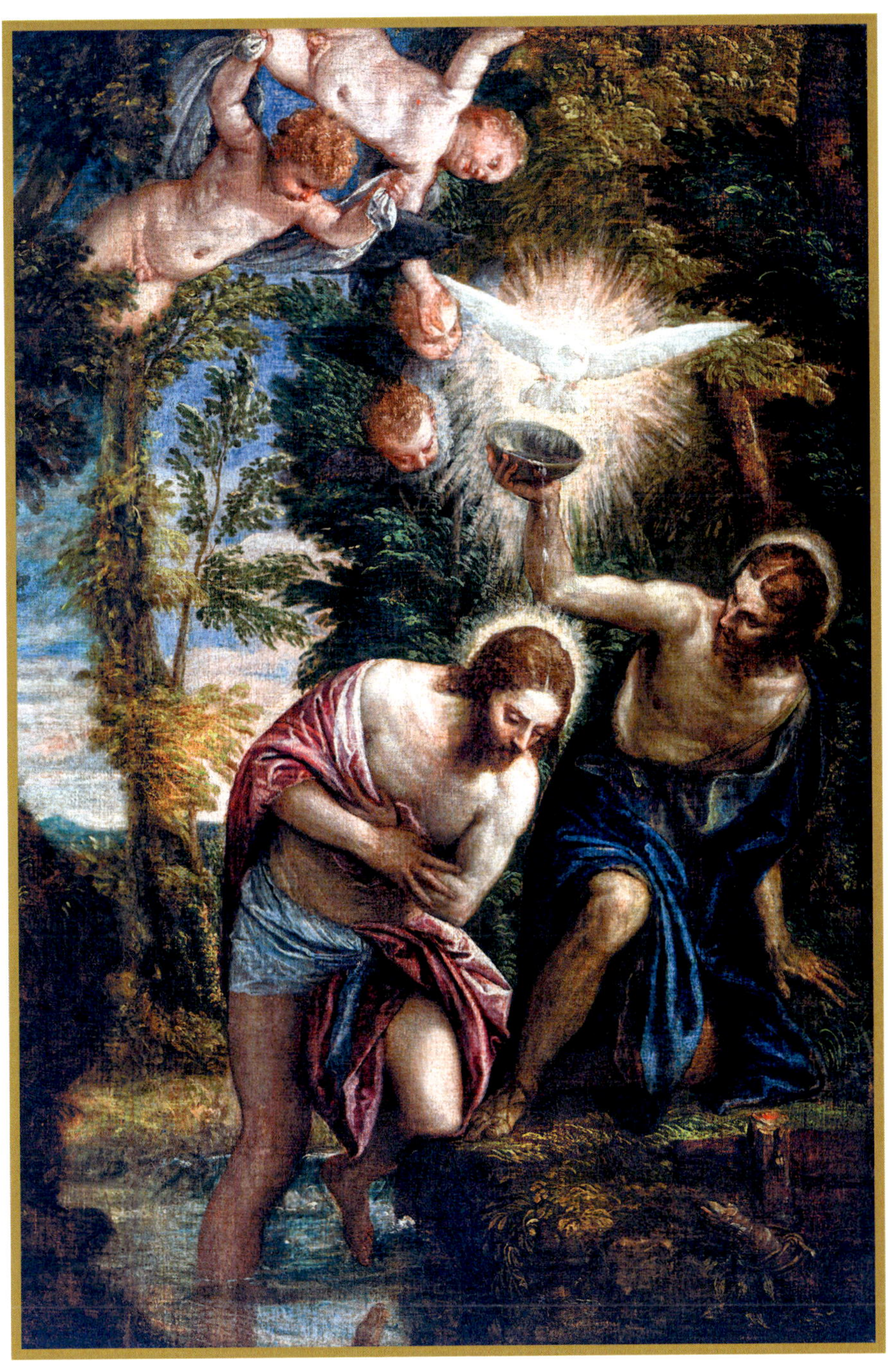

Baptism of Christ, 1584

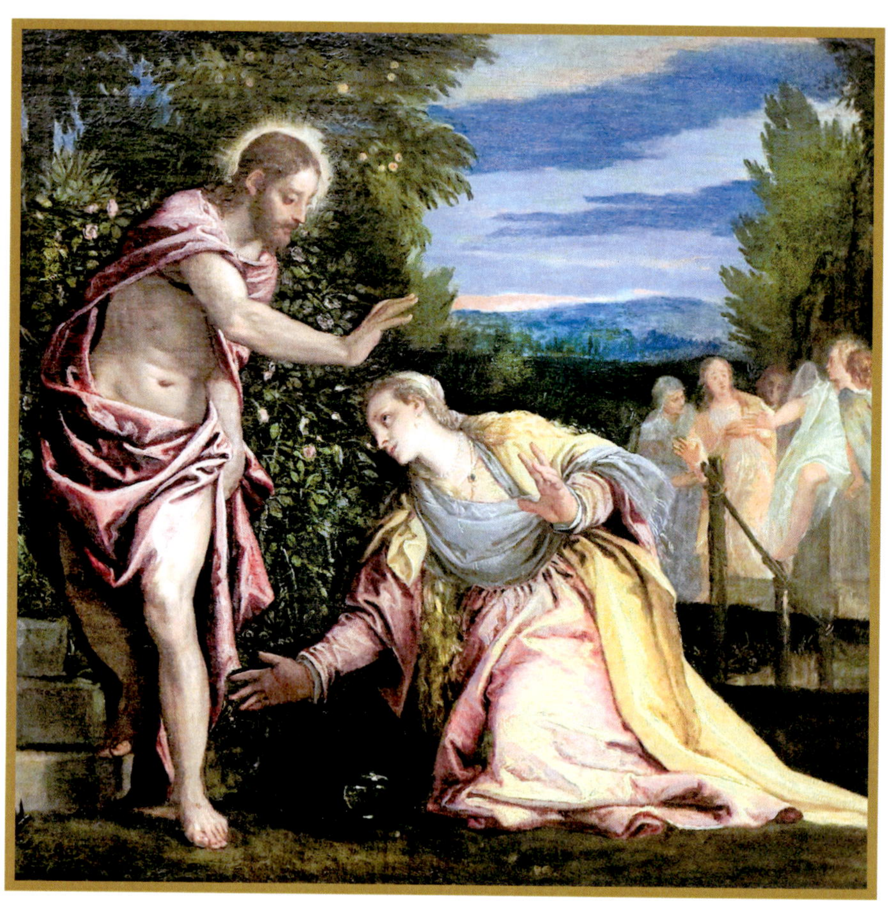

Do Not Touch Me (detail), unknown date

You will be surprised how the lovely "silent voices" of inanimate nature and animate nature alike will respond to your greeting, giving you a greater attunement with beauty and... with God as you hold his hand while walking in the beautiful out-of-doors.

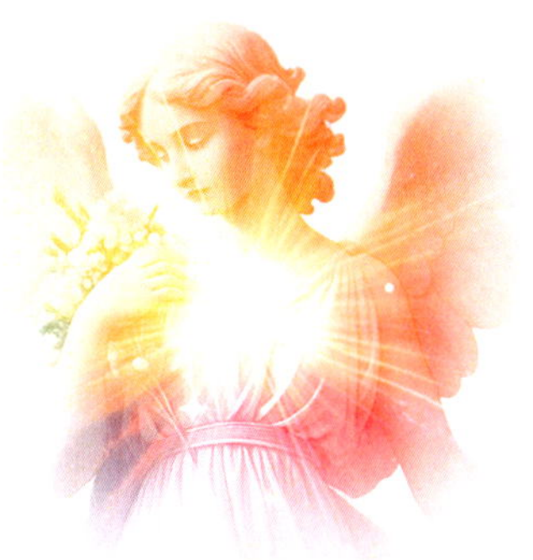

CHAPTER 9

The Fragrance of Love and Liberty

To be capable in thought of actually temporarily entering the consciousness of another lifestream will open the door to many avenues of service and loveliness, providing you use this advanced art wisely.[1]

You become our beneficiaries when you exchange your consciousness with any member of the ascended or angelic hosts, giving us your limited consciousness for a little while as we take yours, inasmuch as human consciousness cannot long abide in our love in action, which will embroider upon it a consciousness of everlasting beauty. You see, true beauty is God, and all things *are* God and therefore are truly beautiful when seen through our consciousness.

Now, when entering the world of the unascended temporarily, much can likewise be accomplished both of a giving and receiving nature, for all have some virtue to give. And so all who bestow healing to another should find some constructive momentum in the mind of the beneficiary that will likewise enrich the benefactor permanently.

Before projecting the mind and consciousness to another, be sure to use your tube of light as protection, then in addition Lord Michael's sword of blue flame and the whole I AM armour of blazing God-light. Upon return to your own sphere, use an abundance of the violet fire.

Now, this is an advanced art, in truth, which while used frequently by the ascended hosts, you may also learn to do, thus fitting yourself for greater service to the light. In past centuries this art was lost because it was used, or rather misused, frequently to project harmful vibrations and expressions to another part of life with whom the individual projecting might not be in harmony.

Such was the activity of the black magicians, who paid dearly for this misuse of God's life, many of them having waited as prisoners in "the compound"[2] until such time as this knowledge of the I AM light made possible the dissolving of that astral chamber of darkness.

The Alchemy of the Pure in Heart to See Beauty

I am speaking to you today from my lovely retreat in France, known as the Château de Liberté. And inasmuch as my release has to do with the projection of beauty into your worlds and all life on this dear earth, I have given you the additional help of the foregoing as assistance in projecting love rays everywhere, spreading the fragrance of love and liberty and the love of liberty everywhere!

You see, although beauty exists everywhere, it remains for the alchemy of the pure in heart to see it. ("The pure in heart shall see God-good everywhere."[3]) The development of this art is the prerogative of those who serve on the third ray. And of course as The Summit Lighthouse is an expression of love, it is imperative that the love of wisdom and the love of love, or the true wisdom of love, be revealed in all its majesty to those who will accept it into their worlds.

In my life as Paolo Veronese, many people visited me in my studio, where I was able to create many very wonderful works of art. Some people came for the appreciation of my art and some for curiosity and the desire to be near fame. (For, you know, outstanding men and women in many fields never lack for their admirers.)

Today, however, those who visit our retreat in spirit will come (I am ever so hopeful) so that they might absorb and then radiate out the Cosmic Christ understanding of true beauty and thereby learn the art of bringing into their worlds and the worlds of all whom they contact an enrichment of Spirit that is permanent and contagious.

To Be a Co-Artist with God

I feel that all conscious chelas of every ascended master should be a co-artist with God, drawing forth the energy of light and designing and molding it so as to daily create constructive and lovely forms and thoughts that will lend a cosmic variety to life and its harmonies.

I call to your attention that the privilege of creating beauty is the joy of those cosmically above you. For your master uses this divinely given prerogative, as do the devas, builders of form, the nature spirits, elemental life, the archangels, the Elohim, and upward unto beloved Helios and Vesta[4] or Alpha and Omega[5] in the Great Central Sun, and on, ad infinitum.

As the possession of true artistry is a quality with which the entire hierarchy is blessed, it would appear that the unfoldment of this creative talent in your own consciousness—and the natural development and awareness of symmetry, beauty, and loveliness—would be ever so desirable for all to learn, and for all who possess it to some degree already, to improve upon it.

The Power of Life Correctly Used Is God in Action

Long ago Saint Paul the apostle, now the beloved ascended master Hilarion,[6] said, "Whatsoever things are true, whatsoever things are honest, whatsoever things are just, whatsoever things are pure, whatsoever things are lovely, whatsoever things are of good report, if there be any virtue, and if there be any praise, think on these things."[7]

All of the goodness, all of the beauty and loveliness of life came into being by the power of some thought from someone, somewhere. As life evolves here, many will begin to understand that all things of an ugly nature were likewise created. Many will begin to know that the power of life correctly used is God in action, and incorrectly used it becomes destructive, unhappy energy, which itself (being of the nature of God) longs to breathe free again—the release of destructive forces in nature being the going home, or release, of misqualified energy from its earthly prison, a groaning, as it were, to find freedom and release. Saint Paul said, "The whole creation groaneth and travaileth in pain together until now."[8]

Man, having been created, the Creator becomes the authority in man's own world to create a garden of Eden where he can eat of (behold) every good fruit or be banished by the consciousness of Good and Evil—the consciousness that alternates in the use of the one energy, flowing destruction at times through the consciousness and thus descending that consciousness to the ground, where by the sweat of his brow it brings forth or creates in the nature kingdom, where the unprotected acts of creation are often choked by the weeds of past karma.

Now, by turning from this human consciousness to the Presence of God I AM, which is the Tree of Life, man eats the fruit of righteousness (right use), goodness (godliness), and joy (spiritual exaltation), receiving the seed within his heart that will grow (expand) right into everlasting life and beauty.

Right here and now I ask each and every one of you: Could God and the masters, in all justice, permit the existence permanently of the ugly? Can you not see why life is as it is—an opportunity to find the true meaning of life in a search for eternal beauty?

Bless Every Electron with Your Love and Light

Now, one way you can commence enjoying the daily benefits of my instruction is to walk hand in hand with the consciousness of God-beauty every day. Make a point of seeing this beauty all around you.

Think of a series of wooden steps. By them you are able to mount higher with less expenditure of energy. Yet atomic substance must remain immobile so that you may have this service rendered to you. So beauty is also utilitarian in one aspect, and renders service. Thus service becomes beauty in action.

Now, to blaze the light of God through these inanimate steps is to bless every electron within them with your love and light, blazing that love through these physical appearances. Jesus long ago said, "If these should hold their peace, the very stones should cry out."[9] Do you see?

Do this likewise with your garments—bless the warm, woolly fibers with the Christ light—and your homes, automobiles, and all you contact. As you tread lightly along the cobblestones and walks beneath your feet, commune with the mineral life of God present there. Commune with the trees and the nature spirits and builders of form.

You will be surprised at how the lovely "silent voices" of inanimate nature and animate nature alike will respond to your greeting, giving you a greater attunement with beauty and likewise a greater attunement with God as you hold his hand while walking in the beautiful out-of-doors.

You see, all this energy is as much a part of him as your own physical bodies, which you treasure so highly. From the dust they came, as Genesis says: "And the LORD God formed man of the dust of the ground."[10] "In the image of God created he him; male and female created he them."[11]

Walk Daily with the Realization and Awareness of the Beauty of All Life

Ought not the electrons composing all life, being part of the body of God, be blessed for the service they render to life? And will not this hidden blessing you bestow (naturally you will do this in the silence of your own beautiful heart, hallowed as it is by the immortal threefold flame of life blazing there) help to free all physical life from the appearance of distress?

Now, because all life is a unity, will this not help you to win your own freedom, all the while giving you a marvelous blessing and attunement every day of your life?

Will this not be a way of silent service that even the more timid ("the meek shall inherit the earth"[12]) can joyfully render, accomplishing thereby an increased consciousness of beauty and by like token having more happiness in their own worlds?

Walk daily with the realization and awareness of the beauty of all life. Enjoy better health by blessing the cells of your own body, which happily drink in the radiation and light of the ascended hosts and of your own Holy Christ Self as by attunement you bring its benefits daily into your world, creating more lovely physical forms right while you lovingly express that radiation and light here.

Did not the scripture say, "You shall be changed from glory to glory, even as by the Holy Spirit of the Lord"?[13] Does this change not transform all your bodies—physical, mental, emotional, etheric?

Liberty in Nature

By visiting me in consciousness here at the Château de Liberté in France, you will find it possible to absorb a great deal of my understanding, which is difficult to put into words because it is of a very high order of things.

As you walk with me in my garden or enter the Château and see a few of the many masterpieces of oil and canvas, it will unquestionably inspire some of you to study art. If your inclination is strong, call to me and I will help you. But first ask your Holy Christ Self if it is part of your life plan.

Yet everyone can benefit by applying their mind in a godly way to assimilate beauty. It will inspire them to use good taste in surrounding themselves with inspiring and harmonious objects d'art in their homes and places of business. The same objects can be magnetized to draw the radiation of the ascended hosts and thus become icons of light.

While you are here with me, come to the Fountain of Flame, where the liberty flame raises its pulsations high into the atmosphere. Remember the words of old, "Now the Lord is that Spirit: and where the Spirit of the Lord is, there is liberty."[14]

Here are a few of my sentiments on liberty in nature:

Every snowflake scampering down,
Every drop of rain,
Fills my heart with joyous hope,
'Tis Liberty's refrain!

For on Liberty's great steed you may ride far out into the beautiful, eternal sea of life and observe the infinite meaning etched into the environment, which now surrounds you wherever you may presently be. On the returning tide you may bring back those thoughts that will enrich the lives of all who may be close to you and all you shall contact. Thus you will presently increase your awareness and sense of beauty until you can create boldly on the canvas of life, by the sure and safe guiding fingers of love, a masterpiece to equal those of the ascended hosts and to eclipse even our works when we were yet unascended. Did not Jesus so lovingly and yet truly say, "Greater works than these shall ye do, because I go unto my Father, the I AM"?[15]

In the name of eternal beauty and the God who would see us all create it, love it, and be it, in the name of love itself, which is oh, so beautiful, I salute you with my Christ radiance and its outpicturing artistry, which I am calling forth into swift expression in your world today.

I am your fellow craftsman, the ascended master Paul the Venetian, Paolo Veronese.

January 28, 1959

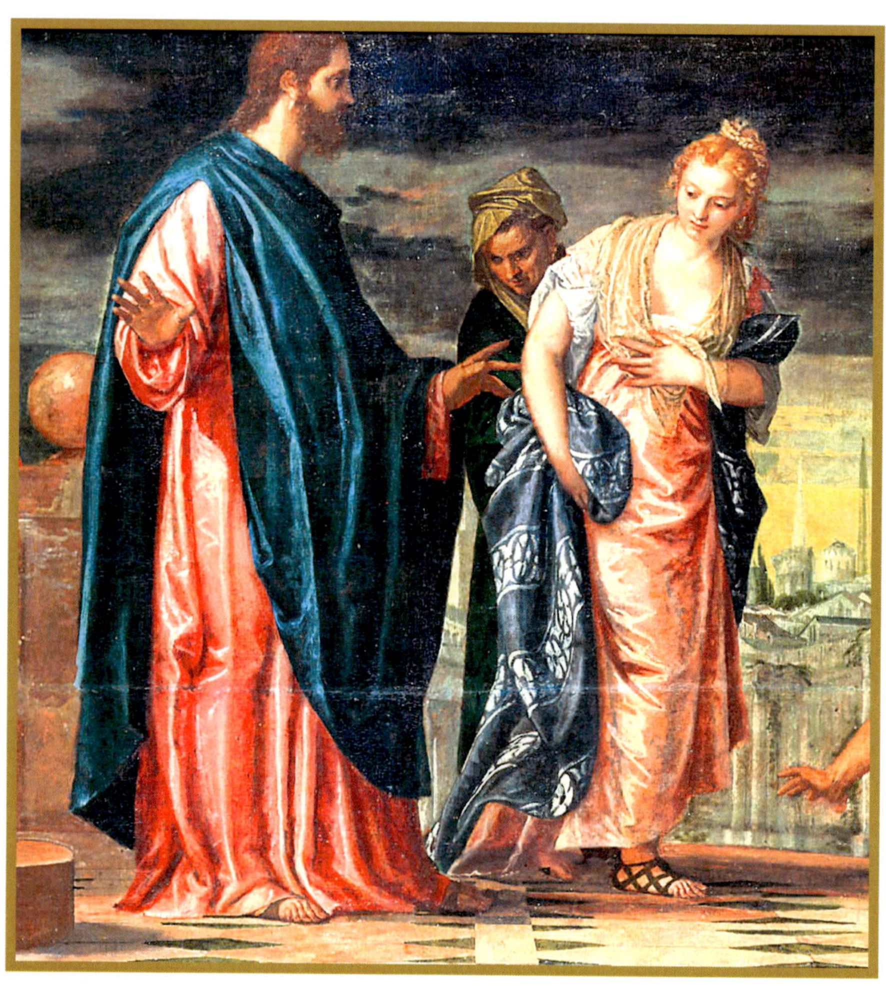

Christ and the Adulteress (detail), c. 1585

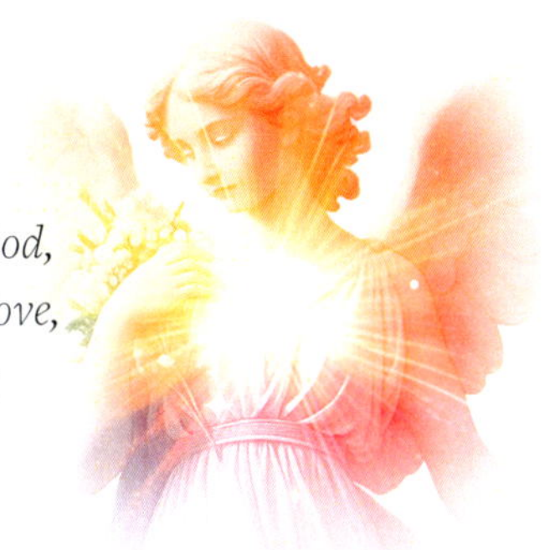

It is our wish to break our bread with the multitudes, to gather them together neath the wings of Almighty God, and to make all one wonderful nation of pure divine love, wisdom, and power that is dedicated to the expanding of the immortal flame of liberty—the conceptions of a divine culture in a golden age of enlightenment.

CHAPTER 10

The Constant Presence of Life within You

O constancy, thou luminous and shining orb, let us proclaim the beauty of constancy—a constancy, beloved ones, that is expressed best in your own mighty I AM Presence and is best expressed in the universal order of perfection as it proceeds from the heart, the head, and the hand of the All-Father within the Great Central Sun.

I, Paul, am come to you this day charged with the beauty of the eternal radiance and the full knowledge of that beauty and that perfection that is the life present within each one of you and within all.

How sacred, then, is the Lord's table. How sacred, then, is the communion of saints. How sacred, then, is the precious offering of each moment, sanctified, as it is, with each heartbeat—the voice of God speaking within you and saying unto you, "I AM thy life! I AM thy life! I AM thy life!"

This sustained, constant Presence of life within you is the gift that your own mighty I AM Presence has given you. To cherish it, to adore it, to give your all to it—to life, to God—is the supreme sacrifice that is beautiful to behold because there is no sense of sacrifice. There is only the sense of sweet surrender whereby the individual, commending himself unto God, finds again a home of such infinite love as to bring peace everywhere that one walks.

The Jewel of Immortality

Beloved ones, I would like to extol this morning the beauty of many of the treasured offerings of life. I would like to extol those offerings so that you might build a momentum of reverence for them and thereby draw unto yourself more of those chaliced gifts that heaven has given you.

Precious ones, life *is* an opportunity. It is an opportunity of wonder, a wonder of expectancy whereby each moment unrevealed holds the hush of expectancy to the waiting soul—waiting for the quickening of the manifest will, love, and intelligence of God into that moment.

Mankind, bored as it were by the empty nothingness of human vacuums, have come to realize that in the search for themselves they find the full beauty of life, the full-orbed splendor of the divine radiance. And mankind, basking in that radiance, are charged with the light of God that does not fail, the companionship of those ascended ones who once wore mortal form and now wear immortal vestments.

Know then, beloved ones, that the heart of God longs to bestow upon all the treasures of his illimitable storehouse, a storehouse surfeited in splendor, charged with magnanimous grace, and oh, far more wondrous than the heart and mind of man can conceive of.

Abiding, then, within this wondrous jewel of immortality, know, O man, that in the beauty of the present, in all the splendor of the past, in all the nobility of the past, all the grandeur of noble lives and of splendid spiritual accomplishments is yours as the treasure of this moment. And beloved ones, all of the treasure of the future is yours, beheld by you in the Presence of life mirrored there. It is yours today—yours to treasure, to share, to hold, to have—*yours,* and no man can take it from you; *yours,* and no man can sunder this treasure from you.

Let No Man Take the Beauty of Thy Crown

O beloved ones, I would speak to you today in the glory of that love, with only the solemn note of warning to let no man take the beauty of thy crown.[1]

Beloved ones, there are still in existence upon the planet men and women devoted to the stealing of mankind's light and the harnessing of that light for purposes of creating shadow and deceit.

These individuals, whether they be few or many—I do not choose to reveal the quantity of individuals practicing these arts of deception—have no power in themselves, and I choose to give them none.

But I speak to you today because it is necessary that mankind should know enough about the Law that they can stand guard and hold the beauty of the crown of achievement within their Presence.

You are a privileged few this day, seated here within the hearing of the sound of my voice, seated here within a circlet of my arms of love. And yet there are multitudes that ought to be here. There are some who are a part of this group who are not here this morning. Perhaps it occurred to them that they could not avoid their absenteeism.

Well, beloved ones, I tell you, if they are not here because they are bored by the sameness of our offering, this is to their own hurt. For the wonders of eternity, which are mirrored in the perfection of our worlds, are the graces of heaven that saturate the finer bodies of those privileged to sit in our radiation and develop within them the divine arts and graces that enable them to be blessed by the treasures of the saints.

Those, then, who are shadowed individuals project shadow, project boredom, and project feelings of sameness into spiritual groups in order to discourage the individuals from imbibing the fountain of divine grace. And yet the beauty of heaven pierces through, shining as the Holy Grail and blessing mankind with the living Christ-conception of immortal truth. These shadowed ones have no power. The power of divine beauty excels all others, and those who sup at the LORD's table are the privileged few.

But, beloved ones, it is not the wish of the councils of the Great White Brotherhood to see this remain the forte of the privileged few. It is our wish to break our bread with the multitudes, to gather them together neath the wings of Almighty God, and to make all one wonderful nation of pure divine love, wisdom, and power that is dedicated to the expanding of the immortal flame of liberty—the conceptions of a divine culture in a golden age of enlightenment, where men (no longer learning or mastering the arts of war, turning their pursuits into channels of peace) find, in a spirit of divinely dominated domesticity, a home and fireside where God is enshrined daily and hourly, where the chiming of the mantle clock is a call to prayer to the household, and where the Angelus[2] is heard in the hearts of men who bow in prayer because they love.

Genuine Reverence Evokes the Presence of Life Within

Beloved ones, if you pause now to think and to meditate, you will recognize that there is an affected reverence practiced by mankind, and there is a genuine reverence. The genuine reverence may not always be distinguishable to the outer eye, but to God, to the ascended masters, it is the only shining reality.

A human heart, having elected to pursue the divine art—the pursuit of the Beloved by the beloved—magnifies God within the forcefield of their heart and causes them to yearn for him, for their own mighty I AM Presence, to yearn to expand the flame that is within them. And as they bow their heads, it is with sheer joy for the privilege. And a genuine reverence evokes the Presence of life within them, floods them with immortal concepts, and makes them one at the LORD's table. "Drink ye all of it. Drink *into* it. As ye drink this cup, do it in remembrance of me."[3]

The chalice that I created for the Lord the Maha Chohan[4] has brought happiness to the ascended hosts. But it was charged with my love for God, for my own mighty I AM Presence. And the mighty I AM Presence of each individual ascended being rejoices and will continue to rejoice in this chalice offering of my being.

You all have so much to give. If it were not so, you would have been told. But, beloved ones, you are being reminded today, humbly and graciously by myself, of the much that has been given you, that you might in return bestow much upon that Divine Being, who has given so much unto you.

Your Own Mighty I AM Presence Yearns to Bestow upon You the Fullness of His Love

Precious ones, can you deny that life has bestowed grace upon you? Would you deny it, if you could? I think not. You would affirm it, and the best affirmation, beloved ones, is to do the commandments of the Most High God.

The commandments of God, in basic simplicity, extol the idea of loving your mighty I AM Presence first and above all, and then loving your neighbor as yourself.[5]

When you do these things, you do it in remembrance of the living Christ. The shining robes he wore begin to envelop your form as you make come alive his conceptions of beauty, his conceptions of the Father, his conceptions of the mighty I AM Presence.

Your own mighty I AM Presence yearns to bestow upon you the fullness of his love. As you open up the floodgates of your being to receive the mighty tide of life, this tide will sweep over you, envelop you in the divine currents, and you will find no time to be bored, no eternity to be bored, and not a moment to be idle. But you will find, rather, that the opportunity of life is beautiful. And as you bask in those beauties that are life, you will desire, as I do, to create lovely articles, lovely concepts, spiritual ideals. You will recognize that you are a co-creator with God, that you are entitled to exercise the privilege of your divine artistry and to express those talents wisely.

But, O precious ones, as I part from you this day, as you no longer hear my voice or the pulsations of my energy flowing through you, remember especially to endow your creation with the living truth of God.

Many create a graven image. It is graven and stamped with the vibratory action of their outer self. Those who are sensitive see in it a twisted, a warped, a confused, and imperfect concept. If it be offered in ignorance but in divine love, it is accepted by their Presence. But the sensitive know that it does not represent the best offering. Like the fruit of Cain, it is not the best and most acceptable offering unto Deity.[6]

Learn then, beloved ones, as Abel of old,[7] to offer the fruit not made as a graven image but the fruit that is stamped with the divine seal of approval—the genuine qualities that represent the artistry of your Divine Self.

Let the currents of that Divine Self penetrate through the very core of your creation, and it *will be immortal.* It is the stamp of immortality that makes it so.

I thank you.

March 17, 1963

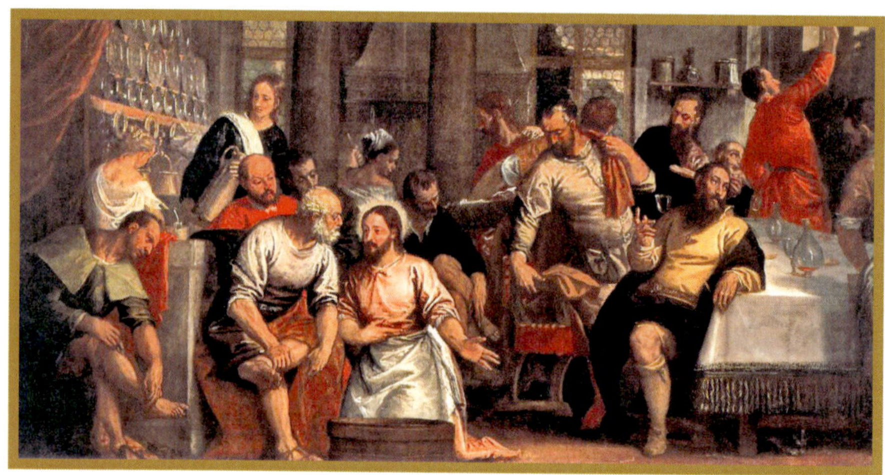

Christ Washing the Feet of the Disciples, c. 1580

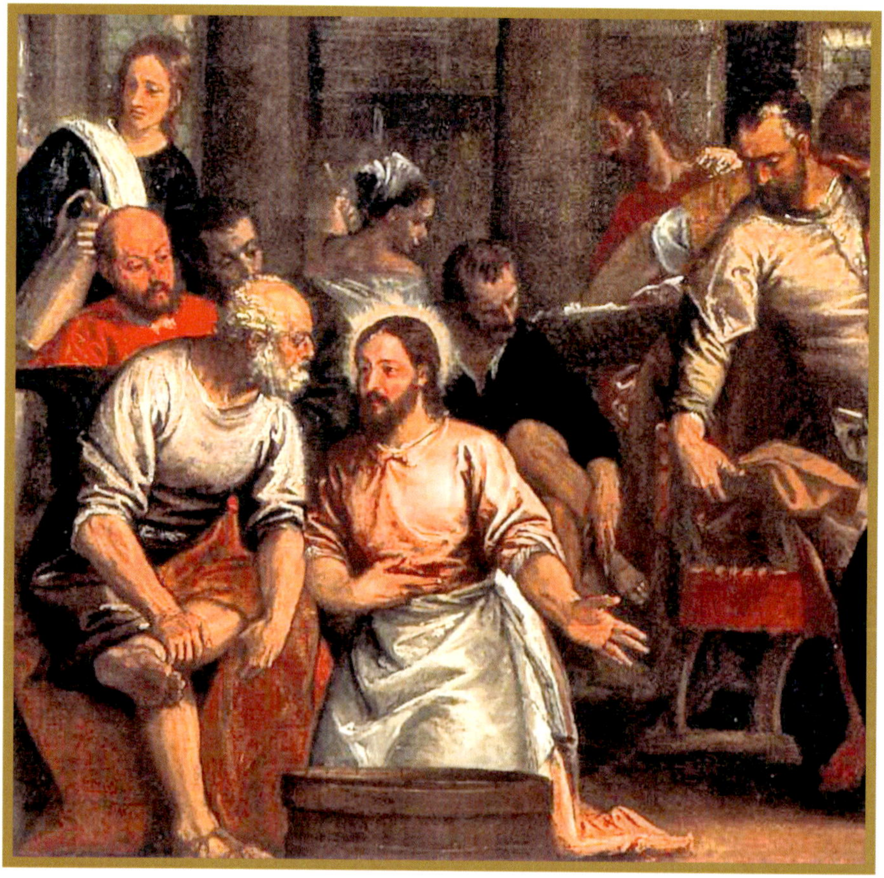

Divine Motherhood—that great eternal privilege—continues to be the blessing conferred upon those miniature replicas of the Divine Mother, the human mother. May she be enshrined, then, and held. . . . May she be honored, as every immortal son ought so to do.

CHAPTER 11

A Tribute to Spiritual Motherhood

I bow my head and I bow my heart in radiant adoration of that blessed Mother, the Goddess of Liberty, to whom I pay tribute this day for her service so magnificent on behalf of life everywhere.

Mankind today, with their seeking hearts, pay allegiance to an earthly mother, and it is well and just and proper. But it is my great privilege to pay tribute to a heavenly Mother, the Goddess of Liberty.

Liberty is, to all mankind, of greatest value, for it enables them to choose divinity. It enables them to cast aside and spurn lesser treasures, that mankind may turn and embrace all of the treasures of God locked in one heart—the heart of a supreme Mother.

Blessed ones, you who are so treasured by all of the ascended hosts know with great certainty that the love of cosmic beings is incomparable. Mother Mary, the Goddess of Liberty, Kuan Yin,[1] and all those blessed spirits borne to heaven in clouds of glory and immortality are indeed supreme upon the world scene. All history, especially spiritual history, pays them tribute, and all history ought so to do.

Beloved ones, motherhood is a glorious opportunity but one seldom properly exercised in a proper manner by the average individual given this great privilege. For although there be so many benign intentions in the hearts of mankind, it is seldom, in this present hour and day of turmoil, that they are able to bridge the gap between their blessed intentions and the realities of daily living.

I am come this morning to pay tribute, however, to the spirit of noblesse oblige, to the attitudes of spiritual motherhood and the divine intentions that are currently, and in the past, present within the heart of every mother. For these divine intentions are there, although in embryonic state in many. I pay them tribute so that I may amplify, in the holy name of God, all of those qualities that are spiritual in nature and cause them to expand, even as a beautiful flower unfolds from the bud.

My Gift to All Expectant Mothers

Precious ones of the light, those of you familiar with my lifestream, those of you who know of my record as Paolo Veronese, will recognize that I have some familiarity with painting, with art, and with sculpture. You will recognize that I have in my consciousness a great affection and affinity for those molding concepts of beauty that enable mankind to externalize a part of the God-design.

Precious ones, I reverently, then, this day, execute in spiritual artistry a portion of the divine design of cosmic motherhood, and I place it as a miniature shrine within the hearts of all expectant mothers upon this planet this day as my gift to life.

You, beloved ones, who have thought upon it, have recognized the great beauty of Mother Mary and other spiritual mothers. You have actually reveled in the thought of these blessed beings.

Well, precious ones of the light, consider, then, the gift that I am bestowing this day upon all expectant mothers. I am bestowing upon them a spiritual matrix that will enable them to tune into many of the thoughts and feelings of beloved Mother Mary such as she carried in her heart during the time of gestation of beloved Jesus.

This, precious ones of the light, will enable the more sensitive to externalize a greater measure of selfless devotion and spirituality into the precious lifestream that those mothers are carrying. And thus those thoughts and feelings will give an impetus to that lifestream and shall cast that lifestream aside somewhat from human moorings and move that one toward the great sea of life, where those valiant souls and Christed beings walk to bestow peace to the hearts of mankind, to ease their burdens, to bring out the beauty in life and spoil not the handiwork of God.

The Perfect Outpicturing of Divinity upon the Canvas of Life

Precious ones, today there has been much discussion concerning art in the world, and many among mankind are concerned about the trends of so-called modern art. Well, precious ones, even ascended beings do not desire to criticize, and therefore free from the desire of criticism—for although some might deem me a worthy critic of art in this present hour—I do not choose to do so. But I do choose and shall exercise my divine privilege to speak to you today concerning these matters from a standpoint of adviser and spiritual counselor.

Truly, beloved ones, there is much dissonance and discord reflected in so-called modern art, which causes the disturbed conditions present within the psyche of the artist to be expressed upon the canvas.

These conditions, then, beloved ones, take the form of engrams, as it were. And when individuals behold upon the screen this outpictured discord, it does not key a response within their being that is calculated to exalt their soul, but rather it pulls them down into the discordant trend of the artist unless they stand their guard.

It is true that mankind must today, and at all times until mankind's discord be permanently healed, stand their guard against the intrusion of discordant music, art forms, worded expressions, concepts, and even invisible thoughts.

Mankind must learn to stand their guard. And it must be the prerogative of every mother and every woman who shall bear a son or daughter to engender with her thoughts the idea of cosmic protection within that precious lifestream of God-design so that she may be able, blessed ones, to assist that lifestream through all the days of that individual's life to be a more perfect outpicturing of divinity upon the canvas of life.

To Honor One's Parents

Precious ones, some of you are aware of the statement made by Abraham Lincoln that he owed everything to his blessed mother. This is not a new concept, for many great men and small men (by mankind's judgment) have recognized all that they owed to their parent or to both parents.

But, blessed ones, I would like to point out to you that many have felt contrariwise, having felt that their parents deprived them of many of life's blessings. They have chastised rather than honored their parents. They have in many cases justly defamed the character of their own mother from the standpoint of human values.

But I tell you, precious ones of the light, that when the understanding of the concept of true Christ radiance is conveyed to the son or daughter, they will understand the meaning of forgiveness. They will understand in the story of Magdalene[2] that forgiveness must be externalized and that those individuals born into the world of form of so-called unworthy parents are not always proper in blaming their parents for this experience.

Many times it is a fault of the son or daughter's own lifestream for inequities committed against other parts of life in previous embodiments. Then again, it is for another purpose, as a test of their own character, that they may rise above the seeming stigma of name to exalt the principles of divinity upon the pages of history and to bring mankind closer to the outpicturing of the purposes for which they came into existence.

Perfect Love Is Perfect Beauty Inherent within the God-Design

Blessed ones, that precious spark of life that is within you, which is your own Divine Self, may not be pictured upon canvas but it is pictured in life. It is apparent in the lines of character drawn upon your faces, blessed ones. When you have fear in your world, it etches into the lines of your physical countenance the appearances that we can so easily interpret as a manifestation of fear.

Bear well in mind, then, that perfect love casteth out all fear and torment.[3] For perfect love is perfect beauty, and this beauty is inherent within the God-design made and created by God in the Beginning—God who created this perfect, tiny form, embryonic in nature, and who created that blessed threefold flame of your being, your Holy Christ flame, blessed ones. And it is your responsibility to expand that Holy Christ flame, that in perfect balance and beauty it may be upon the screen of life an active manifestation of the Christ principle.

Blessed ones, the tiny, infant body that you once wore was also a thing of beauty, created wondrously and fearfully made. Blessed ones, you must recognize this blessed body as an outpicturing of the mind of God and also feel that the pulsations of life within it are the voice of God speaking to you and saying unto you daily and hourly:

> Be renewed in beauty.
> Be renewed in duty.
> Be renewed in responsibility.
> Accept your cosmic opportunity.
> Hear my voice calling to you and be all that I AM,
> all that you shall be.

Recognize Yourselves as Divine Ideas of Beauty as Conceived by the Cosmic Mother

Recognize, then, your privilege. Recognize, then, that this day is a day that God has made. Recognize that every day is a day that God has made especially, beloved ones, for you, each one.

Mankind are too prone to feel that they are alone, that they themselves are separated as an island from the consciousness of God and that God is not too concerned with them individually. This is not true. That which was created was created not only for the *allness* of God but for the *oneness* of God. And the oneness of God manifests in no greater manner to the consciousness of man than in the individual himself, who is a perfect replica of the divine idea.

You, therefore, ought to recognize yourselves as divine ideas of beauty, clothed with beauty as conceived by the Cosmic Mother. For you are, beloved ones, the product of your heavenly Father-Mother God. Both had a part in the shaping of your form. But you, blessed ones, must recognize that your destiny, although guided by them, is yet in the hands of your blessed free will—a free will that may choose to create either ugliness or beauty, either pain or joy and freedom from pain.

Blessed ones, let all, then, master the creation rather than be mastered by outer appearances. Let all take on the prerogatives of the ascended masters. Let all feel the freedom to shape their own destiny in accordance with cosmic patterns. Let all feel the drumbeat of divine love within them, sustaining their heart and mounting within them as a fervor for life rather than despair.

Beloved ones, despair is only a human feeling, as are all emotions of human creation. They bring about conditions of chaos and disorganization. You, blessed ones, must free yourselves from human creation. You must take on *divine* creation. Divine creation must be a creation of beauty and must, then, be a joy forever.

I have reminded you of this in previous talks given to you, but I must this day reiterate it and state it again because of the valiant truth inherent within it.

The Birthright of an Immortal People

If mankind will recognize their divine rights, if mankind will recognize their divine privileges, if mankind will behold the matrix of the divine around them, they will no longer be subject to those outer conditions that are a part of human creation and human chaos. They will cast this aside as a shroud and they will embellish themselves with the garment of Christ-beauty and accomplishment.

These are far more than words, blessed ones. I am speaking of a tangible garment. I am speaking of a robe of Christ unity. I am speaking of a birthright of an immortal people who are here for a season in the schoolrooms of earth so that they might master the problem of their own identity and find in the identity of God, their own mighty I AM Presence, the identity of themselves masquerading for far too long as a human and appearing for far too long as a puny individual.

Man must cast aside *all* that is of his human self and recognize that he does not lose his cosmic birthright by so doing. Neither does he lose in any way. For you can never, beloved ones, lose anything by giving all that was given to you back to the heart of God.

Truly, he who seeks to save his life shall lose it.[4] But he who loses himself, even his identity, for the sake of obtaining his divine identity shall find it again, and in a more grand and noble manner, until the purposes of life shall be fulfilled everywhere as God intends.

Be What He Is, and You Will Find Your Freedom

Gaze not upon the appearance world, the misshapen bits of marble, the canvases smeared with the feeble attempts of man to paint. Gaze not upon mankind as the finished product. They are but in the embryonic state. You need not mimic or copy them, for they are still students in the schoolrooms of life.

Gaze upon the perfect pattern of the Master Painter, the Master Creator, the Master Builder, the Master Artist. See what he has wrought and be what he is, and you will find your freedom. You cannot find your freedom in the pages of earthly history but you *can* find it in the pages of divine identity.

Going back before the dawn of recorded history to your own divine identity, when it was yet a spark of the cosmic fire dancing within the heart of God, there, blessed ones, you can find it, recognizing itself as individualized in part and yet unseparated from God. It spoke, speaking the name of God, I AM. Each tiny spark spake thus to one another beholding the Self and said, "I AM."

This is as it should be today. Then there would be no conflict between your outer ego and your Divine Self. You would not be in conflict with one another or with your own mighty I AM Presence. You would be swimming with the current of life and moving down the great river that flows from the throne of God. You would be obtaining your freedom each moment rather than denying it, and thus you would be affirming the Christ consciousness of your birthright.

So it is and so it ever shall be that the law of life, the law of liberty, O Mother Liberty, is held within thy hand, cradled within thy arm, the great Book of Life that reads the law of freedom for each man's being. This is a document that man must obtain—by *sacrifice* if necessary, by *study* if necessary, by *denial* if necessary, by *affirmation* if necessary, and by whatever other measures their own soul may require until they stand before the face of their own God Presence and behold their Presence as both judge and lawgiver of their life.

Then man will know that all that came forth from the heart of God was beautiful and beheld by him as good, and that each soul is no exception to this rule. For the rule that was handed down for the one is the rule for the many.

Divine Motherhood Continues to Be the Blessing Conferred upon the Human Mother

The law of life is firm. The law of life is supreme. The law of life is just. It is also the law of motherhood. And Divine Motherhood—that great eternal privilege—continues to be the blessing conferred upon those miniature replicas of the Divine Mother, the human mother. May she be enshrined, then, and held. May she be esteemed by man. May she not be spurned by them or held in disrepute. May she be honored, as every immortal son ought so to do.

May all emulate Saint Germain and stand, then, and behold in the maternal situation a manifestation of the great law of life. May they honor and crown the Mother, as the angelic hosts do, until Motherhood Divine becomes transferred from heavenly realms and octaves to this earth, borne by a mantle of pure, snowy-white light and containing within it immortal flowers from the bower of God.

This, then, is our conception. This, then, is *God's* conception. This, then, is an activity of good. In it is no darkness, for it is the life that is the light of God that never fails.

Beloved hearts, to this end were you born and for this purpose came you into the embodiment of life, that you might be a living Christ in manifestation, a Son of God, a Child of the eternal Mother.

In God's holy name, I thank you this day and pay my final adieu to my mother, the Goddess of Liberty.*

May 12, 1963

*The Goddess of Liberty is the spiritual mother of Paul the Venetian.

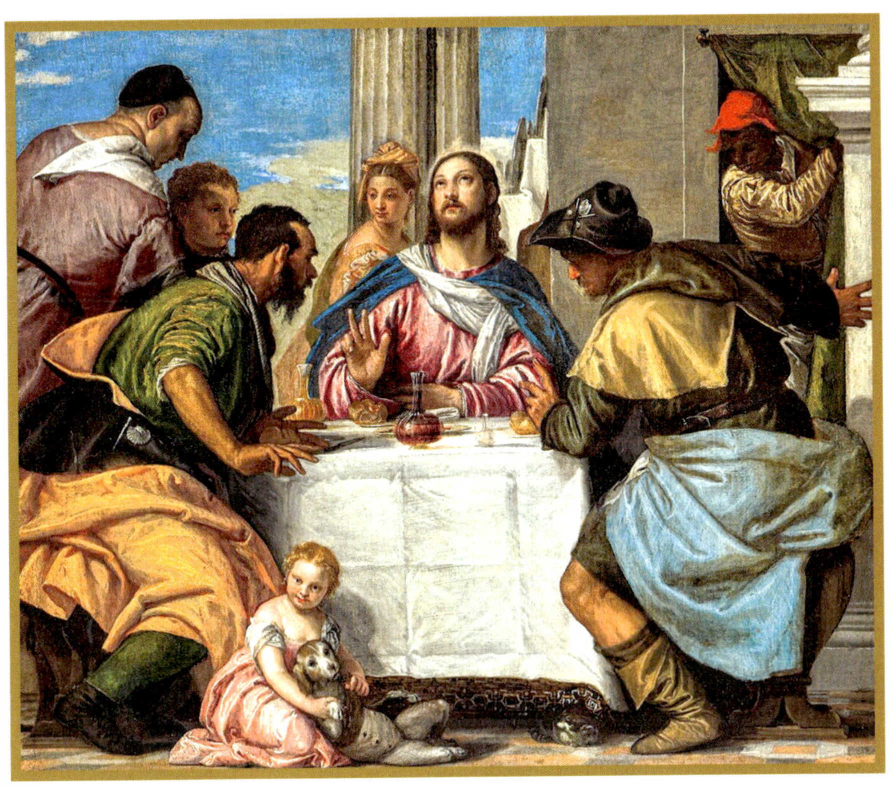

Supper at Emmaus, c. 1565–70

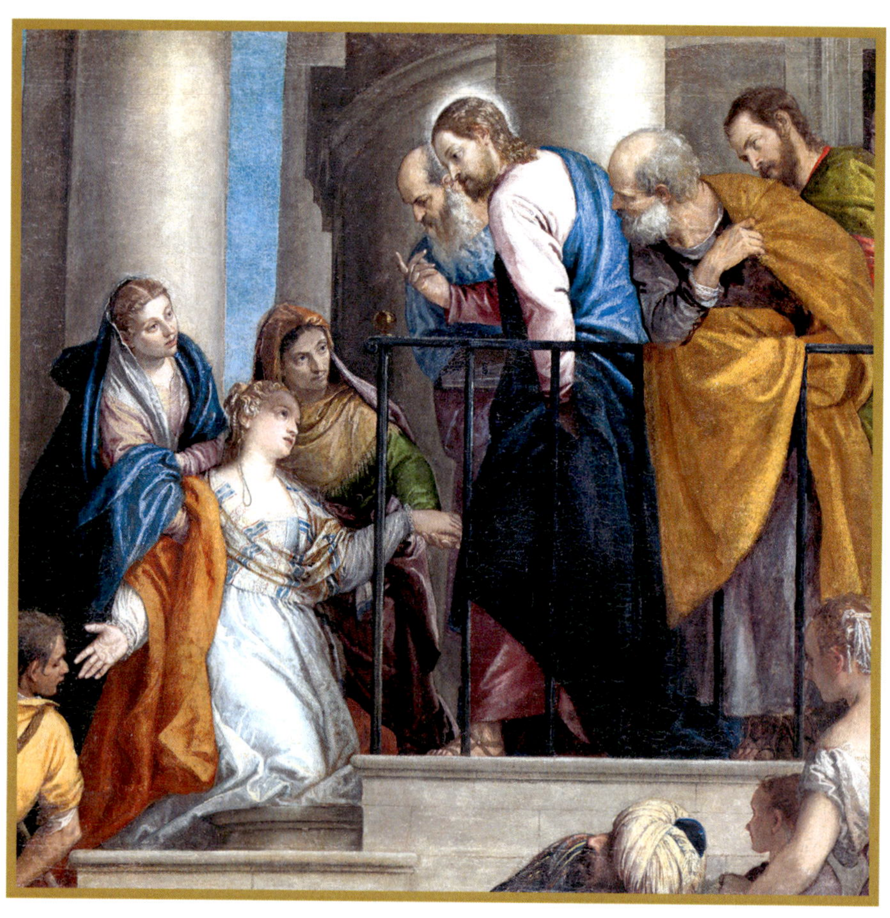

The Raising of the Youth of Nain (detail), c. 1565–70

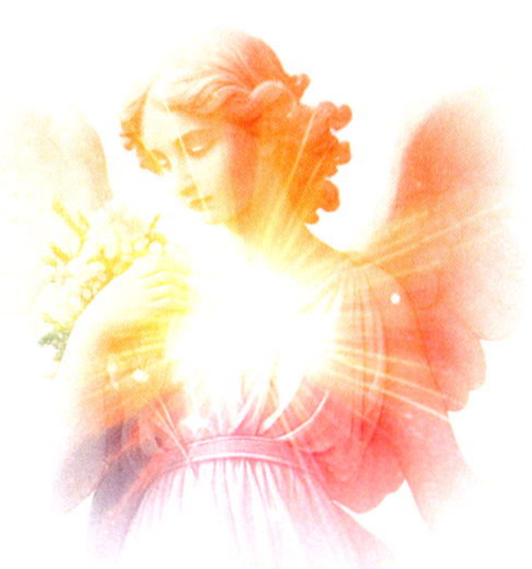

I refer here to the mysteries of religion and the mysteries of life—the mysteries of mankind's journey in seeking the pathway back to the Divine Source. There is not one answer, beloved ones, that can be revealed to mankind, save the answer of the Divine Self.

CHAPTER 12

The Wonders of Soul-Artistry

Beloved and precious ones of God's devotional heart, how priceless is the treasure of welcome—to be able to greet in the spirit of divine friendship those ladies and gentlemen who, in courtly conduct, understand the meaning of divine love translated into active participation in the affairs of mankind and in the affairs of heaven. These truly have one hand in heaven and one hand upon earth.

The earth has ever been enriched by the lives of such as these. And I salute you, then, ladies and gentlemen, who have truly devoted yourselves to the calling of the ascended masters for reasons of that devotion of your hearts and for reasons of your determination to not let anything stand in your way as you pursue the selfsame path that many of us did who are considered by mankind today as artists.

Beloved ones, the turmoil of the outer world frequently becomes most discouraging to the sensitive at heart. And as they recoil from the currents of turbulence and disturbance that manifest in the outer world of form, they sometimes tend to seek the quietness of the monastic life. They yearn to find their peace in a cloister apart from the world, where the stillness of the halls is broken only by the murmurs of prayer, and the atmosphere is penetrated only by the sweet fragrance of incense rising as to heaven.

Some of these dear hearts, having come apart from the world and having entered into the silence and bliss of this monastic life, have found that all was not quietude or peace there, for they found that they carried with them the turmoil and conditions that were indeed of the outer world. The conditions were in their own consciousness, and they found that they could not shed it even after twenty years of living apart.

Others have had a reverse situation, beloved ones. There have been those who have thoroughly enjoyed the world and who were, for reasons best known to God and to the great Karmic Board, suddenly thrust apart from the world, contrary to their will, and conveyed—by reason of inheritance, position, or even ill health—to some distant place apart from the crowd, there to find the tragedy, as they termed it, of aloneness.

Some of you have heard the ascended masters, such as myself, refer to the state of *all-one-ness* rather than that of *aloneness.* And it is this state of mind that all must come to—the ability to find within themselves the quiet peace of divine dominion that is able to encompass in consciousness the wonders and glories of the world. And then when face-to-face with temptation—either in the desert, with all of its despair of aloneness, or upon the mountaintop of vision where they perceive the glories of the world—these are able to hold inviolate the divine principles of heaven's law and mold within their character, firmly implanted by the Creator's master touch, those qualities that shape their ends to be of greatest service to the hierarchy and to the Great White Brotherhood.

I would like to point out that the vocational leanings of mankind pertaining to spiritual vocations are so frequently charged with human emotions. Individuals, of course, have strong feelings about their own calling. And this is understandable because callings are from God, and callings are from the world and from the outer self. Mankind must learn to distinguish between the callings that are from the earth, earthy, and those callings that are heavenly in nature.

As the blessed Christ-discrimination of understanding is revealed to the silent heart waiting upon the gentle ministrations of the Divine Presence, there comes a peace stealing into the consciousness that tells the then turbulent lifestream, prior to its quieting attitude, that all is well. For it does not make any difference. As long as there is a sense of struggle, the individual can say to himself, "Shall I turn to the right or shall I turn to the left?"

But it is this sense of struggle, as beloved Saint Germain has told you, that makes the struggle. And so you continue to feel oppressed and you continue to feel pressed to make a decision favorable or unfavorable, but born of some hidden necessity that seems to drive you onward. This is not *always* the better part of wisdom. Sometimes the secret of solving your problems is not so much to make a decision when you are uncertain, but to rest in the peace of the moment and to await the hour of revelation.

The Trials of Obscurity

Now I speak to you because of some of the canvases that I created. There were times when I felt pressed through the need for my livelihood to create on canvas some wondrous object in order that mankind might be able to glory in it. And yet I was driven, in a sense, to a pensive mood whereby I could create at will a masterpiece, only to find that when I came to create it, the inspirational spark was not present. And I found it could not be invoked. And I found that the harder I tried, the more difficult became the decision as to just what I could paint. For I could not paint a commonplace item. It must be stirring and magnificent. This, then, is why I so well understand how the human hearts of men at various times, when the crossroads of life seem particularly difficult, stand in wonder and amazement as to just which way they shall turn.

Beloved ones, at times such as those, I myself, finding that I was indeed stymied, ceased to resist the condition—and not with a sense of indifference or aloofness or despair but with a sense of realization that God works in strange ways, mysterious and wondrous, to perform his will. I determined to cease and desist in the struggle and to rest in his compassionate consciousness, knowing that with the tides of time I would find an answer to the searching and probing question of the hour.

And then my peace would come in great flowing waves. And with the coming of my peace and my quietude, there was reestablished a contact between myself and those masterful, divine beings who ensouled in my pictures the very essence of their own life. My angelic friends of light—those messengers of hope who guided my hand in its craftsmanship and artistry—were able to express, then, in the stilled muscular control, that which they could never do when the tensions of the hour took their toll over my mortal frame.

I, therefore, urge all of the students to recognize that there is a time to tense and a time to relax. There is a time to pray and a time to wait. There is a time to be devotional and a time to repose in God's devotion.

I would like to remind all who are here that after you have poured out all of your love to God according to the capacity of your own souls, then is the hour when you should await expectantly to receive the love of God in return. It is as though an emptiness comes to you, for you have given your all. And then that "all" comes back to you charged with his love. The love of God flows in mighty waves, sweeping o'er you as the beating sea against the cliffs of being. And the foam intrigues your consciousness as its breakers of many patterns unfold—multitudinous and wondrous spraylets of beauty.

O beloved ones, the wonders of God come from the infinite ocean of his Being. During the trials of obscurity, when the so-called dark night of the soul trembles upon the consciousness, mankind must recognize the knowledge of the coming dawn. But they must not cognize that dawn with tension, as though they would invoke the dawn. For the dawn will come without human interference or invocation.

The dawn will come with quietness, power, and majesty stealing over the very horizons of life. Its light upon the mountaintops will illumine each hill and clearly delineate each tree, until those forms that are traced before the waiting vision will stir the heart with such God-beauty as cannot be put into words by anyone. The *silent* beauty—the majestic feelings of grandeur that flood into the soul of mankind—this is more wonderful than ever has been painted by *any* human hand. Even we in our octave are no substitute for the natural and magnificent power of God in his Allness manifesting to those waiting to receive him.

The Hand of God Steadies the Wheel of Life

Millions of individuals in times past have journeyed to sit at the feet of great yogi teachers in the Far East. Some—and I say *few*—have entered the retreats and temples of the Great White Brotherhood. All of the wonders of the teachings of yoga, in those eras when these teachings were prevalent to mankind, could never be a substitute for the fullness of the teachings of the Great White Brotherhood. For the teachings of yoga are a part of the knowledge of divine union, and the *whole* must be fit together.

They are like a giant jigsaw puzzle. And I refer here to the mysteries of religion and the mysteries of life—the mysteries of mankind's journey in seeking the pathway back to the Divine Source. There is not one answer, beloved ones, that can be revealed to mankind, save the answer of the Divine Self. Man, then, who knows himself—"Man, know thyself"[1]—is ever the victor, and the human creation is ever the vanquished. The vanquished foe is the very child of your own creation. You yourselves, at one time or another, have created the phantoms that face you in the present and have faced you in the past.

It is true that by the interaction of great cosmic forces—and human forces, too, working in this great alchemical laboratory of the schools of earth—mankind have created karmic conditions toward one another, which must be set aside. But mankind need not be detained by these conditions, and their freedom need not be ultimately delayed. It can manifest much sooner than mankind might dream of, if they will give to their own God Presence the preeminence and opportunity of working out their salvation within them.

I do not say that there are not moments when you must place your hands upon the wheel. The Captain of Life, as he steers the ship of life over the raging sea, will turn to the young disciple and say to him, "O soul, I AM the Ancient Mariner. You have watched the steadying of my hand upon the wheel of life. You have observed my movements as I have coped with the fury of the storm. Take now your hands, O gentle chela. Place your hands upon the wheel of life fearlessly, for you shall stand this watch."

And then when the turmoil becomes too great and the individual can no longer avoid or refrain from crying out for mercy and assistance, the call goes forth, "Father, into thy hands I commend my spirit."[2] And so the wondrous Presence of Life, taking command, brings forth the resurrection miracle. And the soul is raised again, and the hand of God steadies the wheel until the time comes when the chela can once again perform the act of mastering the seas and the furies of life and obtaining the glories of victory.

Divine Assistance Comes through a Relaxing of Tension

I have spoken much on artistry in the past. I have spoken much on beauty. Today I am speaking to the souls of men of the means whereby they may paint a picture of divine merit in their own lives by accepting the challenges of the hour and by mastering those challenges with God-victorious freedom, with God-victorious adoration, with God-victorious divine love! Divine love, then, flows forth from my heart this day, and it flows forth that I might instruct you, one and all, in the mysteries of developing a world consciousness, and then in understanding that *you* are given dominion over that consciousness.

While I am speaking to you, night falls upon a part of the earth. The sun is going down, and mankind are kneeling in prayer. The bells of evening are tolling in parts of the world. In other parts, the sun is rising and dawn is breaking. The cathedrals of the world ring out the signals of the hours at various times. And the hearts of men in many climes, of many races and many faces, struggle against seemingly overwhelming odds.

It is well if you think of other people in other lands. One of the wonders of your own century is the travel by air, whereby in one day you are able to cover so much of the earth's territory, and in landing to find yourselves in strange places, with new faces and the miracle of life all around you.

When you travel, then, in these places and then return to your homes, your consciousness is different. And some who have suffered either nervousness or disease have found that through travel they have effectually cured themselves. Have they stopped to inquire why this is so? It is because of the dissemination of divine love and the dissemination of interests. Too many people, beloved ones, become so inverted toward their own personality that they fail to actually hold on to the Captain's hand as he attempts to guide them and show them during their watch at the helm how to steer a straight course.

In their trembling and fear, they fail to recognize the omnipresence of God and his extreme willingness to guide them. All these conditions, then, create tension, and tension effectively closes the door to divine assistance. Divine assistance comes through a relaxing of tension, through a resting in the arms of divine mercy, through an accepting of the gift of true, divine love.

O beloved ones, how can you imagine that God, whose concern for a sparrow is great, would not care for thee, each one? How can you imagine that he is not concerned, that he is aloof, that he is afar off, when he has drawn nigh again and again, only to be repulsed by human tension.

Tension, beloved ones, is so related to *attention.* By turning your attention to your Source, you may find your freedom. But too many think that they must turn their attention toward their Source and then do so continually. They do not recognize that having *once* faced the mighty light of God, they may then relax and let the light bear them up. It is as though individuals would reach up to the Master Mariner and guide *his* hands, in preference to letting him guide theirs.

This is why, as I am speaking to you today of the wonders of soul-artistry, that I am advocating that more and more of you come to put into practice this principle, which is so simple, so sweet, so loving, and so kind. It is kind to yourself, and it is kind to your fellowmen. For while errors will occur in the course of a day, the mitigation of those errors will come more swiftly as the hand of God is more evident upon your own. It cannot be evident there unless you encourage it. God will not resist if you push his hand away, even though you do not know that it is his hand that you push.

God Does Not Intrude upon a Closed Door

Beloved ones, God is love. You have heard it said that divine love is not intrusive. God does not intrude upon a closed door. Remember the words, "I am the open door which no man can shut."[3] You yourselves have frequently shut the door. No divine manifestation can shut the door, beloved ones. No man can shut it. But do you understand that human free will can close the door?

Do you understand how to break the scriptures, the bread of life, so that you do understand the inner meaning of that which is spoken? There are so many scriptures that are not thoroughly understood. Mankind wrestle with them, as Jacob wrestled with the angel.[4] And they do not find all the answers but they continue to seek to do so.

Never contend, beloved ones, in earthly contention over these matters. If mankind are convinced that a law is right, you cannot change them by a word. It is true, however, that the receptive ones will ask, whereas those who are determined that they are right will tell you.

Beloved ones, your own Divine Presence is your friend. Friendship with God has been listed in the scriptures as enmity with the world.[5] This does not mean that you are to be an enemy to mankind. It means, beloved ones, that friendship with God, your own mighty I AM Presence, will find enmity in the world of human creation, which is contrary to the laws of God—which creation you yourselves have ignorantly created. It means, therefore, that you are an enemy to a part of yourself, to a part of your creation. And it means that this part must be transmuted and the middle wall of partition must be broken down.

The veil of the temple of being must be rent in twain,[6] and man must attain entrance into the Holy of Holies within his own heart in order that he may see the flame of life blazing there and assimilate from it the necessary guidance that shall secure for him the rights of life, of liberty, and the pursuit of happiness.

O my beloved, master thyself! Master God-control! Do not give vent to displays of temper or anger or anxiety or fear or confusion. See the guiding hand of God assuring you of your eternal liberty.

This [pointing to a painting of the Statue of Liberty] our masterful Goddess of Liberty has outpictured for all time, for mankind, for the three Americas,* and for the world. The Goddess holds high her torch.

Accept God's Liberty and Be Free

Ladies and gentlemen, will you join me now in holding up your own right hand in honor of the Goddess of Liberty, right where you sit? Hold high your torch. You hold high, now, the symbol in your hand, but will you pledge it to God as a recognition of his guiding light through the night of being? Will you let him guide you as you attempt to execute a work of service according to the divine design? Will you have the wise Masterbuilder for your own instructor? Then accept God-liberty and be free. This is your own gift from God's heart.

Lower your hand, beloved ones, and bring it to your heart. Clench your fist very tightly for a moment, until you almost squeeze the moisture out of the center of your hand. Hold it there for a moment and see how little could be placed in your hand. Now extend your hands and open them. Form them into cups.

Recognize now, beloved ones, that the pitcher that holds the light of your being must be smashed in the name of the LORD, as Gideon of old brake the pitcher,[7] and the light that is in you must shine forth and not be neglected.

Place in your hands now the consecrated gift of God's own holy Eucharist—the manna that came down from heaven. Think for a moment that you are a part of God, a wonderful part of the Divine Whole. Materialize in your consciousness the manna.[8] Take your other hand and reach down into your hand and lift this manna to your lips: "Take, eat: this is my body, which is broken for you."[9]

Hold your hands out now and receive the chalice. Bring the Holy Grail of Being to your lips. In this Holy Grail of Being is the wine of the New Testament,[10] the new wine of spiritual devotion that makes of the body of God upon earth one.

Though men drink of the Communion of our Lord a million times, unless they partake of the realities of this Body and of this Life,

*North, Central, and South America

they have no life in them.[11] Drink ye then the cup of immortal life, the elixir that comes from God's own hand.

As Christ fed the multitudes by the sea, so have I today given you substance of eternal substance. Discern the body of God and you shall find such change affecting your lives as shall make you a part forever of the mystical body of Christ.

I, Paul, have given you this afternoon my concept of the world, of the world's cup, of the cup of world unity, of the cup of spirituality, of the methodology by which you may obtain for yourselves a greater measure of divinity from God's own hand.

I shall stand in the higher ethers with others of the ascended masters and lovingly wait to behold your ascension. But I shall also wait for those first acts that must precede that ascension, the results of this consecration today, and the results of each day's consecration.

Ladies and gentlemen, in the holy name of that wonderful spiritual Brotherhood, in the holy name of that compassionate Presence of Life, I say with *all* my heart, I thank you.

July 6, 1963

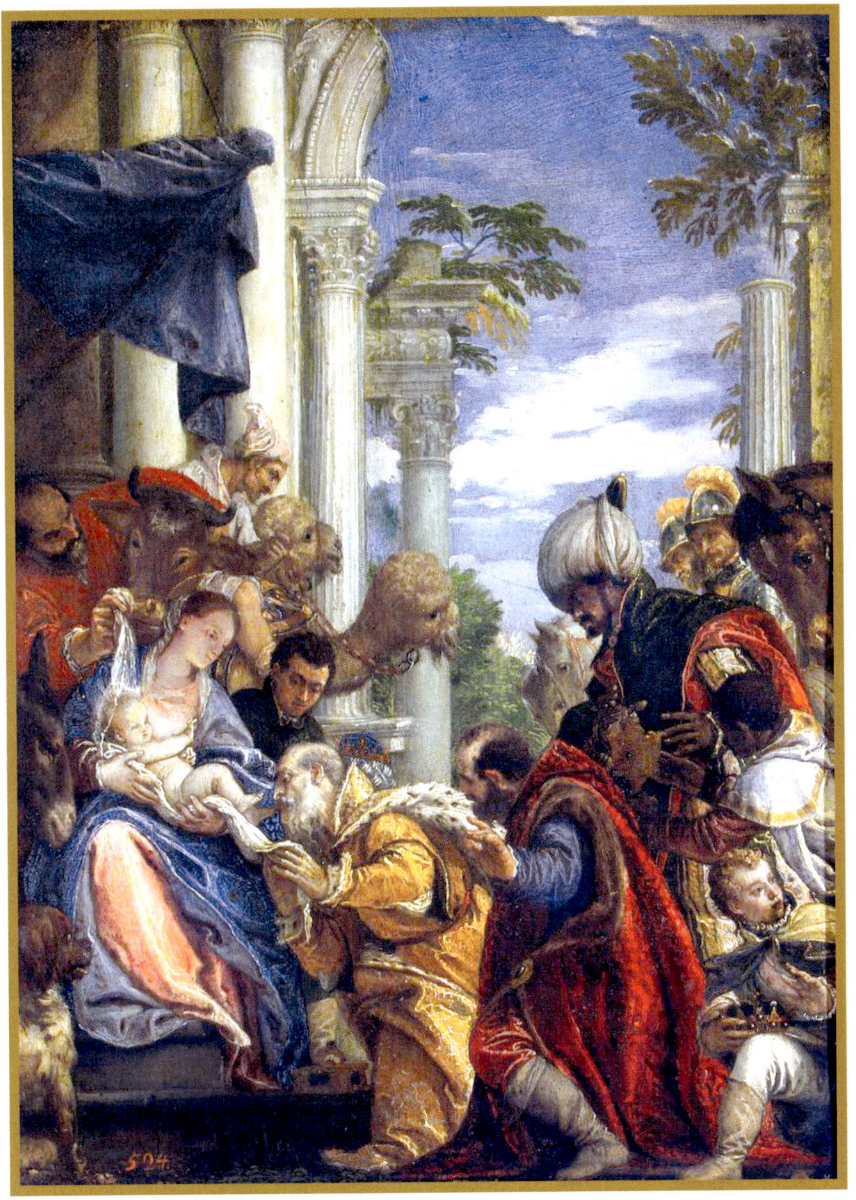

Adoration of the Magi, c. 1570s

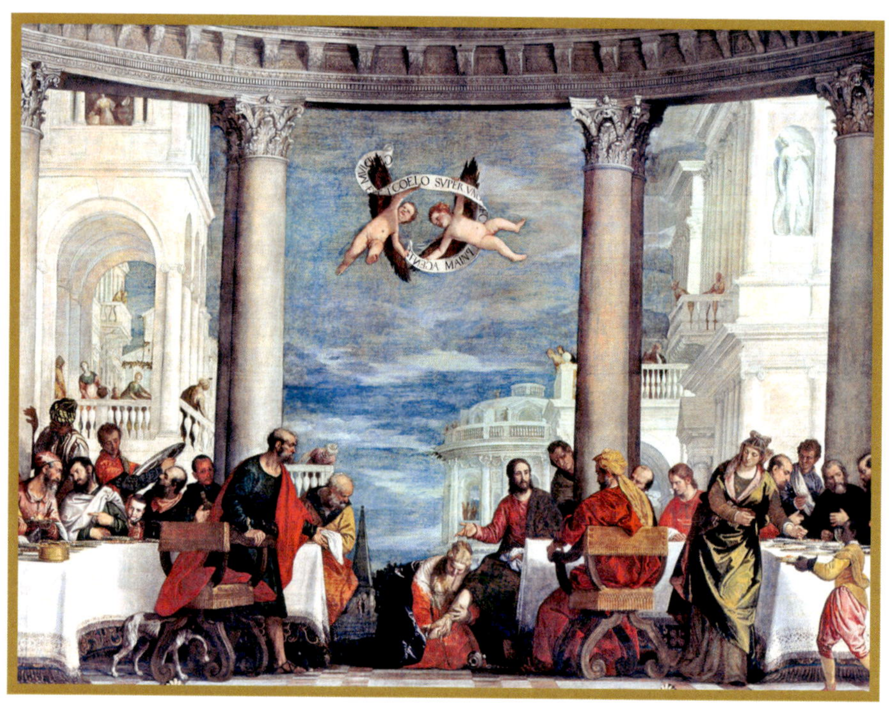

The Feast in the House of Simon the Pharisee (detail), 1570

The threefold flame... is a manifest Presence of God anchored right within the human heart. It is there to sustain a focus of beauty within the forcefield of yourself.... This is your flame, the great treasure house of spiritual power, knowing, and love. It is yours to nourish, sustain, and expand. It is a gift of the eternal Father.

CHAPTER 13

THE FABRIC OF ETERNITY

Ladies and gentlemen of heaven, I salute the great God flame that is within you, and I ask that you be exalted in consciousness to come with me into the spiritual octaves of light, where beauty shines in its great, eternal effulgence, divested of mortal substance and shining with all of the joy and the jewels that the angels have woven into that manifestation of God's own holy treasure.

Precious ones, the flame of liberty* pulsates within your heart, and this flame of liberty, in all of its exquisite beauty, is a drawing nigh unto your worlds of the substance of our octave. When the flame of life that is within you is amplified by your conscious attention to this flame, an expansion occurs that brings to you a greater sense of the power of God, the will of God, and his faith.

When you become aware of the pulsations of the golden element of this threefold flame, the holy pulsations of illumination do rise and you feel inspired to understand the universe as though your mind were one with God's own. But when you enter into the third portion of this triune aspect of your own liberty flame—the flame of divine love, the pink radiance over which I preside as chohan—you become aware of the great love for God and the great love of God for his creation.

*The flame of liberty is synonymous with the threefold flame (see p. 276 in the Glossary).

There is an affinity, a duality implanted within love, which causes the created thing to also aspire to love the Creator. And there is within the heart of the Creator a manifest token that will not let him forget that he himself abides within the warp and woof, the very fabric of temporal creation.

As I gaze at the splendor, then, of the higher octaves, I call to each one of you to forsake the concepts of mortality, which have not brought to you the fullness of that release of spiritual victory that God intends for you all. The substance of heaven and its precious treasure is your own, but only when you make it so.

We ourselves have labored in the past to outpicture the fullness of God's beauty upon earth. When I was embodied as Paolo Veronese, I did indeed engraft upon canvas the substance that caused mankind to admire and to love the more cultured treasures of the world and to drink in that culture so that by inward realization, the wonders of art were for the ennoblement of the mind of man. And to the present day, these concepts remain.

As I have told you since, when I gaze backward through the power of memory and see that which was wrought, although recognized and acknowledged by mankind to this present hour as a work of splendid achievement, I do feel that it is poor by comparison to genuine spiritual beauty. And I say to you today that if your eyes could see as I do the wonders of the immortal octaves of light, you would hasten the day of the appearance of your victory, signified by the pulsation of the liberty flame within your own consciousness, and you would find less inclination to dally in the lurid and sensational archives of mankind's own feelings and abortions of the divine intent.

Many Authors Have Contributed to the Downward Pull upon Mankind's Desires

The corridors of human memory are open unto me, and I can walk as freely in those corridors and hallways—those dead-end streets that lead nowhere—as I can walk in the celestial galleries of light and love. And for a moment I would tell you something of the avenues of disservice to which mankind are often committed by reason of an abortion of the art and literature of the world.

You know, blessed ones, that many famous and widely read books are indeed the creations of mortal mind, and yet by reason of their acceptance by multitudes of people who have read them, meditated upon them, and given them their attention, the contents have actually been expanded so that in the realm of thought, the fabric of that material (much of which is sordid and destructive) is spread abroad in the mass consciousness of mankind. When individuals read this material, they drink in all of the sordid aspects of the mind of the author, together with the similar thoughts of those who have read this material. And therefore they are pulled down into a denser pattern rather than brought up into airy patterns of light and understanding.

Now I would like to point out that many of the authors of the world have contributed to the downfall of mankind. Of course it is a matter of spiritual record that many among mankind have also contributed to the upliftment of mankind, and these we bless. But those who have contributed to the downward pull upon mankind's desires are sought after by the youth of the world, who are thereby trapped in these corridors of mankind's sordid memory. They find, as though they were in a dream state, that they cannot extricate themselves therefrom. And they feel a sense of helplessness and a hapless feeling, which is contrary to the pulsations of Liberty's flame within their being. And because the flame of immortality within them seeks to express immortal freedom, there is a continuing sense of struggle and restlessness in their heart and being.

They do not know the ways of peace, and they cannot find the avenues that lead to God because they are walking continually in those directions that are away from him. When in some way, through the great laws of the mercies of life, an emissary of light is sent to them, they spurn this emissary in almost every case. For they who have need of salvation often do not seek or pursue it, and those who are already upon the path of light are those who snatch at every gem and make it their own treasure. These, then, are adorned with splendid spiritual jewels and shine as the sun in splendor, whereas others walk as beggars and paupers across the highways and byways of life but know it not.

Of such as these the Word of the Christ has gone forth, "Ye are naked, and ye are poor and ye are blind, and ye are helpless";[1] "depart from me, ye workers of iniquity, for I know you not."[2] Of a truth, the Christ image, in all of the splendid beauty that God has implanted there, does not always appear to those who have need of him. You may wonder, then, why we continue to pour out our love upon those of you who seek a greater anointing, to add to him who already has and to take away from him who hath not that which he already has.[3] This is a fulfillment, blessed ones, of the master plan of the universe, and it cannot be altered but it must be understood.

The Law of Mercy

Those who walk in darkness and fear the evils of darkness must someday come to the awareness of their lack by their own free will. As long as the goods and treasures of spiritual light are bestowed upon them, they continue to walk in their own iniquitous ways and to wander farther and farther from the ways of truth. But when the Lords of Karma, in the great spiritual realms of light, do set into motion the return currents of that which these individuals have sent out, and when that energy comes to them for redemption, it can be received as a splendid and wonderful opportunity if it is understood correctly. For it is the fulfillment of the law of mercy that prevents and curbs wrong action so that individuals do not utterly destroy the very fabric of their souls.

The mercy of God, when it is understood, works not only in the bestowal of divine gifts and graces in a manifestation of love and wonder, but also through the misqualified media of contrast, showing up in a glaring manner to the consciousness of mankind those unlovely and unwanted qualities so that they might recognize that which they ought to desire and so that they might feel in their emptiness and aloneness a measure of need for the power of light and for the power of heaven.

This, then, refers also to the fact that the very heavens should be shaken and the stars should fall from their places.[4] For mankind have, in the figure of some of your poets, "hitched their wagon to a star" of nothingness and they have sought after false goals. They have not known the way of peace and the way of righteousness, but they have continuously imagined evil and that which departs from God. They have abided in a realm of shadow, and they know not eternal peace.

Now then, let us recognize how the Law works. In the space of a few short years, through a just application of the karmic lash—even though it might be extended over several embodiments—the chastening of God can successfully prune human tendencies and cause individuals to exercise the passion of right desire for God. Is this not, then, the fulfillment of beauty in the life of the individual, and will not all thereby come to their appointed place and the correct understanding of the Law?

Thus by experience mankind come to love the rod, which when bestowed upon them is the fulfillment of his Word, "I chasten those whom I love."[5] For God loveth all creatures both great and small.

Wear the Garments of Light as You Walk among Mankind

As Kuthumi has said to me (standing in my presence now),[6] "God's love is spread as mighty wings over all, and those who know him and those who know him not are also beneath his rod." His rod is a "magic wand" to bestow the wonders of the infinite stars upon man's being, compassion without limit and to the farthest reaches of space and time. The web of continuum and continuity encompassing man is the very fabric of God woven upon substance, the great light of immortality. Only the interweavings of eternality are present, and these weavings are unparalleled in their loveliness.

Those who are able to see into this octave are eternally blessed, for they are blessed with the fabric of eternity, and there is a difference between time and eternity. The difference is one of light and shadow. And I tell you, blessed ones, that the media of the light, which the light requires for contrast, is provided amply by individual spiritual attainment. For "as one star differeth from another star in glory,"[7] so individuals in the hierarchical scheme of things do not all manifest the full brilliance of the Son of God's Being but are positioned according to their development down the scale of the white light. There is a co-relative measurement, a co-measurement of Spirit, which shows to all the great need as well as the power to draw from higher dimensions the requirements of immortal realms. By this I imply to those of you with understanding that there is a need for you to wear the garments of light here and now as you walk among mankind.

You walk forth, blessed ones, clothed upon with the fashions of the times. You attire yourself so as to be in style. But if you were summoned this moment to stand in the presence of the elect, there is no human fashion or mode that could serve to hide you from the eyes of Deity and the presiding power of the Lords of Karma. For you would be, as it were, naked before them, if you were not clothed upon by garments of light.

Do you think it would avail you to come there attired in the most shapely garments of the day? I tell you, nay. For loveliness of mind, beauty of soul, compassion of consciousness, purity of motive, ordered service, devotion to truth, and the qualities of heaven are both garment and jewels to those who walk according to the tenets of our order.

Our Intent Is to Bring Every Man His Freedom

We cannot, then, in the spirit of light, ignore the needs of mankind. And so when we speak as I have spoken this morn and this day, it is for the sole purpose of bringing you into greater awareness of the great heavenly galleries of life. For artists abide here also, and writers. Men of science abide here, but these are men of heavenly science, versed in all the arts of mankind but oh so blessed with all the divine arts as well.

These are indeed sons of God. You can make them, then, your own closest friends, for they stand ready and willing to serve your needs. But the Law must be fulfilled, and you must inquire of them as to whether or not they will step forth and serve your needs. Just as the magic lamp had to be rubbed by Aladdin, so mankind must consciously summon the powers of light and fulfill the law of being.

We do not enter your homes or consciousness simply because you might have a weak or strong desire to improve yourselves. We come when bidden, and we stay as long as we can comfortably abide in the aura of your thoughts. When your thoughts abide in concepts of loveliness and exaltation—*gloria in excelsis Deo*—we are then able, through the consciousness of God, to sustain an elevated momentum in your own forcefield.

When through your own purpose or design or through happenstance you depart the higher concepts and enter into the vibratory action of the sordid and destructive, we must of necessity excuse ourselves and bow out, for we cannot remain there to nurture and to foster such types of action that are contrary to the holy purposes. Therefore, understand that this is not an act designed in any way to harm you, nor is it one of aloofness or discourtesy on our part when we do not remain with you. It is a necessity, for we cannot sustain or amplify those qualities that are not noble.

Take, then, this holy truth and make it your own. And draw, then, all of the ascended masters into proximity to your forcefield and receive from us those incomparable treasures of light that are ours to bestow upon you with joy. You know, precious ones, that you will abide in our octaves, or at least out of your physical form, far longer than you have abode in this form. Therefore, it is necessary that you understand that it is our intent to bring to every man his freedom, his great liberty this day.

The Threefold Flame within the Heart of Man

Of all the objects of loveliness that I have ever painted, the most beautiful painting I have ever made was a simple attempt to duplicate the threefold flame within the heart of man. For this threefold flame, in all of its radiant outpicturing, is the design of God himself, fashioned of the power and faith of his being, fashioned of the divine intelligence, fashioned of divine love. It continues to spring up as the fabled fountain of Ponce de León. It is a manifest Presence of God anchored right within the human heart. It is there to sustain a focus of beauty within the forcefield of yourself. It shrinks when you turn your back upon decency and loveliness, and it expands as you approach the Deity. This is your flame, the great treasure house of spiritual power, knowing, and love. It is yours to nourish, sustain, and expand. It is a gift of the eternal Father.

If I were to make an individual portrait of you, each one, and if I were to make a portrait of you that had the power to bestow upon you the qualities of immortality and true liberty, I would draw upon that threefold flame within each of you and I would fashion that portrait as the True Self. Human dross is not thy Self. On the contrary, it is thy refined gold, thy illumination, thy expression of reality that leads thee Godward.

Many Shall Find Their Freedom

May the great golden eagle from Venus[8] speed thee heavenward and lift thee up and bear thee toward octaves of cosmic purity and thought and motive. So shall noble men stand forth upon earth, recipients of our holy charge. So shall the kingdom flourish. So shall many find their freedom.

Ladies and gentlemen, I bow to the God flame within all of you. Ladies and gentlemen, I commend you to the keeping of the One who has taught you that all life *is* one.

Good afternoon, in the bonds of divine love.

September 27, 1964

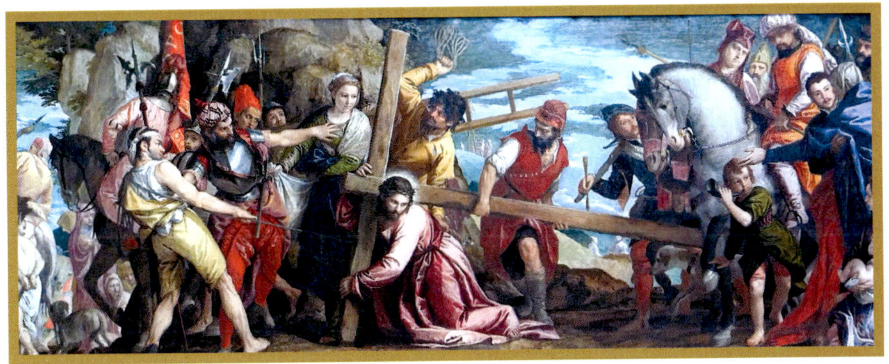

The Bearing of the Cross, c. 1571

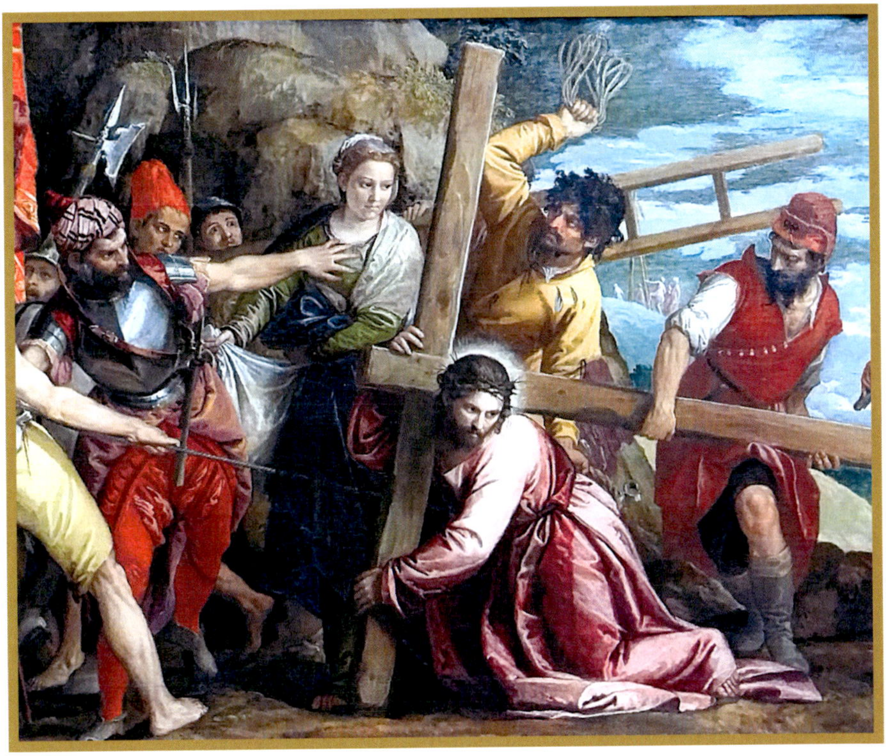

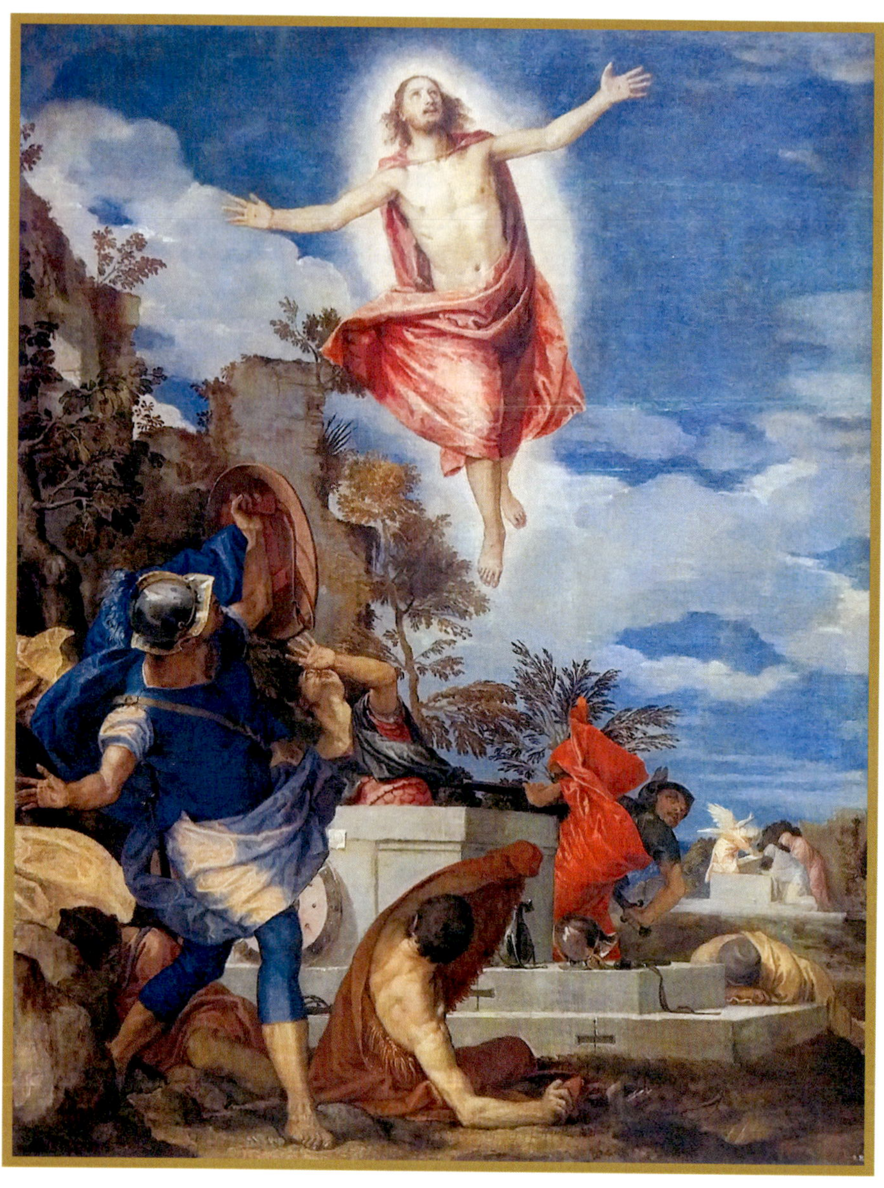

The Resurrection of Christ, c. 1570

The sun will burst upon your soul, with all of its rays and radiance, and the light that maketh the universe whole will come to full glory and expansion in your world here below, as Above.

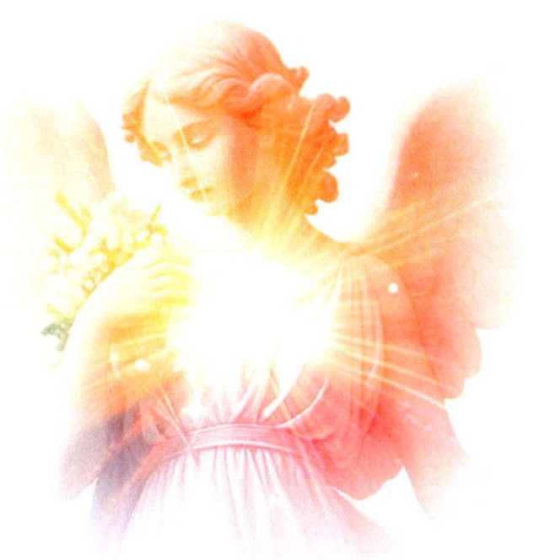

CHAPTER 14

The Great Abiding Presence of Beauty within the Human Soul

Gracious ladies and gentlemen, I recall through the process of memory how that many years ago when in the city of Paris (for I kept a small home there, to which I would journey on occasion), I walked one night at sunset alone to a peculiar little area near the water and stood watching as the twilight descended.

Far from the madding crowd of the city, my thoughts flew as on wings out over oceans and continents to other lands. And I thought of the vastness of the world, as no doubt you too have mused. And I sensed the great abiding presence of beauty within the human soul, and I knew that in my solitude and aloneness there was a great blessing, which could never have been realized had I been among the multitudes.

The Christ long ago also demonstrated his desire to be apart from the multitudes. But all these withdrawals were for purposes of strength, that the bond of grace and immortality could then become boundless in sense.

Man, you know, is often prone to render a situation grave. And I would take the gravity out of a situation and teach the art of buoyancy to you, whereby you sense that behind every veil and all seeming mourning there is the sun that lights the cloud with gold and silver and a tip, a little touch, of heaven.

The tiny concept of a babe, whether in Bethlehem or elsewhere, with rosy cheeks and bright eyes showing the freshness of heaven, not only gladdens the hearts of mothers but of all people throughout the earth, who are often pulled by the radiance come late from heaven to their consciousness.

And so as I mused by the water and beheld the lamps of evening lit, and as my soul flew Godward to muse upon color and upon the part that the rainbow spectrum plays in the manifestation of reality, I gave thanks to God in a silent petition offered upward for his gift of color relative to the rainbow of promise, which in our artistic minds we often employed in order to gladden the hearts of mankind with simple scenes executed with such talent as God gave to us.

Today, in mankind's kindness and because time has passed, lending enchantment to the view of our art, they choose to praise us and to think of us as great men. Michelangelo, Raphael, Titian, and many of the other greats of the past are considered to be artisans of tremendous ability. But I would remind you of that Great Painter of the sky itself. I would remind you of the angels who make the color of morning and evening and the brightness of the sea and the foam.

There Is an Inner Sense in Art, a Transparency of Spirit

You recall, perhaps, how there came from France to a South Sea island a painter who dwelled among the natives there and who was fascinated with the joy and the sense of the joy. May I now, then, give a criticism from the ascended octave of his work? You perhaps did not fancy me an art critic at this stage of my development. And perhaps it is best that I do not directly refer to him by name, but I am sure that you can easily ascertain the one of whom I speak.

This individual captured something of the bizarre in France in his sketches upon tablecloths and other common items. He became quite famous, and mankind were not quite aware of the fact that part of his work was a perversion of the third ray of divine love. For he was never able in that embodiment to discover the delicate and radiant sense of Michelangelo. This was because this individual was enamored with womankind in the manner of the ordinary, and he did not understand the proper regard for womanhood.

Now, my reason for referring to this painter today in criticism from a spiritual octave is not to direct energy against his blessed lifestream, but it is to point out that there was a certain garishness about his work and that this is ever the case when the lack of purity of soul does not permit the angelic radiance to come through. And I cite this not to harm him but as a guide to future individuals of the skill of brush and craft so that they, taking warning, may recognize what they ought to do and what they ought not to do in the realm of art.

There is an inner sense in art, a transparency of spirit that views the body of man not as filled with arterial canals or bone and skeletal framework but recognizes all of the points of balance where the skeletal framework would be, seeing it all as light and retaining its complete form as though there were nothing there to hold it except light. And in this transparent sense, man is able to frame the body and fashion it with brush in hand in a more delicate manner. For the angels do not have flesh and bone. They do not have a musculoskeletal frame to hold together their being, and they are composed of light.

The Ascended State Is But a Beginning, and There Are Many Octaves Beyond

And you also in the ascended state will be composed and held together by light. And the internal organs, many of them, will not be necessary to your existence at all. Certain focuses of the glands, of course, will remain, for they are jewels of light placed there to remind you of the call from higher octaves. These jewels will always remain with you unless you choose to be completely absorbed by the Great Central Sun. And then, of course, you would offer them for cremation upon the altar of God through the process of the highest nirvana.

This is usually not required, for most individuals are happy to perform some service to life in a blithe manner, as the angels do in the various octaves of life, even far above the ascended state. For the ascended state is but a beginning, and there are many octaves beyond, reaching toward the Godhood and the Godhead and the center of all that is.

But the servitors of light are required in the ascended state, and holy men and women of dedication are required there and are needed. And there is a great service to be rendered even in the higher etheric realm, and also in many realms yet unknown to the mind of man.

You need not fear or ponder or become exceedingly curious, for all is linked with being, and being is linked with God. And you may rest secure, as a babe in the arms of its mother—a babe who knows not of the concerns of the world nor has yet learned letters and is content with an inner contentment to sleep upon her bosom in the quiet sleep of infancy. In comfort those of mature states may also rest in the arms of the Holy Mother and be aware that the concept of the Holy Family is one not just for this earth but for heaven also.

The Engendering of the Cosmic Sense of Art within You

Did not our Lord Christ recommend and commend to you the concept of the Father?

The heavenly Father, then, is made more real to you by reason of his mission, by the sublime joy of God, never holding any conceit but only the immaculate conception. You see, precious ones, the idea of *conceit* is somewhat related to the idea of *conceive,* but it is a wrong conception.

I point out many things to you this morning, that your thought may not necessarily flit about but that you may recognize the tenor of that which I am driving at, as you say.

For I have a purpose withal in all that I say to you this day, and that purpose is the engendering of the cosmic sense of art within you that is not confined necessarily to three-dimensional form. It takes into account the four dimensions and therefore enters into the octave of God-purity, where the Goddess of Purity[1] and the Great Silent Watcher together hold conclave in revealing the immaculate concept of each individual person (or monad) to that individual, so that individuals will not see themselves as bone and flesh and muscle or see themselves as an ego bobbing upon the waves of life like a cork. But rather they will see themselves as a stable factor in the universe, a spark of the great sacred-fire wheel—the wheel of life turning in all its dynamism, the wheel of the sacred fire and the wheel of the Law.

It Is by Contact with the Great Wheel of the Law That Man's Ills Are All Cured

Take note, blessed ones, how the vibratory action of *wheel* is affinitive to the vibratory action of *to heal*. For it is by contact with the great wheel of the Law that man's ills are all cured and God mends every flaw, else sin and its inequities would be endured. And the world would stand in awe of that rightness of inheritance, which God would see all secure.

Strength, then, must not diminish but enfold all, and compassion stretch forth its bonds on wings until, as songbirds with heavenly melodies, the hearts of men can sing and hold such love in view as shall improve the lot of men and still the elements of strife—those tones that are a din rather than the voice of immortal life.

I say, then, let strife end all,
And let love expand over all
Until God has removed every pall—
The strength of sin.
All nature then shall sing,
And freedom's bells shall ring,
And compassion shall enfold,
Making the world so old, so new,
So fresh to view,
With colors rare
And sounds so fair
Heard ringing upon the air,
As morning light breaking forth everywhere
Ends the night of despair
And creates a new sense of virtue and liberty.

If You Shall Move Forward in the Light, You Must Win in God's Great Fight for the Victory of Each One

I am come, then, this day to remind you of the words of the Master, who preceded me: "I am come that they might have life, and that more abundantly."[2]

The outer sense, O precious ones, has never brought the freedom of expression that the inward one does. Blessed are ye among men and women, O children of the light. For you have the rare jewels of ascended master compassion and understanding.

I know full well how you differ in your appreciation of art. Not all of you have the same development. But it matters little (as you have been told in this class) if progress be made. For ultimately, if you remain unafraid and shall move forward in the light, you must win in God's great fight for the victory of each one. And then the sun will burst upon your soul, with all of its rays and radiance, and the light that maketh the universe whole will come to full glory and expansion in your world here below, as Above.

And this is an understanding factor in the Godhead itself. For with what measure of understanding shall mankind measure their strength if not by the divine standard?

If they shall measure their strength by the human standard, shall they not all vary? If they shall measure their strength by His strength, shall they not all become one?

And if one, then I think, as Saint Germain would say, the work shall be well done. And if well done, then, victorious servants, you shall become that which God would have you be—a part of the ascended hosts. And this is the most glorious state that you can ever imagine.

The Great Golden Strands of Heaven's Light Shall Shine Forth

Precious ones, is the divine art not worth waiting for? Is the divine art not worth possessing your souls for? Is the divine art not worth all? And if these things be so, then let us gather together the children of mankind in wielding the sacred powers of the Holy Spirit in order to capture the divine idea in stone and bone and canvas and substance, as well as in that which is above. For all that man doeth below must be executed in love.

And if so, then, as in the early days of ancient Greece in the Age of Pericles, the great golden strands of heaven's light shall even shine forth in the land in constitutional government and the voices of freedom will ring out.

Men like unto Paul Revere alerted the people in days of old. Today this task is sometimes left to the ascended masters. We do not, however, say that your assistance is unwelcome. We welcome it. For I think that there are many of your brethren who would heed your voice even more quickly than our own, for they have not yet understood how we may speak and come unto them in this fashion.

They have forgotten the old prophets of Israel, and they have forgotten the gift and true art of prophecy and spiritual attunement. And false prophets are abroad in the land and world, not directing mankind toward God but toward Magog[3] and toward destruction.

Truly, blessed ones, the dawn of thy immortal inheritance pulsates as a flame within thy heart. And if liberty is ever to be enshrined in this land and upon earth, it must be enshrined in the hearts of the people.

Will you now—under the direction of those who sing among you and your pianist, and as I radiate Liberty's flame over this city and call to the Maha Chohan to bring ten thousand snow-white doves to this city, to bring the light of purity to this city and its government—will you sing to the old, familiar tune of the French national anthem, the song of liberty, "La Marseillaise," while the doves come with the angelic hosts over Washington, D.C., as wings over the world—wings to raise, to elevate, to purify, to ennoble, to bring a message of the new culture that shall be, that shall make men of liberty a part and of God's light forever free.

I thank you.

October 11, 1964

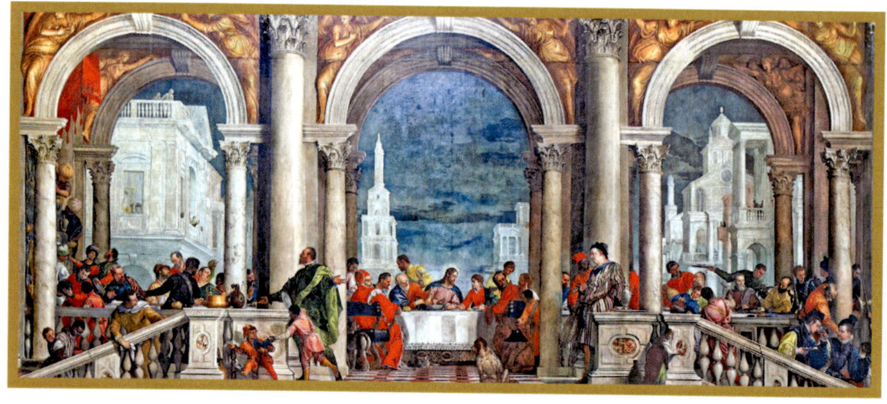

The Feast in the House of Levi, c. 1573

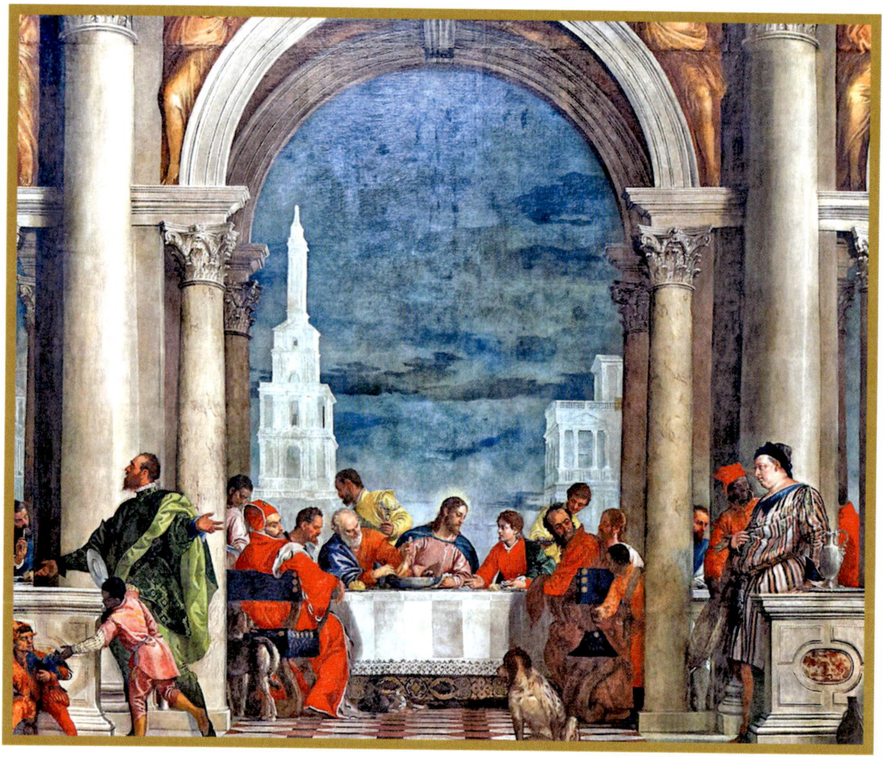

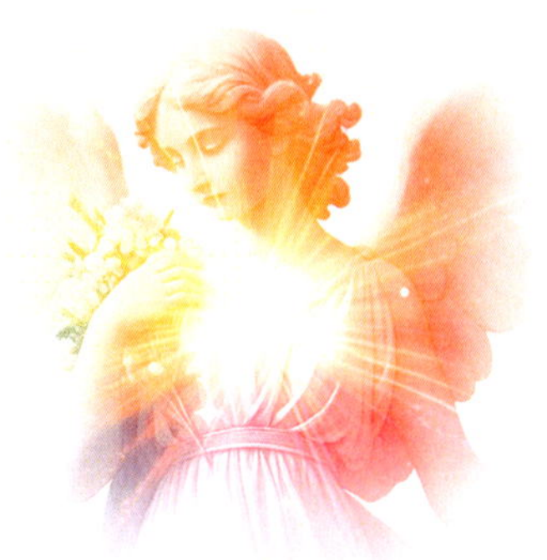

Listen to the sound of the angels.
Listen to the crescendos of their hearts of gold.
Listen to the anthem of the ages.
Listen to the anthem of the free.
Hear it echoing from the depths of eternity.

CHAPTER 15

The Beauty of Creation

O flame of infinite comfort, come forth now within the temples of mankind's heart and knit those hearts together in that beautiful release of infinite peace, that beautiful release of the silence of God's love, the power when all is still. For in the beauty of stillness, the calm pool of knowing begins to reflect his radiance. And in that reflection there is born the selfsame beautiful obedience that elemental life manifested when it received the impetus of the Holy Spirit and, directed by the ancient covenants, went forth to accomplish the beauty of creation.

The miracle, solemnized by the archetypal manifestations of God, is indeed beautiful to behold manifesting at inner levels. I think also (although mankind have corrupted much of the pristine beauty of creation through wrong thought and feeling), that the remnant of that creation also holds a beauty (although somewhat faded, as an ancient painting) from the original design. The cracks and flaws, the hardened pigments occasioned by mankind's hardness of heart, have taken their toll. And I think the canvas does, then, not fully manifest the original beauty of the cosmic creation of God.

But that which is within, that light within the heart of the children of God, is beautiful to behold. For although it may seem to be to thee but as a candle in the midst of billions of feet of shallow darkness, the light of that candle is very great when thou considerest it. For it is the essence of thy life, and the meaning of that life is thine to discover.

The miracle of life, then, is in the flashing forth of beauty upon the screen thereof. When the curtain goes up and mankind behold the solemn purposes, their hearts leap from the banal consciousness of bondage into the wondrous spirit of liberty, and the pulsations of Liberty's flame consecrate mankind to holy purpose.

Wedded then to holy purpose, mankind seek constantly to please the beloved, and the flame of life flashes forth in right conduct, right speech, right thought, and the reflected image, which resembles the purity of the original design.

Oh, how intricate are the weavings, precious ones. And I think that if mankind could behold each strand as it is placed in the garment of being, they would realize more fully how important is the placing of each thread in completing the pattern as God intends.

A Miracle of God's Love

Now I recall how a very poor young lad—embodied in France long ago, sometime after the passing of Jeanne d'Arc—did offer unto a poor widow and her sick child a loaf of bread, which was all the substance that he had left, and he did not reserve so much as a crumb of it for himself. And this lad went into a great cathedral to pray, having offered this gift unto the woman, who joyously accepted it as a gift from the angels.

It came to pass, as he went into the cathedral to pray, that the angels of God came and comforted him, and there was given unto him a holy vision. And he saw the land of Palestine and the multitudes gathered upon the hillsides, and to him the great ritual drama of the Christ in his Sermon on the Mount[1] became a living thing—before the advent of motion pictures and before mankind possessed the power to re-create in imagination these designs from the akashic records.

To this boy, by angelic hands, was given this great and precious gift of witnessing in faithful representation every act concerning the Master Jesus in his full delivery of the Sermon on the Mount. "Blessed are the poor in spirit.... Blessed are the pure in heart."[2]

The ringing tones of the Master were heard forth from him in fluent French, the lad's own native tongue, and the lad's heart was gladdened by the miracle of God's love. This young lad felt no pangs of pity for himself because he was anhungered, and he rejoiced in the opportunity of having been the donor of some grace to a part of life.

Re-Creation and the Power to Create Is a Thing of Beauty and a Joy Forever

What a different message this is, precious ones, to that sorrow that occupies the mind of some, who in base self-pity do feel that their lot is not a happy one, whereas God has given to them a scale of opportunity whereby they may rise from the sands of the present upon the desert (or seeming desert) of self and find that at the command from on high the land bursts forth into blossoms. And the rose and the essence and the perfume and the flowers and the magic of light and loveliness kindle the desert with blossoms.

And the dust mingles therewith, and all is God's light, a sea billowing with angelic forms—a sea of splendor that like the flowers of the grass will ultimately pass from the screen of life but not from the screen of consciousness. For as a field of wheat waving in the wind, as the living wheat that the disciples took and did eat as they passed through the wheat fields,[3] so in the blessed memory of mankind, re-creation and the power to create is a thing of beauty and a joy forever.

In the divine imagery, in the divine image, mankind awaken to a dream of immortality and its reality. In the divine image and the image of consecration, the fires of Almighty God are banked upon the shores of man's consciousness, and mankind, coming then to a new land of self to discover, find their freedom in the I AM Race consciousness.

I Come to Reconsecrate a Flame of Beauty to the Earth

"America, we love you." These words pour forth in this blessed land consecrated to Saint Germain, consecrated also by the power of the Goddess of Liberty's flame. And I think it shall be my privilege to stand above this place in the upper atmosphere when she speaks her words to you on the morrow[4] and I pour my adoration down upon you as she rekindles the torch of your being in accordance with the divine design.

Now as a flower opes its petals to the sun
To drink the beloved radiance
That falleth as the gentle rain,
So do I ask that once again
Ye shall consecrate your being
To the magic of a lute
That like an entrancing flute
Blows and pipes its notes anew.
The consecration, oh, so true
That brings a sense of beauty, too,
And loveliness beyond compare
A blossomed immortelle so fair.
God's own face to thee is shown,
And thou dost know thou art not alone
But ever surrounded with radiance fair,
The power and love of a maiden's prayer
To gladden then the very air
With a sense of beauty beyond compare.

I am come this night to reconsecrate
A flame of beauty to the earth.
The sense of beauty is gone;
The house of God is desolate.
The people's hearts are affrighted
And they tremble
As though peril were in the cup.
And the poison of iniquity is spread abroad in the land,
And greed and selfishness are on every hand.
And men in the barrenness of their soul
Do fail and fail to reach the goal.

The old boundaries of sin and stain
Continue to wreak the havoc of pain.

And mankind know they must find the way
To break the shroud
Of death that cries so loud:
"Come, play with us
And feel our dust,
For we eat, we drink, and tomorrow we die.
We perish and our life will fly.
So let us, then, drink the cup—
The cup of happiness complete
That comes from mortal substance sweet
And despises God's own law and truth
And findeth naught but pain in truth"—
Because they understand not the Way.
I AM the Way, so let us pray:

Our Father dear, hear our prayer
And consecrate these people fair
Whose face is like an angel's prayer, in reality.
O thou dawn of God, eternity,
That everywhere does show, disclosing,
Reveal the forces, then, opposing
All that is the light of God.
And let Babylon fall that is not the Law,
And let men's hearts then turn in awe
Because the truth of God is plain.
It is the life; then don't complain
But do thou, O thou children wise,
The acts of God, and don't despise
The chastening of his blessed rod
That leads you, calls you back to God.

On bended knee,
Let mankind see
I AM the power to make you free.
Then call and call and call again
And let all bondage go indeed,

For God will be with you as you speed
Your prayer of love to his own throne,
And you shall feel no more alone.
Self-pity gone, your soul will be
Consecrated to the free.

The Way Is Thus Made Plain

Precious ones, I call to God, to his Almighty altar, that you understand clearly what I am speaking to you in the beauty of poetic release, that you understand that the Way is thus made plain, that you may be consecrated through the power of inspiration and the song of joy within your own souls to awaken from the constant threat and shadow of the pall of mankind's own iniquity.

You know, precious ones, mankind continue—and I do mean continue—to repeat the old mistakes continually. And they wonder why they do not learn divine artistry. They wonder why *they* do not become painters of divine beauty. They wonder why they do not find their freedom. It is because sometimes, unbeknownst to them, there lurks within the darkness of their thought something of which they are not wholly aware, and it is urged upon them to discover through the power of Christ-illumination all that needs correcting within their world.

Many times I have come to you and I have urged upon you the sense of beauty. I come now, this night, to urge upon you the sense of beauty of soul. When you stop and pause, precious ones, to consider the goal that is before you, the majesty of Christ—and I regard him as having a visage that is not mean but one that is indeed filled with the radiance of victory and God-determination—then I say, let all who will emulate him find the will to stimulate themselves by divine fervor, to determine to overthrow all that hinders and opposes the victory of their life and world.

God's Word Is Consecrated within You

You cannot know, precious ones, until you are willing to shatter the human matrix, just how much the human matrix has done to oppose the freedom of your soul. You think sometimes, precious ones, that a little thorn has no meaning, and yet how great a beast can be brought low in whimpering, howling madness because of the pain of one thorn when placed between the toes.

And therefore I think, precious ones, that you will recognize how gracious it is when you spend your life in a beautiful way:

To free others from strain and sin and pain
And fill them with the vigor for the fight—
Not, precious ones, to scatter among mankind fear and fright.
It is so easy for tumult to be spread abroad in the land
And for fear to appear at every hand.
And then I think that if he could
Almighty God would shed a tear,
But because his perfection is so clear
He holds the soul and doth revere
All that is his divine plan—
The plan of God for every man.

O precious ones, listen, and listen clearly,
For I have been told by an angel
Who had the boldness to speak,
That the bells of heaven shall ring this night
And can be heard audibly
By those who have the courage
To lift high their ear.
In the upper atmosphere right here,
The joy bells of the LORD are ringing clear.
A sound of joy and peace will be heard then,
Throughout the world by the power of God's Word.
His Word is consecrated within you;
It is beautiful. It is lovely. It is a joy forever.

Listen, then.
Listen to the sound of the angels.
Listen to the crescendos of their hearts of gold.
Listen to the anthem of the ages.

Listen to the anthem of the free.
Hear it echoing from the depths of eternity.
As I am speaking to you,
This beauty is pouring out all around you.
It is like a series of lights that glow.
It is like welcome fires here below.
That which comes from above the plain,
The truth that lives as Christ shall reign
Within thy heart, where I AM free,
The power to know is given to thee.

Will ye, then, remain all bound
When by God's law and holy sound
The tone of OM resounding then
Is like a prayer, a great Amen?
The angels' voices in the air
Do now make music everywhere.
And life Edenic then is born.
'Tis like the beauty of a cosmic morn,
When the birds do sing
And joy bells ring
And freedom maketh all a king.

O God, let thy kingdom fair
Now appear to every heart.
Let the eyes of the heart expand;
Let the eyes of the soul understand.
And let that darkness that has covered the land
Be broken, the iron band!
Shatter it now in God's own name!
I say, let *all* claim
That victory that God would have
Descend upon the souls of men!

O, blessed ones, awake, awake!
And feel the beauty, for God's sake!

For he has given his all to thee
That thou mayest breathe his air so free
And know that *I AM liberty!*
Thy flame is flashing in the air!
That flame is heavenly joy so rare!
Oh, take it now
And to the light bow
And feel that God is ever thou!

Blight Shall Disappear as God's Beauty Appears

Ladies and gentlemen, in the name of liberty's holy flame, I say to you in honor of America and in honor of the true France—for I was once a dauphin thereof—that the flame of liberty shall this night expand in this place and in the hearts of those who will receive it, until beauty shall take the place of ugliness, and blight shall disappear as God's beauty appears.

So go and do thou likewise. In God's holy name, I AM, and for the sake of the prayer of the Master Jesus: "All that thou hast given unto me, I have kept, and none of them are lost."[5]

Father, I thank thee.

Pax vobiscum et spiritu tuum.

Adieu.

April 15, 1965

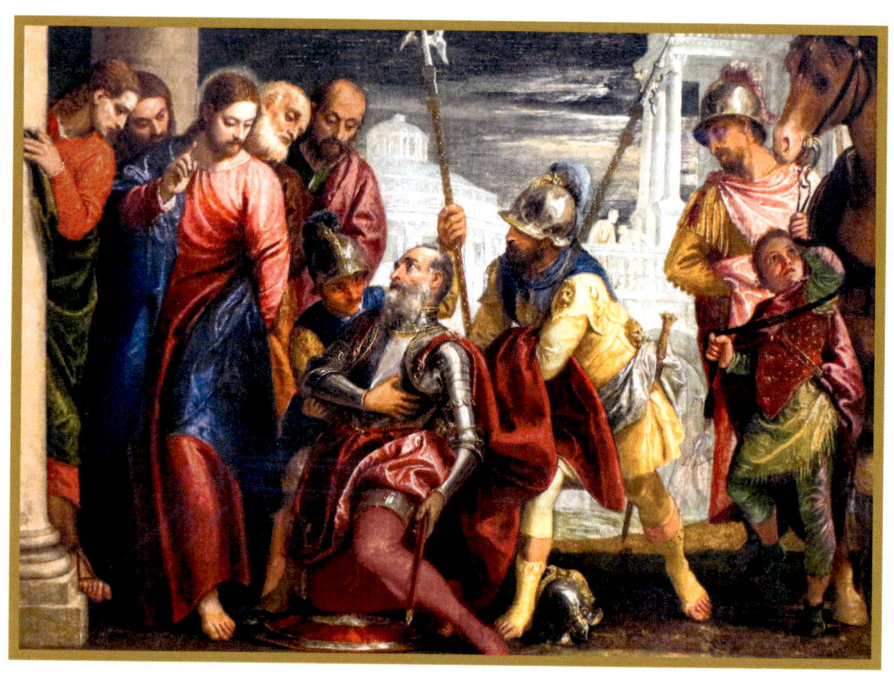

Christ and the Centurion, c. 1575–80

This is that type of beauty—the love that gazes in the eyes of the child to his mother and speaks to her these words: "Thou art my mother forever." In this closeness there is no growing up, no conception of the flow of time. There is only the little blessed delusion of a frozen, eternal moment.

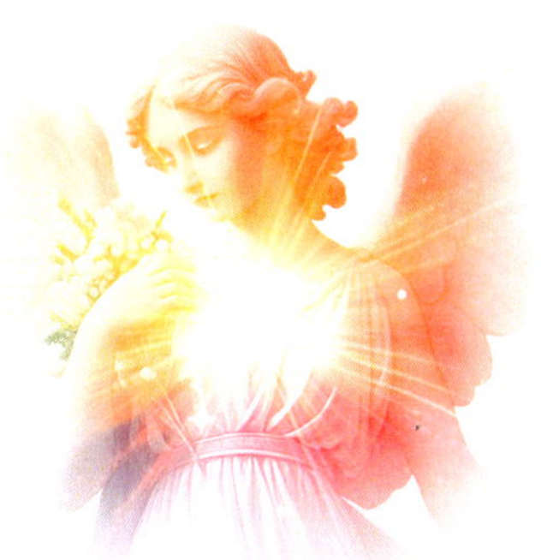

CHAPTER 16

BEAUTIFUL CONCEPTS OF THE HEART

Gracious ladies and gentlemen, from the heart of God you came, even as did I, and together we journey on the way of return.

Will you this morning stroll with me, then, in my garden at the Château de Liberté? Will you come this morning into the way of peace and love? Will you forsake the delusion of the senses and feel the reverence of the God flame within your heart for the beauty of life, resurrecting in infinite compassion all of the feelings of grace that you have ever known, that we may enjoy this period together as one of gathering more of infinite grace into our consciousness?

By so doing, the way will be made plain. We will see, as never before, how infinite love comes forth into the finite world, manifesting in the heart of the artisan, the craftsman, the individual who performs a labor of love for mankind.

Accusations have often been leveled unjustly against the artists of the world, and there have been those who would accuse these artists of having the desire to perpetuate themselves, to perpetuate their own name and fame and the desire to seek only gain.

I am certain that, as in every craft, there have been those who have served only for mundane purposes, executing skillfully in order that they might be thought wise. But certainly the few have nobly encompassed themselves roundabout with divine grace and have sought the lofty, not for the sake of worldly ambition but in order that they might spread abroad those beautiful concepts of the heart that first drew them to the field of art.

The Eternal Purpose of Spreading Beauty unto Others

As I come to you today, I want you to hear the soft tinkling of the fountain that is in my garden. I want you to realize that in the flow of the water element, guided carefully so that it is not a disturbing factor, man may find purity and release from all disturbing conditions. The water element is indeed blessèd to contemplate, and the mystery of the sea is one of great depth in the being of man.

Truly, precious ones, your physical form is for the most part composed of the water substance, and your minds and feelings do indeed gravitate to the water element. For even in the mind there is an element of great respect for the flow of water and the calmness of a mind that is like a still pond.

Will you, then, as you come into my garden this day, permit yourselves to be calm pools of knowing that God, in his infinite love and grace, desires to create a concept of beauty within you, that this lofty beauty may flow out to the world and cause the youth of this world to attain, through spiritual proximity to your aura, some realization of the hidden wellspring of great beauty and depth within you? And I ask that this be done not for your sake or mine but for the sake of eternal purpose—the eternal purpose of spreading abroad beauty unto others.

The Meaning of Reality

You and I may together contemplate beauty today. We may bask in the sun of holy radiance, of understanding. You and I may sweep aside fear. We may sweep aside doubt and questioning. We may hold ourselves in the purity of the angels. Our minds may be clean and lifted as on wing of holy prayer. But we must convey this thought, this feeling, so that it does flood upon the air of the earth and come to many hearts with a message that seems to be within themselves, that seems to be from themselves, that seems to be a whisper of themselves and of Reality. Only as we do this, only as divine love is spread abroad as forthright action, can the youth of the world understand the meaning of Reality.

That which today enamors the mind of the youth of the world is not reality in God's name. It is a vicious cycle of never-ending destructivity, and it has no true savoir faire. It has no true culture. It is not of the Spirit and of gracious art. It is a thing that is transitory and enervating, that passeth away with the fashion of the times and brings no permanent mark upon the reality of the soul. Today, then, we seek to stir those latent qualities in mankind that will give them an appreciation of beauty and an understanding of what beauty is in reality.

Beauty is ever-present in nature, and it must, then, have been fashioned by nature's God. The Deity is beauty, and he is mirrored as the breath of life, frozen into the beauteous patterns of the snowflake or a star or a dancing fairy with wand aflame to gild the flowers and the field with the ever-changing wonder-magic of color and grace from the laboratory of God. All of this surrounds mankind day in and day out. It is but an outer symbol. It is but ephemeral too, for behind it there is the spiritual, immortal color of life that is woven of the fire, just as the outer is woven only of the earth and the water element, with a tinge of the fire of the sun passing through nature's magnificence.

Let us, then, understand that that which is here below, that which passeth away as the fire passeth through it in the circle of time and space, is not the real. The real beauty is that which endureth forever, which is the master pattern—the master pattern from which nature itself draws design and form and symmetry. In the fire is the pattern, and out of the fire it cometh into manifestation. It is the light in the eye of a child. The absence of the awareness of death reflected in the eye of the child renders a complete understanding of the Father's love apparent in his eye and countenance.

With the coming-of-age and the so-called illumination of the world and the things of the world, children are taught to fear. They are made aware of the fright that is present in the world. And so the bad dreams of life that come to them are the products of those older and supposedly wiser individuals who are entrusted with the care of the children of the world. And yet beauty goes a-hungering in the hearts of the world's children, and they beg for the bread of spiritual grace and understanding.

The Beauty of the Christ Is Ever-Present in the World and in Life

You, then, to whom so much is given, conveyed by spiritual osmosis—you to whom so much is given by our radiation, who understand the intent of our purpose as we come to you this morning—must understand that the beauty of the Christ is ever-present in the world and in life, but it goes unappreciated because mankind have not schooled their minds and hearts to understand. They have been taught a symmetry that is born out of the imperfect concepts of man, and the symmetry of God goes unnoticed. They do not understand that his hand works through the tiny beings of the elements to fashion and form that which they enjoy. They do not understand that in themselves there is also an outworking and an outpicturing of eternal loveliness, which flows through them as electronic essence.

Mankind do not understand this. They do not realize or cognize that the electronic essence is real. They do not realize that just as the signal is borne upon telephone wires or through the ethers to your radios, so the voice of God goes forth with its great cosmic challenges from the Central Sun as fire of life within the soul, expressing the true beauty that has been captured in part by many of us in past embodiments, who had some of this sense resident within ourselves but were unable to truly capture it all. For who can comprehend the Infinite and compose it into finite form?

You see, precious ones, it is actually the service of infinite time. (I use this expression guardedly, for there is no infinite time but only the Infinite. But to you who are caught in the web of time, it is desirable that I should express it thus, saying "infinite time" as differentiated from ordinary time.) This is a short lifespan, whereas the infinite time of which I reference here is the infinite manifestation, the Absolute, the all-powerful radiation of God released into form as his beauty—not only that which has been, that which is, but that which shall be.

This is the transcendence of God manifesting age after age in a magnificent outpicturing of true Reality, which goes unnoticed before mankind's consciousness but is always captured by the tiny angels and cherubs in some manifestation of beauty. At times it is full of laughter, and then again this beauty is full of such somber dignity as to cause the heart itself to become introspective and to turn upon itself and wonder just what God hath truly wrought in consciousness.

This is somewhat the feeling that we have in the ascended realms. There are often moments when the grandeur of all that is revealed to us causes us to stand in awe of existence itself, and we ponder existence as a miracle. And the commonplace, the smallest little thing, the singing of a thrush, becomes for us a moment when celestial melodies are captured and heard not only in ear but in heart. And it is in heart that one truly hears, and not just in ear.

Those individuals who do not have the necessary training in the capturing of culture and art are often unable to appreciate the wonders with which they are surrounded. They listen to the more discordant side of life, and they are concerned with those phases of their existence that are of so little meaning and reality. For they are concerned only with the temporary supply of physical things to themselves and of the accumulation of the favors of the world so that the world will think well of them and esteem them and honor them.

The Radiance of Eternity

I know what it means to have honor. I know what it means to have fame. But I also know that when one has ascended and gone into the God flame, the fame of the world is indeed become a transitory object with which one is little concerned at all. And one becomes deeply concerned with the favors of heaven—that God dispenses wisdom to us and his sense of appreciation of himself through us so that we may appreciate him more and love him more with this appreciation. And I also think that when this is carried to the powers of the ninth degree, it has a tendency to cause mankind to love one another more. For some of this wonder is captured in every eye and heart and in every being whom God has also molded and shaped in the inward parts in the image of himself.

This grandeur, this celestial loveliness, this tenderness, is present even in the coarse and the gross. Their comprehensions that they express, precious ones, are not the comprehensions of their soul, of their Higher Being. They are the comprehensions of mortal mind, of mortal feeling, schooled in delusion and the warp of mortal conception.

All of this is not the immaculate concept, and thus the wonder of the tiny babe of Bethlehem was, in his immortal conception, the conceptions of his mother's heart. Mary's heart was filled with tenderness as she contemplated Gabriel's message, the Annunciation. "Hail, thou who art favored of God, the Lord is with thee and with thy spirit,"[1] became a musical cadence that she hummed as a lullaby before the child came forth. She knew the meaning of this, the inner flow of Gabriel's fiery words.

The favor of God was the favor of the good and the tender and the beautiful, as a jonquil, as a rose, as the song of a nightingale. All these that speak of beauty thrilled her soul—the glances in the children's faces, the glances that expressed hope in nature, the eternal glance that looks up to the sun as if to say, "Thou art my life forever." This is that type of beauty—the love that gazes in the eyes of the child to his mother and speaks to her these words: "Thou art my mother forever." In this closeness there is no growing up, no conception of the flow of time. There is only the little blessed delusion of a frozen, eternal moment. Glowing with all the radiance of eternity, that moment becomes a thing of beauty and a joy forever, captured in the glance of a child.

Men have tried to photograph these glances. They have tried to paint them and convey them to mankind, the richness of the rewards of a moment. For eternity is grasped in a moment. Eternity is not grasped in eternity, for one could become lost in this unfettered vastness. But it is grasped in a moment, in the tenderness of true love expressed from heart to heart—paternal love, maternal love, all types of love, so long as they are pure.

So long as these expressions are tinged with radiant, cosmic beauty in mortal expression, they embody the radiance of eternity frozen into a moment, a crystal clear, beautiful treasure, which is the fire of the heart because it came forth from God. It does not need to exist forever. The very fact that it can take a given shape and symbol for a moment in itself speaks of the mighty onrush of eternity, transcending itself as it tumbles forth from the heart of God, blown by the wind of the Holy Spirit.

Try the Spirit

We hear the sound of majesty from the mountains, the voices of the angel choirs singing, the people longing in their hearts for the touch of release from pain and from delusion. We see also down into the depths of the graves. We see also into the astral plane of existence, where mankind are enamored for the moment and then tortured by the delusions they have fabricated in moments of ill-conception. We see the hand of the Christ going forth to release them from these burdens, and we see fear destroyed and cast into the lake of fire.

We see all destructive emotions and tendencies cast into the lake of fire, and we see the fire absorb and purify and transmute and release all atoms from that overprint of darkness and malice. And we see from that lake of fire a transcendent violet flame, the very onrush of God's perfection and purity, the original concept of God come forth to wash and purify and cleanse until symbols themselves no longer hold the vacant, empty meaning that mankind have given unto them but are given the perfect, planned radiance that is inherent within the symbol.

The meaning of the cross has been lost to most among mankind. The meaning of all these things is dimly perceived. Now then, try thy spirit[2] and see whether it manifests the light of God, which truly has compassion not only for this hour but for all the days and years and months and cycles that are to come—the cycles when God shall be honored as you honor him, when God in you shall endow you, when through that endowment you shall come to expression, when through that expression you shall come to Source consciousness, when at Source consciousness you shall merge with the oneness of God. And then as the Oneness sees fit to cast thee forth again into some great cosmic triumph, you shall flow forth as a beam of light and shall move victoriously to fulfill his plan.

Thus the eternal cycles transcend themselves. Thus beauty and loveliness are born and perish not but move eternally in the fleeting areas of time. Folded in space, the light of God is hidden in the veil. It can be found and known and captured. It is within. It is available. It is truth. It is the power of the symbol. It is the tone, the joy, the flush of life. It is God... beautiful forever.

I thank thee.

October 31, 1965

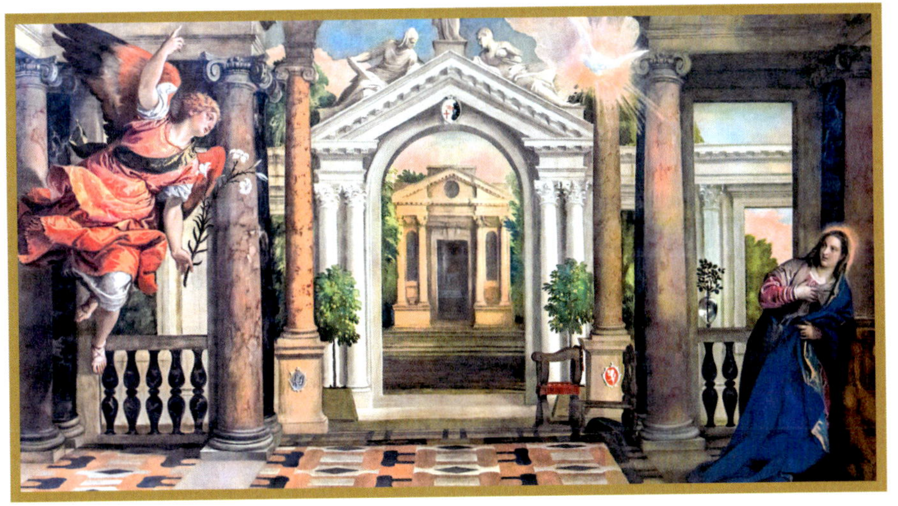

The Annunciation, 1578

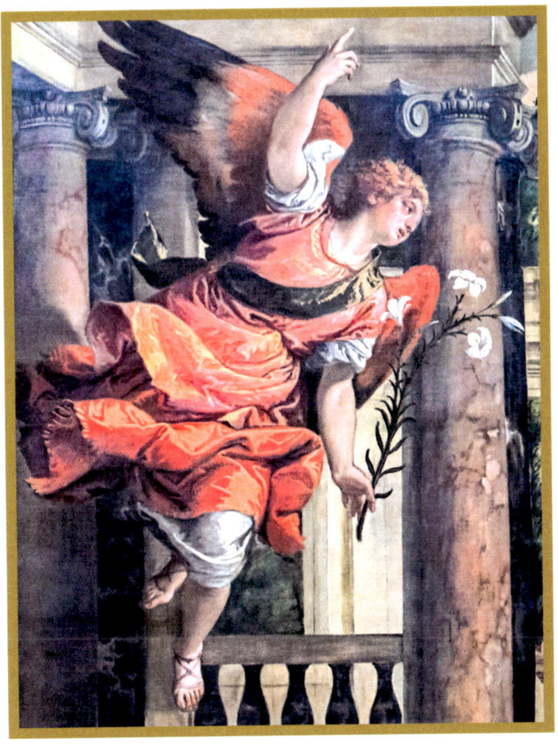

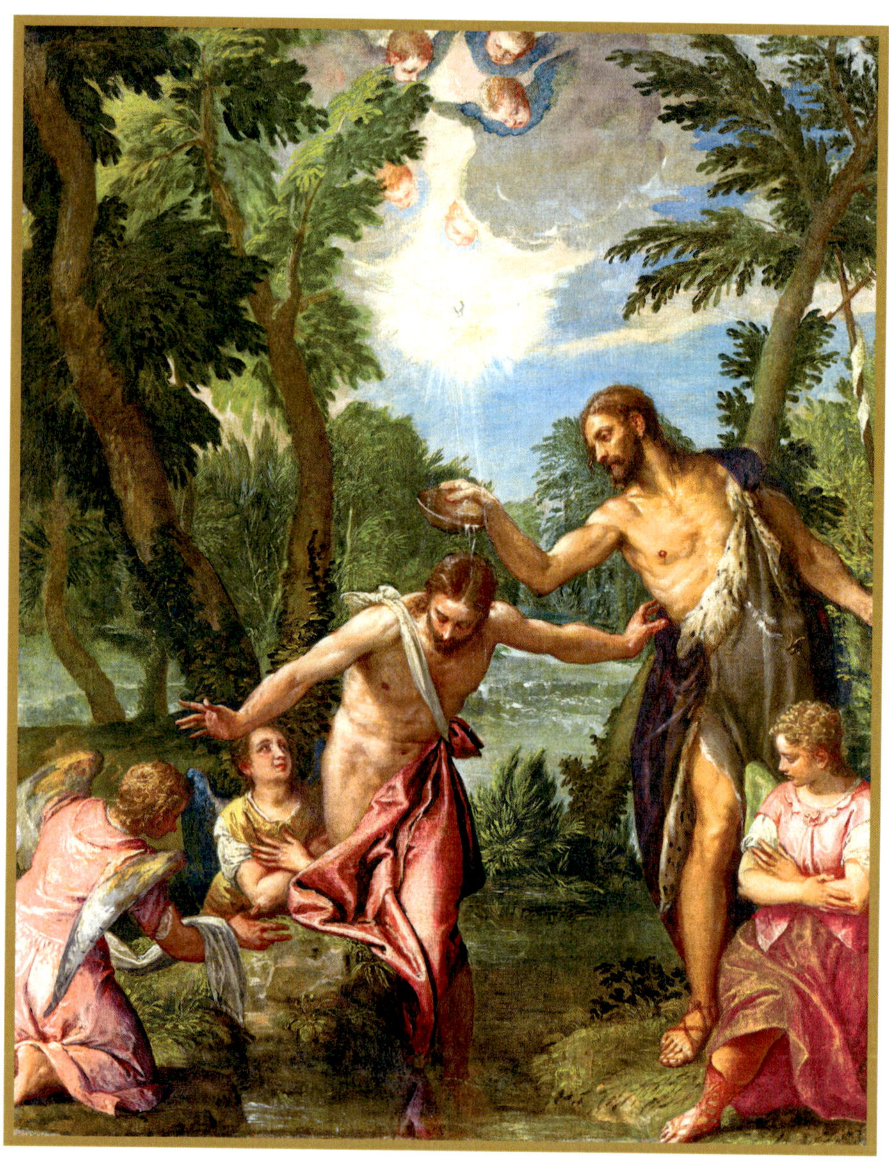

The Baptism of Christ, c. 1580–88

Come with me, then, to the garden of your heart....
See the peaceful, winding pathway, the verdant,
protective hedges, the trellised roses of love, the lacy fern
of form symmetry, the statuary of masterful achievement,
the tinkle of falling water from the fountain of God-purity,
the hush of reverence in angel minds, the sense of prescience,
and the peace engendered by this retreat from the worldly sense.

CHAPTER 17

The Garden of Your Heart

Gracious Ones Who Respond to the Heartbeat of God in Majestic Nature,

Pause to reflect for a moment, for the hungers of the hearts of mankind are never truly satisfied except by their own inward stance of spiritual beauty and its appreciation.

Mounting world distress creates a sense of the desolate in mankind, especially in the more sensitive. As though they were upon hot desert sands, athirst and without water, mankind long for an oasis of peace or the journey's end, where the accoutrements of civilization will once again assuage their thirst and bring them that release they seek.

Now, purity of concept is essential in both material and spiritual victory. For if mankind were to obtain outward respect or stature by vapid or cruel means, the karmic debt would exceed the recompense attained. In spiritual matters, it is impossible for man to acquire by wrong means, for the soul is always set back by the employment of wrong method. It is most difficult, precious ones, for the ascended masters to reach mankind when their own souls are unable to do so!

Have you thought, then, gracious ones, of the hunger of your own soul, made in the image of God, for the beautiful image of the heavenly world and of the Higher Self? Do you know what it means to satisfy the longings of the soul by setting your feet upon a pathway worthy of eternal pursuit?

There are so many byways, so many diversions, so much that is confusion in the world, that a moment's thought will reveal to the honest heart of man or woman—who will take stock of himself and of his aims and aspirations—that vain and repetitive events, even of mortal achievement, cause the human mind to soar to dizzying heights from whence the tired eagle must ultimately drop into the great abyss of unreality and experience the termination of personal aspiration.

Treasure Our Words

Unquestionably, each individual soul would act as self-teacher if its voice could be heard by the outer consciousness, if the sensitizing and purifying action would occur naturally or be encouraged enough so that it would understand the message of the eternal mysteries imparted by the soul.

Now we must face the problem encountered by the ascended hosts in their outreach to mankind via the spoken or printed Word sent forth in your day for your edification and upliftment. Unless you shall treasure our words, as God intends, we cannot assist you any more than can your own soul in attaining that development of right action and right reaction, which is our intent and God's as well.

We must direct our concepts to those of many stations—providing nourishment for all, evolving all, assisting all, and attempting to reach all. Yet the few who find the meat of spiritual sustenance within our words dearly appreciate them and treasure them, one and all, whereas those who have no sense of the value of our contact and radiation unwittingly pass by a great release of love and light, which is in truth the sheen of the soul, the living treasure of their own being shining through from the inner lantern.

Come with Me to the Garden of Your Heart

Come with me, then, to the garden of your heart. Raise the latch of your attention and watch the great golden gate swing inward. See the peaceful, winding pathway, the verdant, protective hedges, the trellised roses of love, the lacy fern of form symmetry, the statuary of masterful achievement, the tinkle of falling water from the fountain of God-purity, the hush of reverence in angel minds, the sense of prescience,* and the peace engendered by this retreat from the worldly sense.

In this garden come apart;
In this garden find your heart;
In this garden is liberty;
Hear the anthem of the free!

Be brave when all the world's in fear.
I AM God Presence ever near.
There is no failure in his plan
Of liberty for every man.

I AM eternal gratitude
For opportunities so good;
The very presence of the light
Hangs in the air so sweet and bright.

As angel faces peep right through
From sunlight shaft of glory's hue,
I see the ladder of the Lord,
The law of love now so adored.

Increase the attitude of right
That pens the law of sacred might
And holds me close to God's embrace,
Exalting the courage of his grace.

I move mid cycles of the years
As beauty's hand wipes 'way all tears;
I see the shining realm of light
From whence I came descending bright.

As God's own hope for victory
Singing the anthem of the free,

---

*foreknowledge

"I go to do thy will in thee,"
A sunbeam ray from higher towers
To utilize thy finest hours
By inspiration's mighty power.

Every precious day I see
As welcome opportunity
To dwell in garden fair within
Where God does triumph over sin,

And find the way that leads me Home
And keeps me seated on the throne
Of oneness with thy purpose rare,
This is my heart's great daily prayer:

"Father, I thank thee for beauty and, more than all,
For the beauty that now and always is within me."

Lovingly, I AM

Paul the Venetian

January 9, 1966

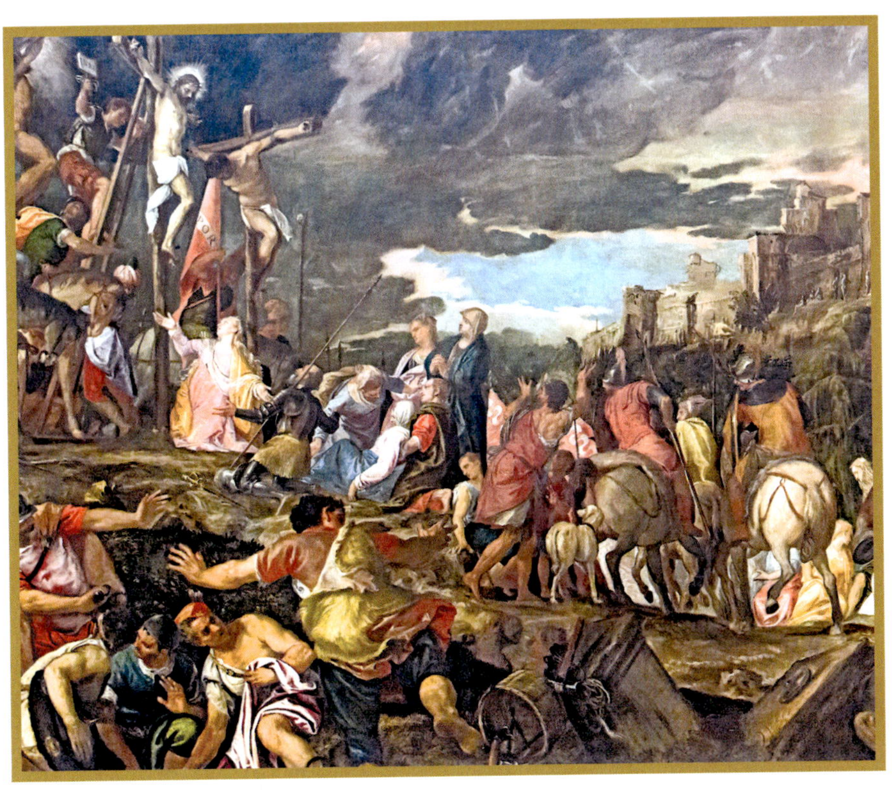

Crucifixion (detail), c. 1580–82

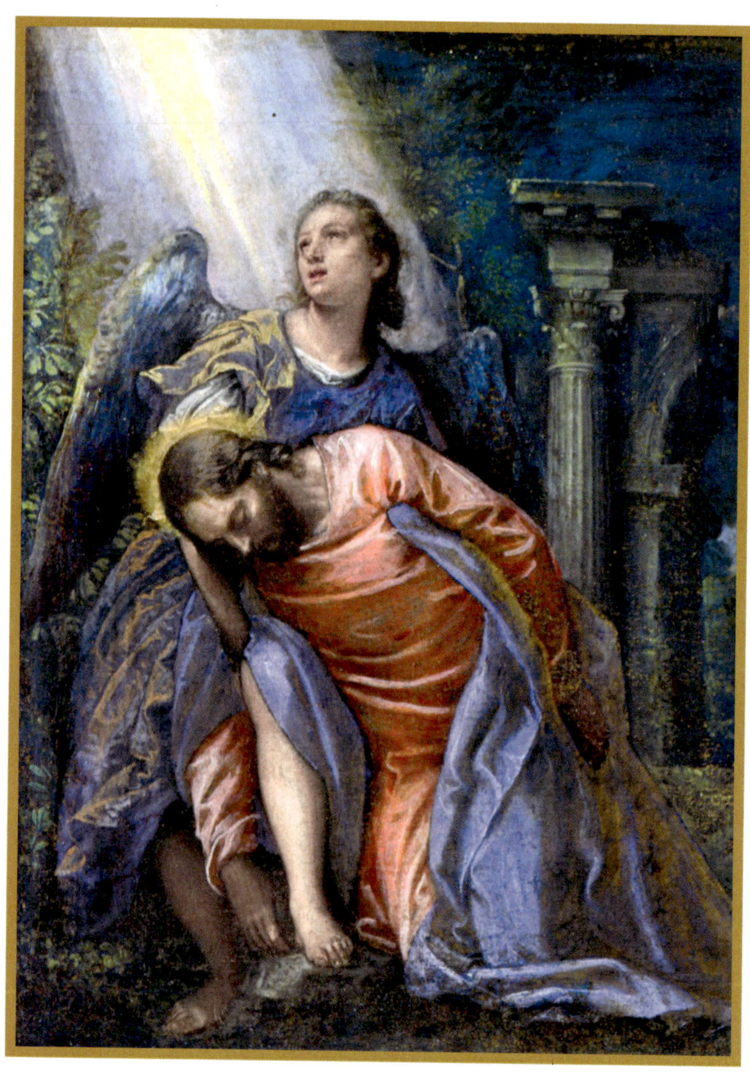

Christ in the Garden of Gethsemane (detail), c. 1583–84

We speak of the reflection of heaven in the face of a babe—yea, in the innocent of heart and consciousness, who by reason of their devotion have embraced the power of heaven and of heaven's truth.

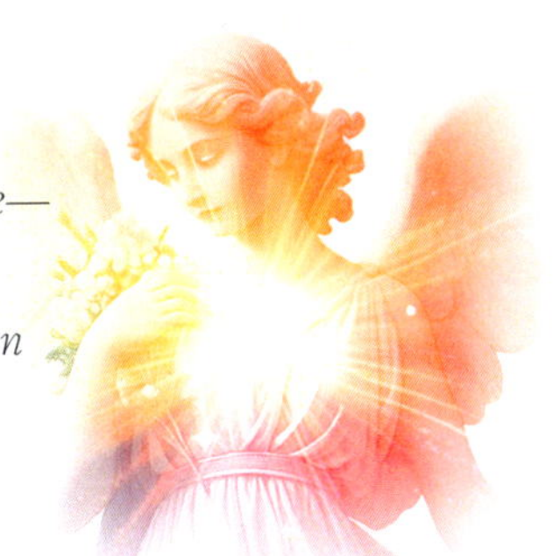

CHAPTER 18

The Beautiful Pearl of Great Price That Is Holy Innocence

The serenity of innocence portrayed in the face of a child of innocence, in all of the radiant outpicturing of the meaning of the soul of God, is beautiful to behold and lovely to encanvas.

In this sense of beauty there is a majesty that far exceeds all of the violence and assertion of temporal power in the world of form. Yet mankind over the years have been subjected to the betrayal of the innocence of their soul and of their being by the clanging and the clashing of the world's episodes of armament and might—human might pitted against human might.

The end result is always stain and pain and those objects of life that are difficult for the soul of an artist to portray. For we do not like, we do not enjoy, we do not find excitement in all of the world's "exciting" battles and adventures, but we find the greatest excitement in tracing the outlines of a rose or of a child's face of innocence. For there we speak of the majesty of heaven—that which *God* hath wrought; that which is true, brave, and eternal.

Mankind may wonder why I reference this idea of painting the majesty of heaven as brave. Does it not require braveness in the soul of man to be able, in an age of materialism and of faith in mortal strength, to portray the qualities of simplicity and love to mankind?

These are not qualities that bring fame to those who seek through art to portray that which would bring them name and fame. Therefore, artists who seek fame often find that the world will reject that which they would bring forth of simplicity and love, and so they seek (as they do in this age) to draw those lines of harshness and bitterness that are reflective of the unhappiness of the times.

Yet unhappiness was also filling the cup of life to overflowing in past ages, and those among the peasants and the peasant classes were often without bread and without the necessities of life that are now held so dear by mankind. Yet the landed gentry and the noble of those ages were also experiencing the bane of unhappiness. For with all of their ballroom dances and the excitement of their control of sectional, national, and world situations, they did not find the happiness that they sought but found only a temporary feeling of elation when they were victors over some world situation.

Gracious ones, the age of innocence has far flown from the world and from mankind, and yet there is a longing in heaven to re-create upon earth that true innocence of Spirit that is reflective of the highest God-qualities.

We therefore, in our release to you this day, speak of the majesty of an angel's face. We speak to you of the great glow of power and of the transcendent love that is in the face of an archangel. We speak of the reflection of heaven in the face of a babe—yea, in the innocent of heart and consciousness, who by reason of their devotion have embraced the power of heaven and of heaven's truth.

Take Hope! Take Faith!
Take Renewed Courage This Day!

Certainly you must understand that we are well informed as to the consciousness of mankind and to the conditions of imperfection that are dwelling within mankind's thoughts. We know that they are far from innocent. But we would bring to you this day a ray of hope, and we would bring this ray of hope even to those whose worldly sense of sophistication is possessed with a complete, or reasonably complete, knowledge of the world's descent into darkness.

We would bring to you the hope of the Christ and the hope of the hand of God, which is able to wipe away from the screen of your mind the banalities of all of those expressions of darkness and shadow that have plagued the world for so long. These are not truth. These are not holy reason. These are not holy purpose. These stem from the ignorance of men, and they create and re-create patterns of pain and darkness, which have no part in the mind of God.

Therefore, take faith! Take hope! Take renewed courage this day! God is able to wipe these patterns of darkness from your mind and to replace them with the innocence of heaven in an age that is not of innocence. This is the plan of God—to fill the world with valiant men and women and to flood into the minds of the youth in this day and age the understanding of cosmic innocence.

The meaning of this is sweet. It is the thought of God reflected in the babe of Bethlehem, the thought of God that penetrated the density of two thousand years with a ray of hope. The thought of God is manifest in each child brought forth into manifestation, who receives the holy breath. With the incoming of that sacred breath of God, the child becomes a living soul, clad with the innocence of heaven until mankind—by their thoughtlessness and carelessness—do cast upon the clean linen of that one the mud of human thought, spackling the clean, white garments with that which does soil the tenderness of the soul.

But God be thanked, and the beauty of God be thanked. For the divine intent reigns supreme forever, and holy innocence is crowned, *always,* with the majesty of the Son of God. Thus the glow-ray of the Supreme One is captured by some artists in part, so that on canvas and by paint and oil, men are able to see the beauty of God penetrating through the sunlight of Reality.

The Pearl of Great Price

As we pause to consider the meaning of holy innocence again and again, we would bring this meaning to the feet of kings and priests. We would bring it to the feet of prophets. We would bring it to the feet of righteous men and even to the feet of the wicked, and say:

"Here is thy lost cause. Clothe thyself now with this, which thou hast once rejected in thy youth. Take it now, and accept it. It is the veil of Christ. It is his countenance, which he has offered to you then and now. Reject it once, and it comes again. Reject it again, and it comes again and throughout all eternity. So long as man shall breathe the breath of God, the thought of God shall come again and again. Men may reject. They may turn aside. But they can never escape the face of their own innocence because it is the face of God."

When men understand that the old image, the old boundaries, the old landmarks of cosmic identity must one day be sought by all, they will hasten to apprehend that which God has apprehended long ago for all—the victory of the free and not the victory of the spoilers, who in taint have continued to ruin the lives of men by their own lives.

Poor examples are they, filling the screen and the stage of life with all the sordid examples of crime and debauchery, reaping in due course of time the full reward for all that they have sent out. They are of all men most miserable, and at inner levels their plight is too terrible to paint, too terrible to reflect upon. For we would rather extend the olive branch of peace and the thought of hope to the world so that the youth of the world may find once again, even in this age of materialism, the beautiful pearl of great price that is holy innocence.

The Spiritual Bread That Beauty Brings

As I speak these words, I see before me the faces of the world's children. I see before me the face of their Holy Christ Self—their angel in heaven, who always beholds the face of the Father and his radiant innocence. As I see the faces of the children and the face of God reflected in the face of their Holy Christ Self, I say to the world:

"How can you betray them? How can you offer to them the horrible lines of distorted forms of art? How can you offer them monster creations and abortions* from the astral world? How can you draw in line, by power of hand and mind, those things that belong in the pits of horror and ought to be transmuted by violet-flame substance, never to be anymore, to vanish from the screen of the universe and to end their existence?"

*monstrosities

When the universe breathes through all her pores the substance of the sacred fire—the fingers of God caressing the screen of life with renewed hope—how can men, made in his image, mar that image?

Yet they do. And it is temporary, for they have no permanent power to despoil the virgin beauty of God! Nor have they permanent power to mar the face of childish innocence! And nor can they take from you, who are adults and who embrace your Holy Christ Self, the beauty of the innocence of heaven that is given to you!

No human sophistry has power over the thought of God and the angels. No human sophistry has power over the infinite hand of Christ and the identity that is soul reality.

I contemplate, then, this day
The meaning of renewed life
As it flashes forth through mind and heart
Of those inspired patrons of the art—
Those who will take their pen or brush in hand
And ask the power of light to command
That they may trace in beauty
Infinity for all to see,
A touch of God to make men free.
O gracious ones, how the need mounts up
For men of courage, wedded not
To gold of human worth,
But wedded to the joy
That takes delight in cosmic mirth.
Peace, tranquility, and light—
These are the substances of right.
Gracious ones, employ them
In all thy doings—
Thy hand and head and heart,
Eschewing evil and embracing good.
So, then, the children of the world may have their food,
The spiritual bread that beauty brings,
And in their hearts to innocence let them cling
And see the face of God.

Precious ones, I am releasing today the substance of the thought of God's beauty into the world. And I am hoping against hope that the thought of the world will also capture some of this thought of innocence and revert away from that which has so destructively laid traps into which the young and tender fall.

The Innocence of Life's Pure and Original Patterns

Precious ones (who love light, who love God, who love truth and whose hearts yearn to see the manifest design of God outworked and outpictured), realize that hope liveth on not only in our hearts but in yours. It is the hope that God-victory will come to all, that they who sit in darkness shall see a great light,[1] that they whose eyes are blind may have the scales fall therefrom,[2] that the power of old that descended to Saul upon the Damascus way[3] may also come to all men's thoughts, to those who pray and also to those who *prey*—p-r-e-y—upon mankind.

Let all come to the "Damascus way" in order to know that it will be hard for them when they kick against the pricks.[4] But through the returning currents of their karma (which I urge the Lords of Karma to direct), they will find that they, who have marred the world and have sought to mar it, may yet turn to serve the light and to utilize their talents for the release of holy innocence into the world.

There is so much beauty in the ethereal realms, gracious ones, that my ascended soul reels to behold it. It exceeds all that I have ever thought it would be, and it is *here,* and it is *there,* and it is *everywhere.* It is awaiting the outpicturing of the chaliced mind and the fervent spirit to portray it so that none may fear life but draw nigh unto God, who *is* Life.

Thus life may draw nigh unto you in the innocence of its pure and original patterns, which are released into the hand of every angelic being and released into the eye of every lover of God, who, in seeing him, beholds himself.

I thank you.

May 8, 1966

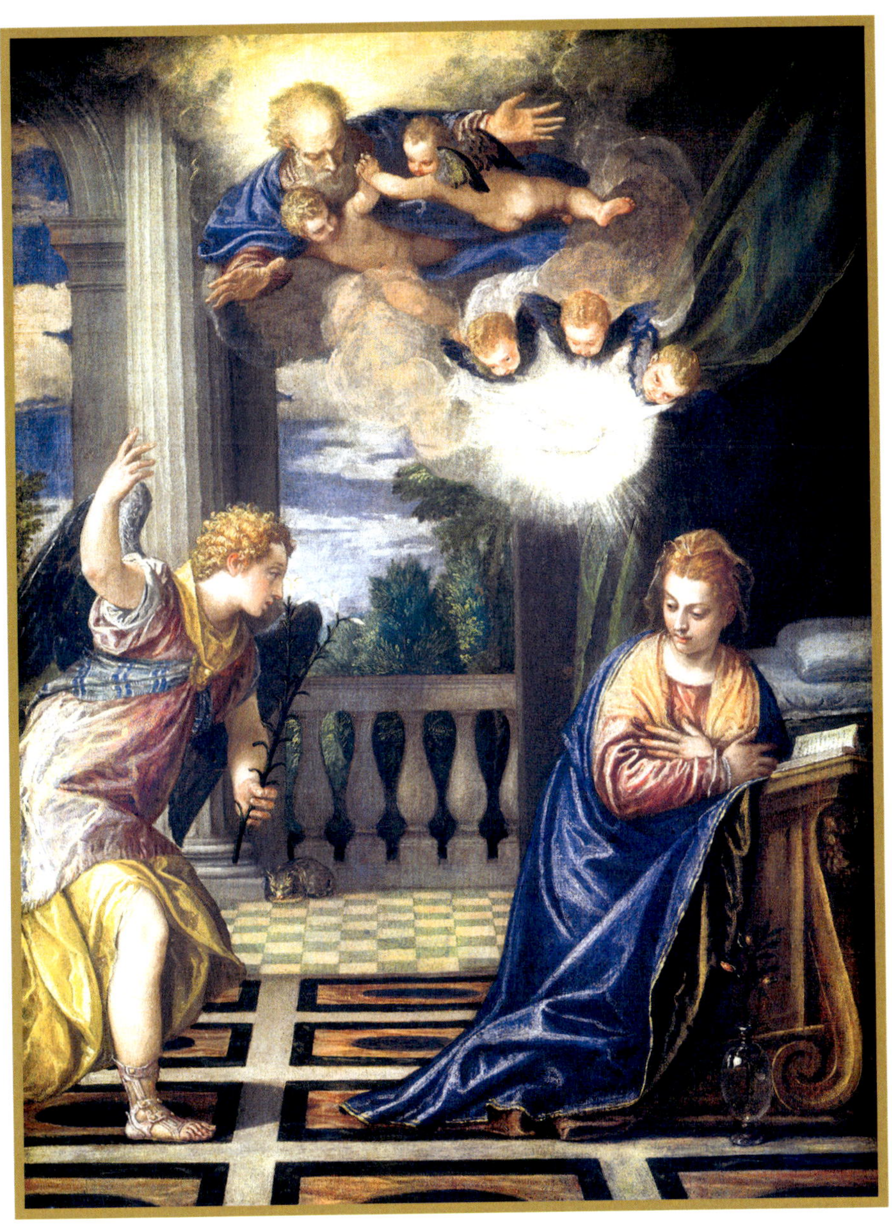

The Annunciation, c. 1583–84

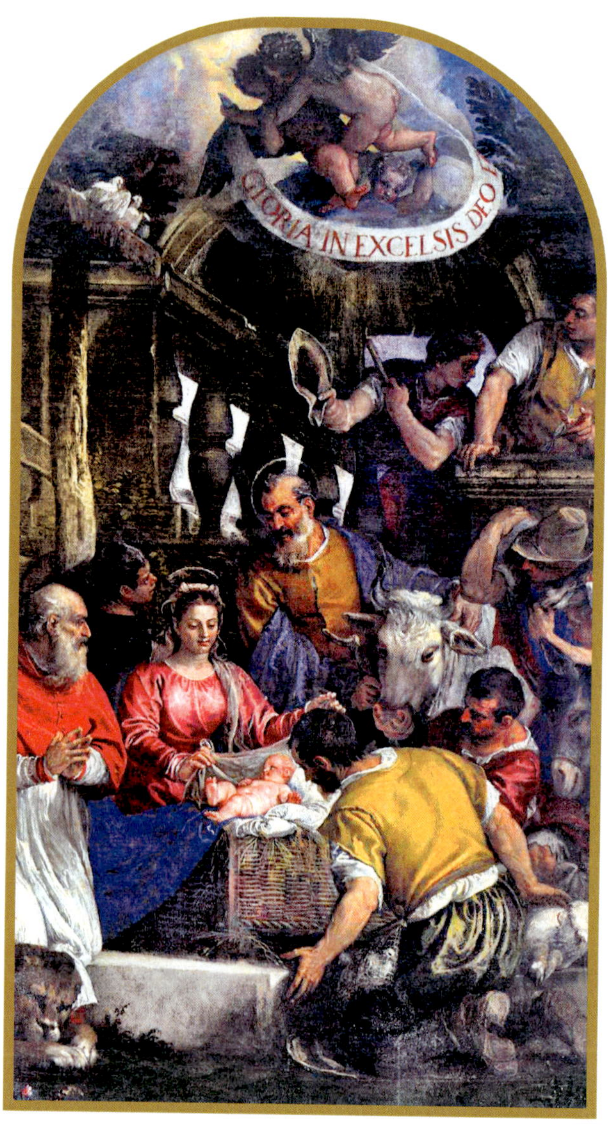

Adoration of the Shepherds, c. 1582–83

My gratitude is to each of you and to all who have thus understood a portion of cosmic beauty within the heart. And to the artist, to the hands that served, is my gratitude and eternal love in the Be-ness of cosmic beauty.

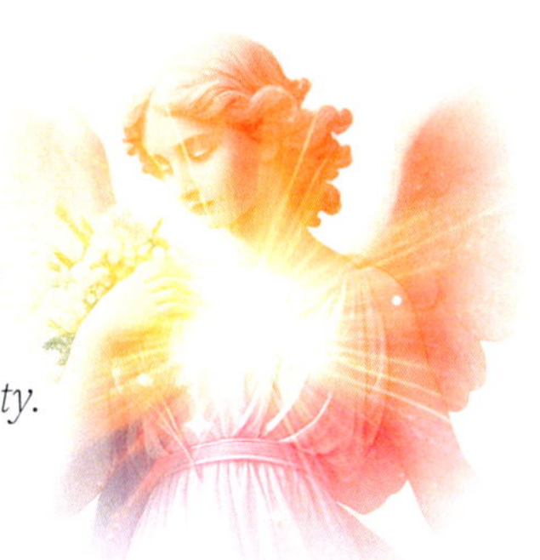

CHAPTER 19

The Hidden Beauty of the Soul

Gracious ones, I speak of the serenade of the soul. I speak of the beauty that the soul drinketh from a wild rose. I speak of the beauty of God as it filters through the air, in the descending waves of energy from the Great Solar Orb. I speak of the fragrance of hearts and of how divine love, compassion, and understanding are wafted as upon a gentle breeze between the shores of men's hearts, teaching them of the hidden beauty of the soul.

With the passing of the centuries, mankind have entered into a greater era of scientific and supposed cultural understanding. But as so many of you are aware, the world is still so lacking in the simple rudiments of the sense of beauty and divine love among the masses that a vast cultural, educational, and spiritual program is needed and required in order to extend to mankind the finer senses of the soul, which will enable them to escape from the raucous manifestation of the world and its sense of dissonance, which it desires to call "harmony."

Men and women, misguided in thought and feeling, are often content with manifestations that at our level would serve to jar the senses. For we would have no portion of that jangle of discord that mankind today have called music and of that jangle of discord that they call art. We know that as the lineaments of soul-magnitude reach forth in the search for divine grace and beauty, the cosmic spell is woven in the mind and consciousness, which causes men and women to be enamored of divine grace and to be comforted by the Spirit of God. They find, then, in understanding the vast "crux" of creation—the cross of light, the mighty power of God descending into form and blending with the horizontal bar, fusing the great Daystar from on high into the consciousness—that *then* mankind have begun to live.

Life, precious ones, does not consist of habit patterns that mankind have created and renewed again and again, unless, perchance, those habit patterns should resemble the consciousness of God and the full magnitude of his love, his beauty, and his sense of reality. To perpetuate the negations of mankind currently in vogue would be to create a race of misanthropes, in a cosmic sense. But to understand the need to shed the paltry senses, the false glitter and the glamour of the world, and to do it with joy and alacrity—substituting the rightful manifestation, which ought in the first place to have taken preeminence—is the work of God and the Holy Spirit. For mankind have built very poorly upon the foundation of cosmic manifestation.

Their breath, their life, their substance, all that they are, comes forth from God, and they know it. Yea, I say unto you today, many of them know it and sense it. Yet even these, the supposed blessèd of the world, are also a part of the nerve-jangling tensions of the world, creating and sustaining by the economy of their life, their person, and purse, all that brings discord to the youth of the world and to those agèd ones who, I fear, would find difficulty in executing the maneuvers of the modern dance.

The Gentle, Emerging Sense of the Christ Consciousness

You must understand, then, that to make a joyful noise unto God,[1] to rejoice in the wonders of his universe, is to receive the knowledge that mankind call *avant-garde.* Is it avant-garde to receive the pure, simple joys of the Holy Spirit? Is it avant-garde to receive the grace of God? Is it avant-garde, is it progressive to receive the manifestations of cosmic love and a sense of cosmic beauty? What a pity that man chooses to call this avant-garde, when in reality it ought to have been their first love and the foundation stone upon which they would have builded the whole structure.

Now, in an era of human discord, man chooses to see progress in spiritual things as though it were far from them, and yet they have a fond hope that one day they might be able to manifest it. Know ye not that the joy of God is in the eternal Now and the manifestation of the eternal Now is today? The words of the masters have ever been spoken, saying, "Why will ye tarry?"[2] And yet the world tarries, and dalliance is still the order of the day. Now then, this does affect the individual and the individual's sense of beauty, even his sense of integrity.

What do you suppose, precious ones, is done to those among mankind who have no knowledge of the light to counterbalance the sinister, shadowed forms that cross their pathway? These are subject to the outer darkness, where there is indeed, as has puzzled many, a gnashing of teeth.[3] For even the youth of the world have gnashed their teeth at the banality of life and the seeming vanity, even purposelessness of life to their consciousness. And in the blackness of despair they have stripped from themselves the gift of life in the awful perdition of suicide.

Understand, then, how very dire is the need for an awakening of the consciousness of mankind to a sense of reality and beauty, which by its Christ light and its strength of illumination is able to give genuine and lasting joy to the world, not only for that embodiment but for all time to come. For it is certainly time that mankind should understand that when they build, they build not for a moment but they build for an eternity!

It is an eternity that awaits the manifestation of perfection from within their souls. Yet they are cut off from the sense of the beautiful and the good because it does not seem to be popular, and there is always the question of tension as the old habits of mortal thought and feeling refuse to yield to the gentle, emerging sense of the Christ consciousness. We understand this struggle, but we know the worth, the supreme worth of magnification of the divine ideal and its replacement in the consciousness of mankind of *all* that is mortal in thought and feeling. You *must* replace mortal thought and feeling with the purity of the divine ideal.

The Hungers of the Soul

Gracious ones, how tender is the love of God flowing through his creation. It is a strange travesty indeed that simultaneously with the beautiful thoughts of God that stir the soul—and with the banners of the Lord waving from Shamballa with the purity of the breezes of the Holy Ghost and with the radiance of cosmic love flowing to the universe—that in the lower strata, the manifestations of old records of human discord and old planetary and solar records of discord and vanity should yet hold some shred of manifestation, those tatters—and I spell it *t-a-t-t-e-r-s*—that mankind hold on to as though they held the whole cloth. And they know not that they are naked by reason of exposure to these horror covenants, which mankind have executed in their ignorance with the powers of density in shadow and darkness, the enclosures that have rendered man stupid and insensate to divine ideas.

You see, then, and you perceive how beauty radiates through the world and through the universe, and mankind do not even catch the first notes of it. They strain in order to hear it, but their ears have waxed dull and their senses do not even measure up to their ears, which sometimes do catch a small strain of the melodies of heaven.

And so as I came to you today, I said unto myself, "Paul, with all of thy getting that thou hast received of cosmic understanding and a sense of beauty, it is needful that thou shouldst impart unto mankind upon the Earth planet the wonderful grace that thou hast perceived and that has given unto thee thy liberty."

And I said, "I will seek to impart to every heart that will listen and manifest the will to learn, the understanding that there is a need to turn from all that is unhappy, that burns in the soul as a pricked conscience." And I said unto myself, "I *will* impart beauty unto the listening ear, and a readiness for heaven, and the security of cosmic domains. For the span of the lives of mankind is very short indeed, and during those lives there is a great deal of struggle."

And I said unto myself, "The vision of great beauty is so fleeting, and the world's shadow and sordid manifestations are so everywhere apparent, that the need is great to assuage the hungers of the soul and to bathe mankind in the liquid, light essence of immortal compassion and freedom."

> And so today as I address you,
> I choose to address the world at large,
> That the world at large may awake
> And partake of the beauty that God intended for all to share;
> That the lispings and sweetness of a child's holy prayer
> May rise from hearts that have attained
> A measure of outer seeming maturity
> But have in reality
> Not even the blessing of a child's security—
> The comfort that "lays me down to sleep," to rest,
> And understands some small measure of the blest,
> Which in later year has flown,
> No more to blossom in the mind and soul.
> O precious mankind of the earth,
> Be thou made whole!

Necessary Growing Pains

As I speak to you today, it is to acquaint you with the domain of heaven and the majesty of God's sacred heart. It is to understand for you, if necessary, what beauty God has imparted unto many of us ascended and to cause you to recognize that all of your struggles in this domain are as naught. The struggles of the flesh are but little pain compared to that which the soul has suffered by its crucifixion in material-sense consciousness. Many times, and oft when mankind seem to be joyous, it is as though it were that God should hang his head, crucified within their sense of dimness and dullness—the Great God of life and light and love confined to the small room of their outer self.

And then I say, mankind cry "pain" when a small prick cometh in order to give them their eternal freedom. And they often do not understand the meaning of struggle, and yet throughout the historical epoch of *all* great men in *all* times past, struggle and pain have been very much a part of their overcoming. And so we could almost say as law that struggle and pain are necessary growing/expansion pains to the soul of man as he becomes more illumined by cosmic grace and light and more able to serve among mankind.

And now as we move in our consciousness into higher expressions of cosmic beauty and love, let us understand that much that is below will change, and necessarily so, in the consciousness as it becomes more divine.

The outlook will change;
The sense of manifestation will change
From a small acorn to a mighty, towering oak;
And the branches of this great Tree of Life,
As in the fable old,
Will stretch across the world and enfold
The soul with awareness of all its many parts,
And expand upward toward the stars.
And so, the senses of the soul will expand
Even beyond the leaves of the tree and the branches thereof,
And the soul takes flight as a mighty bird,
As an electric spark with infinite speed,
Going out to partake of universal mead—
The nectar of God in the universe
That everywhere is quaffed
By souls in whom the Holy Spirit manifests
The fullness of cosmic communion.

My Gratitude to Each of You

Now then, gracious ones, the domain of heaven is the realm of expansion. And so long as the soul is confined to the small, finite sense, it cannot possibly know the great, divine, infinite sense, for it is and has been concerned with many things of lesser stature.

As you pause to think with me about the domain of heaven and man's readiness for wearing eternal garments and casting off the dust of mortal ones, you certainly must realize that this is an advancement, an increase of stature. But unless there be some measure of cosmic fire within thy soul, that which is so vast would seem to thee but an eternal awesomeness and you would long for the confinements of form and sense as being more real than the great cosmic domain into which it is the will of God that thou shouldst enter.

He has not prepared for thee the gifts of smallness but the gifts of the largesse of his cosmic heart, and it is his will to give you the fullness of himself. Therefore, he seeks to stretch the boundaries of thy soul so that thou canst, in thy tent, be as the tabernacle of the Almighty, a covering for all life, and that all life beneath thee may receive the outbreathing of the blessedness of thy True Self as it enters into a oneness with thy wingèd God Self. Cherubs thou art, in a sense. Thou art things of beauty and therefore joyous forever.

It is so easy for me to come to you today, trembling with the beauty of light. It is so easy for me to come to you and to express gratitude for the joy you paid unto me upon the occasion of the unveiling of my portrait,[4] [Congregation rises.] expressing in sketch form some of the light-radiance that is held encased, not as mold but as light within the domain of my form ascended consciousness. My gratitude is to each of you and to all who have thus understood a portion of cosmic beauty within the heart. And to the artist, to the hands that served, is my gratitude and eternal love in the Be-ness of cosmic beauty.

Won't you please be seated.

Know Thyself as a Being of Great Light

There is in the world today, and there has been for a long time within the consciousness of mankind, a fear concerning the world and the universe and concerning their birth as well as their passage from the screen of time. Let me hasten to assure you that the gentle breath that floweth so normally into the child from the heart of God, that billows the sails of life and moves the ship forward for a time, simply returns to the Great Source, and the sails hang limp. This does not mean an end at all to existence, and therefore,

Comfort should come to man
In the understanding of God's holy plan,

To understand the way the soul goes,
That the soul may be the vehicle that knows
The fullness of the love of God
And the beauty that flows.

You see, gracious ones,
It is all a perfect activity that dovetails together;
For except God had given thee the consciousness
That would descend into mortal form,
Thou couldst not ascend;
For that part of thee that is Above
Is always surfeited by his love—
It has no need for anything,
For all the treasures of universal joy
Within that consciousness do ring,
And it is sounding now in thee and also in me.

It is the mutual joy of interaction,
But compassion dictated that a portion
Of this great flame should descend
By love and light in his own name
To be vested with individuality's flame.
And so it was needful that thou shouldst descend
To master form and put an end
To all the density of mortal thought and reason
And win thy Victory in due season,
Rejoicing and rising, ascending, then,
To the place of love from whence thou came,
So natural, so perfectly beautiful, and yet,
The Law with all its wonder and its awe
Could not take from this realm of density
The substance raw and unrefined
With all its human, mortal propensity.
It must of need refine the seed
And generate a noble deed
That wins the laurel with Godspeed

That raises a soul to God's own seat of joy,
Without alloy—without cloy,
Without any substance to annoy;
That paradise should remain paradise
And beauty should remain beauty,
For men have mocked it.

They have said of that which is ugly
And banal and dissonant, "It is joyous."
And if we were to give to them
In their day of darkness
The power to confirm life,
They would take of the Tree of Life the fruit thereof
And perpetuate iniquity;
And God is of too pure an eye to permit it.

And therefore this is why the Word went forth,
"Man must die."
It was not man that God sought to destroy;
It was only that in man which would the Law annoy;
And it would annoy thee also,
For there would be no paradise there.
If mankind were to struggle,
If mankind were to compete,
If mankind were to serve the laws of human deceit,
It could not be, and therefore
It is manifestation that dies
And not man, not soul.
For the soul has gone on in the schoolrooms of life
To master; and to master strife and confusion it shall.
But do not be annoyed
And do not be disturbed by outer circumstances,
For they have no power over the soul
If you will understand the goal
And keep it ever before the eyes of the soul,
For it is most essential in this simple way

That you confirm God's life *today*
For thyself and know—I say,
know thyself as a being of great light,
And *change* thyself, that neither the night nor the night fright
Can disturb the tranquility of thy being.

The Gentle Seed of Beauty

You recall the great drama of the Master in the boat—how he lay fast asleep while the disciples, frightened and in terror, beheld the raging of the sea. This is a painting of great beauty. And you remember how he arose as they became so affrighted. And with no other look than a calm demeanor of majestic command, he stretched forth his hand and said, "Peace, be still!"[5] And the elements obeyed his will. This was majesty, confined in thee as well as in him, but you have not yet paid it heed and recognition. When you do, you will perceive the need to *act, act, act* in the name of God to speed the advent of beauty in thyself, and loveliness, and to do it by turning to God.

Do not look even for earthly examples below except to serve to be one. Do not expect perfection in others but expect it in thyself. I do not mean that you should not perceive it in others as the immaculate concept. I say to you, do not expect it and then you will not be disappointed if it does not always manifest at a given time and opportunity. For I tell you, if you were to examine the records of your own self, you would not be so quick, then, to speak unto others the word to condemn.

You see, it is the love of God in *all* that sows the gentle seed of beauty and the sense thereof, and all must develop it for themselves. And it is the ascended masters' prerogative to develop it for themselves and to convey their assistance to you, not only this day but every day. You have our love. You have our Brotherhood. You have our assistance. But we would like to have yours, because of the awful longevity of mortal persistence in doing its own will while the will of God goes begging.

Then, when the mighty Law comes down and claims divine justice, and karma's activity stretches forth its hand, there is a weeping and gnashing of teeth and mankind resent the halter of the Law as it draws tightly upon their own neck. Let us, then, have respect for that Law. It is the law of mercy and beauty also, for it is the law of your freedom. As the karmic lash falls and mankind recognize by and by what is wrong and they correct it, then the song of life begins and is not ended.

And so shall it always be, for we deal here with perfection and imperfection, with flesh and spirit, with mortality and immortality, with joy and sorrow, with compassion and with hatred. We deal here with the imperfections of man and the perfections of God. When imperfection ends its reign, the power of God shall manifest in all.

All That I Have Said Must Be Studied and Read

That which I have said today shall not climax itself, and I shall not seek for a climax in worded form, although I think you know I am capable of it. I shall end this dissertation with a manifestation of a radiant outpouring of cosmic beauty, and I shall pray that your souls will drink that manifestation and emanation that shall pour forth tangibly into your midst.

But I want you to know that it is *all* that I have said that must be studied and read, not just a part. And while I am on this subject, let me say to you that there are few among you who have yet developed the correct sense of understanding the blessings that you have via these outpourings of ascended master love from the messengers of light.

People are often prone to accept these things as though they were laws they had always known. If you have always known them, why no action? If you have always known them, why so little action? If you have always known them, why is your liberty not already yours? It is yours, but why are you not manifesting it?

Therefore, you have a great and mighty need to understand speedily that you are privileged and a privileged people. We could close this door with a snap so soft that the world would never hear it, or we could close it with a door resounding against the very casements thereof that would shake the foundations of the earth.

I hope you understand that in keeping the door open for man, it is the raging of the great soul of man composite that seeks to free all men in this day and age, that the culmination of the ascended masters' love, long a-gathering, should be a harvest of great light, which would saturate the world now with that perfection long awaited.

So hear me and heed me and study all that I have said, and I think that I shall have profitably conveyed some of this emanation, which in one sense of the word is now sprayed upon you.

I thank you.

July 10, 1966

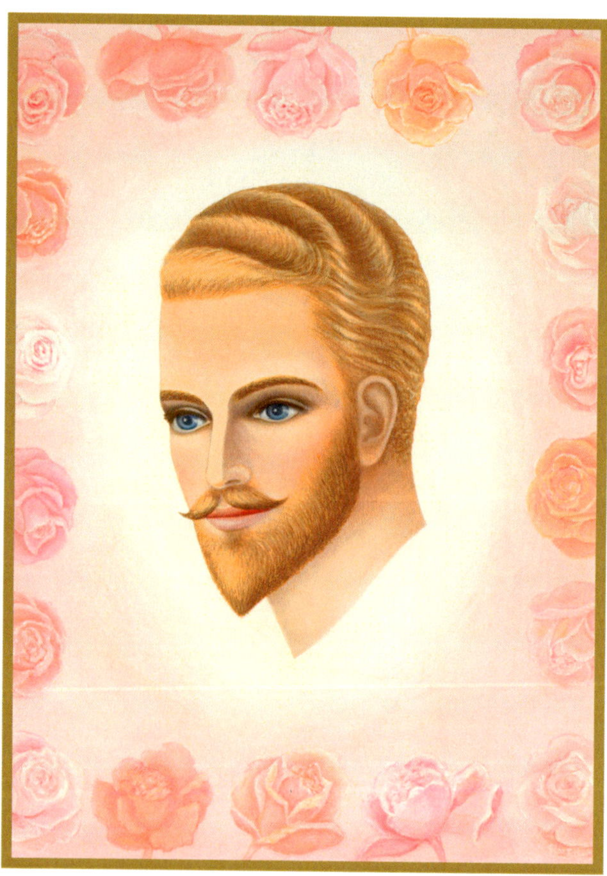

Paul the Venetian, by Ruth Hawkins

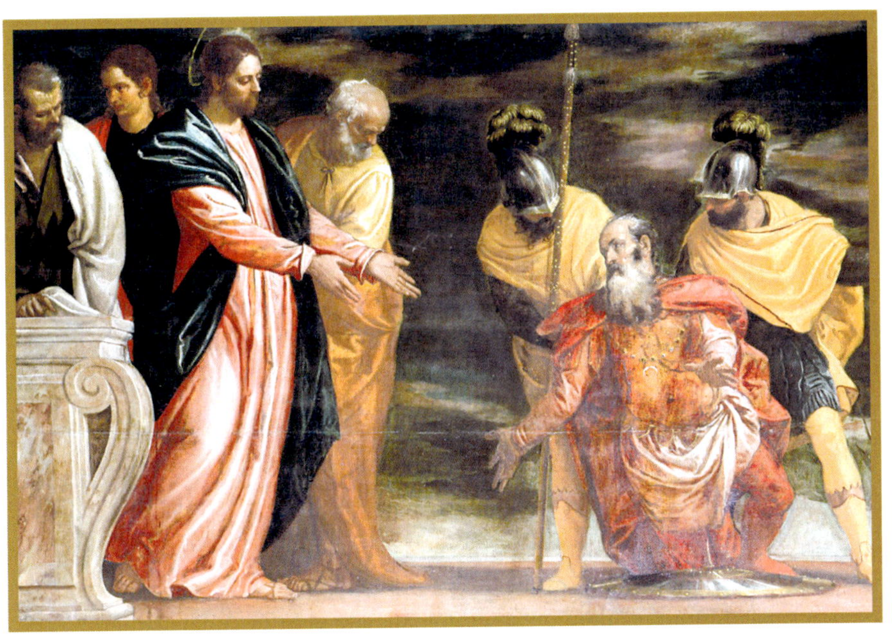

Jesus Healing the Servant of a Centurion (detail), c. 1585

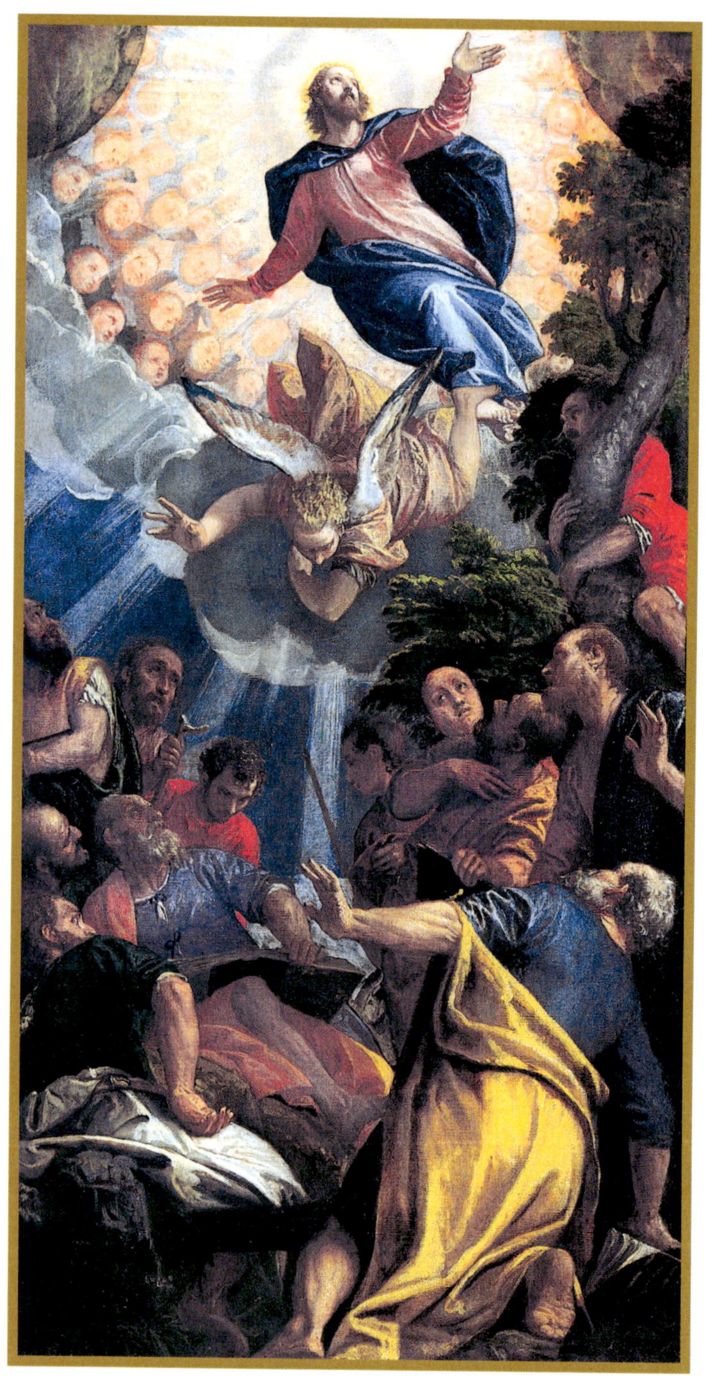

The Ascension, 1585

All souls are derived from the central essence of God and thus are inwardly charged with the lightning of God's love, the beauty of his countenance, and the strength of his wings of light, which raise mankind… into the magnificent goals that intentionally flood all nature.

CHAPTER 20

The Divine Ideals That Produce the Fruit of Immortality

Gracious men and women in search of the divine concepts that were fashioned from the Beginning and are therefore called founding concepts, I say to all of you: When beauty is perceived, the purposes of life are served. And when life is perceived to be lacking in beauty, the purposes of life are *not* served.

There is a very real tie in divine logic as it is outpictured in basic simplicity, which enables mankind, through a conscious effort of the will and the use of cosmic faculties, to strip the consciousness of those thorns and thistles that produce a manifestation of pain and unhappiness in the consciousness.

Now, when the purity of God is sought and when it is pursued, there is generated a certain forward momentum and thrust that enables the individual pursuer to attain elements of grace not formerly present in the consciousness. This is because, as you would put it, certain elements of the ascended master ideals "rub off" on the aspirant and become a part of that one's world.

In a way, it is a pyrotechnic display of cosmic fireworks. And the sparklers, held in the hands of the children of God, are also bathing the consciousness of those who witness this display with the ever-outpictured and ever-outpouring endlessness of cosmic creation. As stars miniaturized, these scintillate with infinite brilliance and continue to flow forth as an electronic stream without end. Man, therefore, finds an inexhaustible supply in the consciousness of God and the ability to enjoy every moment by recognizing naught but beauty in that which surrounds one and is one's environment.

Your Life Is the Life of God

You may ask, "How can this be, when the world itself has so thwarted the divine concept?"

I say to you as a wise counsellor and father: Remember that the thwarting of the divine concept first finds entrance into the consciousness, and when the consciousness is imbued with earthly ideas, these predominate. But when the consciousness is imbued with heavenly ideas, these strong, positive, virtuous, Godly, beautiful concepts are in the ascendancy and take command and dominion over outer conditions.

There are those who can find beauty in what men call ugliness because their consciousness *is* a beautiful consciousness. In a very real way, as I come to you today, it is with the benign desire to create in you a *spirit* of the divine artist—one who is able to accept the saturation of the Holy Spirit and the cosmic grace that floods the moments with the infinite capacity to dominate one's environment by divine ideals thrust forth from the motor of consciousness, by that power that refuses to accept the *appearance* of those elements within the world of man that produce sin, sickness, and death.

Your life is the life of God! It can never be taken from you, now or later, if you will only understand the importance of tying your faith to that concept. For as long as man's faith is tied to divine ideals, those ideals will produce the fruit of immortality and bring the blithe spirit of the beginning seeker, as well as the advanced one, to that place of congruency where the individual, by reason of divine proximity, is veritably manifesting the selfsame qualities that the heavenly Father manifests always and for the son, the beloved one of his heart.

The Consciousness of Separation from God

Human miasma has created the doldrums for those individuals who enter into it, because, I must admit, it has elements of confusion.

But these elements of confusion did not stem from or originate in the mind of God, and therefore they have no permanent reality nor are they able to mar the consciousness of the aspirant, as long as the major thrust is toward cosmic goals.

From a temporary standpoint, one's birthright may seem to totter between mortality and immortality, between faith and doubt, between the ugliness (that at times is in appearance in the world) and the beauty that is always the appearance of God in the world. But the Holy One of all that is Real continues, as the sparkler without limit, to shower forth into the consciousness his energy, purity, beauty, righteousness, love, strength, the flowering of identity, and a mountaintop goal as well as mounting reasons for pursuing that goal.

Now for a moment, as I let the shadow pass across your path, the shadow of the human miasma, I call to your attention that life in the world of form without God is utterly blackened. And phantom shadows of the unreal, which show that the lingering moments of pleasure received from the world of form—where selfishness warps the heart of those whom God made so beautifully—are indeed a treacherous act, shifting sands and shoals that produce no fruit of divine perfection but create separate individuals throughout the world rather than individuals connected to God.

Separate individuals are those possessed with the consciousness of their own separation from God and who recognize that they are far from him and consequently find little possibility of recognizing that they are nigh unto their brother. "I am my brother's keeper"[1] is a concept that stems from the Divine Presence, which I AM.

All Souls Are Derived from the Central Essence of God

Therefore, all who are conscious of the Divine Presence of God, I AM, within the self must recognize—in the faces and consciousness of all they meet, whether it is actually tangibly manifest or not—that *all* souls are derived from the central essence of God and thus are inwardly charged with the *lightning* of God's love, the *beauty* of his countenance, and the *strength* of his wings of light, which raise mankind out of the shadows of human creation and into the magnificent goals that intentionally flood all nature but are simply not perceived by man.

Is life a tangled barberry bush into which the human creation will be caught? Then it will be caught in its own trap. But life is God, and God cannot be imprisoned. Thus when man persists in wrong courses, in wrong pursuits, they will ultimately find that they are running away from life. It is not that life retreats from them, it is that by the erroneous concepts that they hold, they retreat from life.

And thus the planetary sphere today embodies this in the main because of the consciousness of the people. And I am not referencing *conscience,* but *consciousness*—a state whereby little is known of the divine Reality behind the veil, for it is seldom penetrated during the hours when mankind hold the grace of opportunity as the gift of God in their hands.

The Matrix of Christ-Purity

Where are the true pursuers of the divine sense of beauty? Where are the pursuers of the angels of God? Myriads deny the angels of God. They deny them existence and they do indeed deny your existence as well, and even their own feeling that life is not completely real. These individuals reel to and fro between a state of some odd type of faith in themselves and doubt in the Divinity.

How strange it is that mankind should believe in themselves and deny their Creator, when their Creator has never denied them, even when they were caught in the mire and quicksands of the world mind. But the mind of Christ, as a towering figure upon the world's hillsides, produces the blessing of infinite hope in the consciousness of all.

The steps to his heart may be few or many, but he will enable thee to attain thy aspiring goal as thou lettest go of the caked, crystallized, and muddy consciousness that is akin to the world sense but resembles not at all the divine Reality.

The Master was aware that in the multitude someone touched him, for he said, "I perceive that virtue is gone out of me."[2] And a woman came forward with trembling, who had an issue of blood about twelve years, and she had touched the hem of his garment. And he spake unto her and said, "Woman, go in peace; thy faith hath made thee whole."[3]

How beautiful, then, is one's own faith when it is tethered to Reality! How beautiful is one's own faith when it is faith in God that is not moved to and fro betwixt doubt and faith. How beautiful is a stable faith, that even when the appearance world seems to deny its reality, it can hold to the hand of God and know that it is only a matter of mortal time and its passage ere the transcendent reality of God is produced again and again as miracles of wonderment for mankind.

Gracious ones, the beauty of God and the divine sense is so far above the mortal sense that we often wonder why mankind are not literally crawling up the mountain. But we *are* there. We *are* there. We *are* here. We *are* here.

The divine sense, the sense of the beautiful, the Presence of God and the Presence of Christ, is everywhere, even where the consciousness of mankind has marred it. And it only mars the surface of the inner sense, which does not hold the matrix of Christ-purity.

Beauty within Man Is the Symbol of the Transcendent Reality of God

I have come to you this afternoon to bring you the consoling radiance of the cosmic thrust for beauty within man on *this* planet. It is a symbol—a symbol of the transcendent reality of God and of his loving, watchful care for all who aspire to his senses, to his consciousness.

Won't you, throughout the coming year, recognize the meaning behind what I have said?

Won't you, throughout the coming year and all the days of your life, begin the transformation of your consciousness?

For therein lies a great key to the God-purity of the thoughtform for this year[4]—the key to manifestation and to supremacy on not only the personal level of the individual but on the divine level.

For you are dual and will become one. One day the duality, that which is twain, shall become united, and whom God hath joined together, no man *can* put asunder.[5]

My peace I leave with you—the sense of cosmic beauty and the grace of our Father.

I thank you.

January 1, 1967

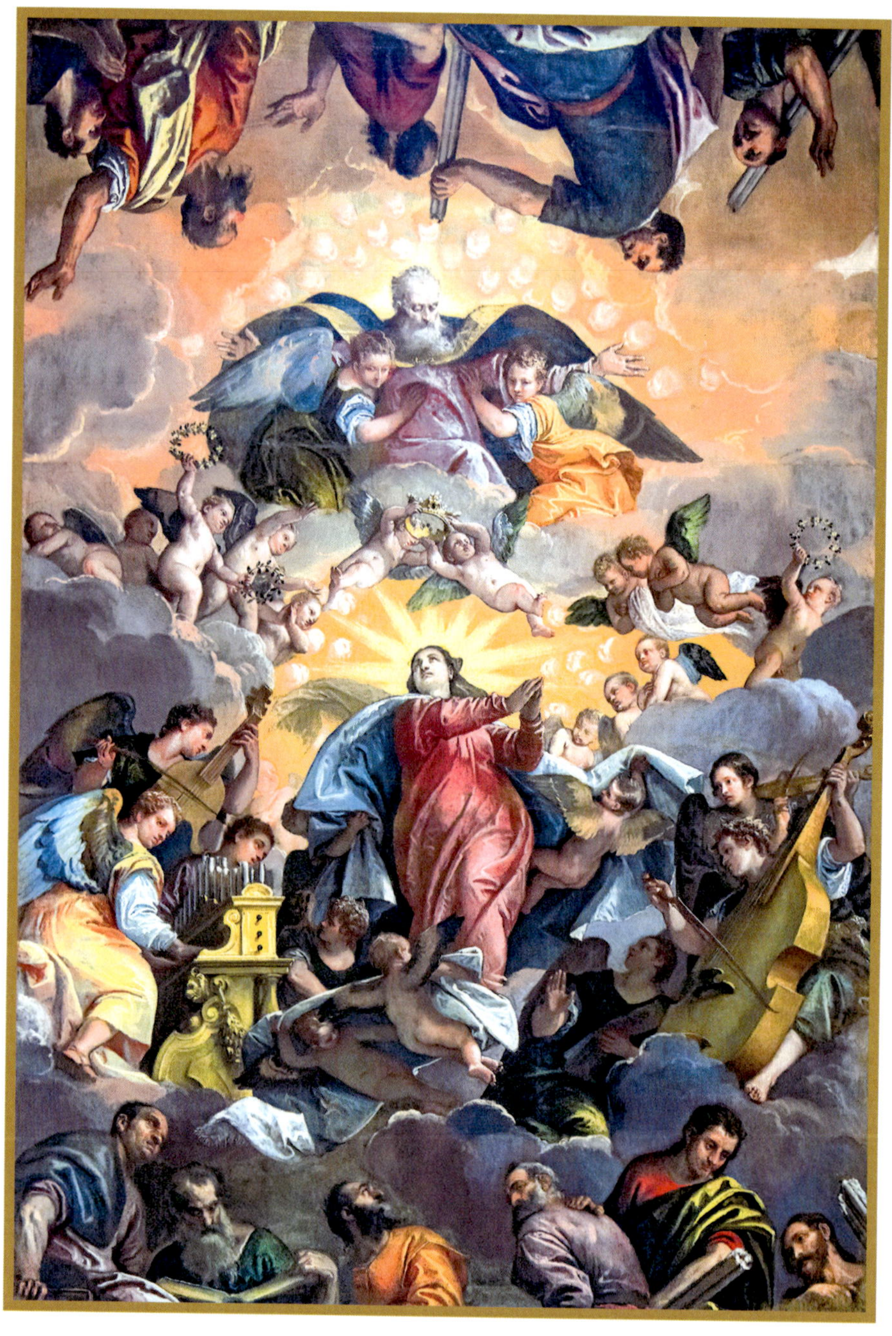

Assumption of the Virgin, c. 1585–87

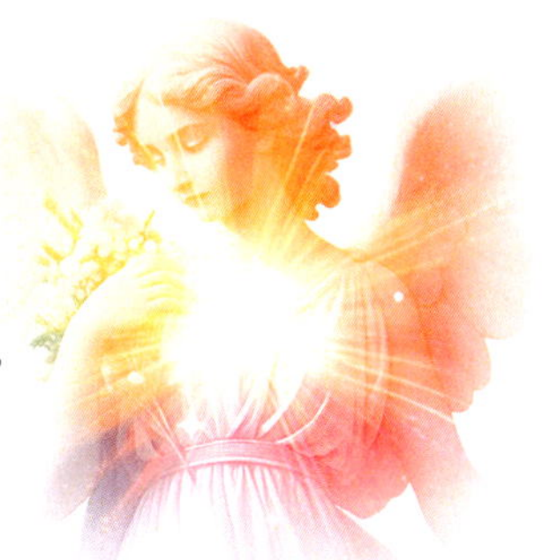

The self is, in reality, a fragile, tender thing.
But it is, beloved—as it opens itself, its tiny eyes unto the light—an ever-widening aperture, an ever-receding panorama, a vision transcending itself again and again, capturing new moments of new hope and faith.
This is the purpose of life.

CHAPTER 21

The Supremacy of Infinite Purpose

Beloved ones, the purity of divine expression is a tender and fragile thing. Let all understand, then, the need to balance in the forcefield of one's identity that magnificent God flame of immortal perfection, tripartite in nature but endowing man with the divine sense of balance by which he is able to achieve a realization of cosmic culture and appreciation for each blessed moment that God gives unto man.

In our Brotherhood the supreme idea is, What is good for the soul? What can still the restless confusions in the hearts and beings of man?

And therefore even in symmetry and form we strive for an expression of loveliness as an avenue to the Divine, that man, beholding our works of art, may themselves be inspired by them and relate themselves to a higher order and form.

The supremacy of infinite purpose, then, is realized at that moment by all who behold art. This art, then, becomes beauty in the eye of the beholder and a many-splendored thing, keying again and again those responses in thought and feeling that are akin to the Creator's own concept held in mind and cherished through the making process whereby God externalizes among mankind, through his instruments and in full view of all life, the methods that will enable them to grasp the thoughts of the Creator and the Creator's good servant—the artist, the musician, the creator in form—those who first create in thought and in feeling the magnificent momentums that come not into full focus in, of necessity, one moment but are betimes the study of lifetimes of service and desire—desire to serve mankind, not for the sake of glory, not for the sake of recognition, but to serve as an artist of the Spirit to create those designs that will afford mankind to see the splendid visions of the future that the ascended masters desire to spread abroad in consciousness.

For consciousness is indeed, my friends, a fertile field where the divine seeds may fall and have a rich and full-bodied harvest of illumination and strength of love and of love for the object of one's affection.

The Expansion of Consciousness Requires Attention upon the Deity

You must understand that love is not only a gettingness but love is also a givingness, that there is a greater blessing conveyed in the sense of the giving than even in the getting that is born of necessity.

For in the circle of lives there is always a return—a return of energies to each precious individual who sends forth into the universe some desire for service and the expression of those cosmic modes that are often expressed most arbitrarily by individuals. For individuals do not always understand these expressions with the full focus of consciousness, but instead they are often simply moved by certain conditions of heart and mind without understanding the whys or wherefores at all.

We are not concerned with any of this, but we are concerned that the divine expression may expand itself in the dimensions of each individual's consciousness. For it is consciousness that has the need to expand as a chalice, not to stay a certain fixed size in a spatial sense but to reach out for an ever-widening grasp of universal thought and feeling.

This requires attention upon the Deity. For while there may exist in the world of form those unfortunate hazards to young life known as mind-expanding drugs, we know that the wings of the Spirit will safely enable mankind, through their own latent inspirations—awakened and quickened by the Holy Spirit—to reach out into the universal consciousness and pulsate vibrationally in consonance with the Divine.

There are many avenues by which mankind may expand their consciousness, and God is not particular to call a halt to safe attitudes that desire to expand into the forcefield of the Divine. For attitudes are most important.

Individuals ought, then, to generate within themselves those tender responses of attitude that are chaste toward the Deity. They ought to understand that faith in the Deity is an essential ingredient if God is to manifest within the forcefield of themselves. They must not only believe that God is, but they must understand that he is the rewarder of diligence.

God's Love Is a Tender Reality of Each Precious Moment

And therefore if mankind are hungry to be fed the divine manna, the beauty and culture of the Spirit, they must sow the divine seeds of culture and beauty as they understand them within the forcefield of their own consciousness. This must not be a nebulous thing fraught with doubt. It must be a specific intent to garner from the field of the world, in every way they can, those thoughts and ideas that will produce kinship with the Divine.

Pre-essence of the divine intent is also a valuable adjunct to the seeker. To grasp in thought and feeling that God's love is a tender reality of each precious moment does itself create a sense of divine beauty and eminence, the eminence of the Divine.

"God will draw nigh unto you as you draw nigh unto him"[1] is not a platitude but a formula. It is a formula whereby you may bridge the chasms of doubt and distress and walk safely across into a radiant field where the light stands in all of its joyous appearance, a mighty thing of wonder. Moses saw it and said, "I will go apart and see now what this thing is, this bush that is aflame that is not consumed."[2]

And thus there are many ever-present realities in the field of art, of science, of philosophy, of religion, and of many departments of life whereby individuals are able to go apart and to see this miracle of infinite creation that surrounds the world, even as the ocean surrounds the little fishes in the sea.

Faith in God's Purposes

Let mankind, then, understand that everywhere there are miniature breaks in the garment that opaque the light, and through these rents in the veil the gleams of the Spirit do shine and bring renewed hope to those who will recognize this Reality as nigh unto themselves.

Blessed are they who are the pure in heart, for they shall see God.[3] To see God within the form of self, to see God within the mind of self, to see God within the emotions of the self is to bring about and effectuate a tenderness in the entire schema, a tenderness of thought and feeling that trembles in delight and ecstasy as to just what each new moment will bring forth.

Will it be an essential manifestation that will carry the soul forward, as a cool mountain stream? Or will it be a temporary stagnation for reflection in a calm pool of being? Or will it be the cascading rapids that move the consciousness on, ever upward, ever downward, rising and falling, undulating, because in the relative sense there is no up or down but only movement—flow, as Meru has said,[4] of the cascading consciousness of being.

And what delightful surprises are just around the bend for many who will summon the faith, who by faith in God's purposes elect for themselves a higher walk, who are not satisfied with outer conditions, who are not satisfied with the past but yearn to move forward into that glorious, veiled future that God tenderly reveals unto his children because their love flows out to him as the connecting link between that great eternal Presence and the self.

The self is, in reality, a fragile, tender thing. But it is, beloved—as it opens itself, its tiny eyes unto the light—an ever-widening aperture, an ever-receding panorama, a vision transcending itself again and again, capturing new moments of new hope and faith. This is the purpose of life. It is a great tragedy (and no comic purpose whatsoever) that causes mankind to fail to perceive reality when it is all around them.

Listen Closely to the God Within

And so tonight my plea to all who hear with the inner ear is to listen closely to the God within who speaks to each soul, the God within who caresses each consciousness, the God within who is also the God without.

He is beautiful of heart. Beautiful are his feet that have moved in the world of form to leave permanent markings of infinite love and light right where man is so that man can grasp these hopes again and again and break the matrices of old and callous actions, understanding the need for recognition of the purity of the divine seed within themselves.

There is no sacrifice in offering one's all to cosmic purpose. There is only the blending, the harmonious blending with the light that is everywhere and yet is nowhere unless mankind perceive it. For if the light goes out in the human consciousness and purpose seems dim, it is because Reality is not contacted. And there is, then, one solution and one alone, and that is to come by faith on a journey on the great boat of reality to where Reality is.

If this requires movement, well and good. If it requires a stationary activity wherein the movement is from within, well and good. For both are necessary. There is a time to move and a time to be still, and mankind must understand the need to perceive which time is in readiness at a given moment.

We, then, tonight, will give you these simple thoughts based upon the great purposes of the light, because it is the light of divine love, and divine love alone, that will serve as a beacon for those who open the doors of their consciousness to that sublime Reality that is captured within the countenance of the newborn and sometimes is caught as the dying light on the face of the aged, whose hopes are reaching out beyond for a new beginning, or *la fin* to a career of service to the Most High.

Great is the universe—wide, magnificent.
Let your grasp be as wide as the universe,
As magnificent as God's mind,
And then the sea of Being will encompass thee all around,
And you will see that life does by fire abound
To create a matrix ever new,
To make you one of the very few
Who elect to be and see their God,
To understand the might of rod
Of cosmic law that chastens some
And moves man forward till they are one.

I thank you.

September 24, 1967

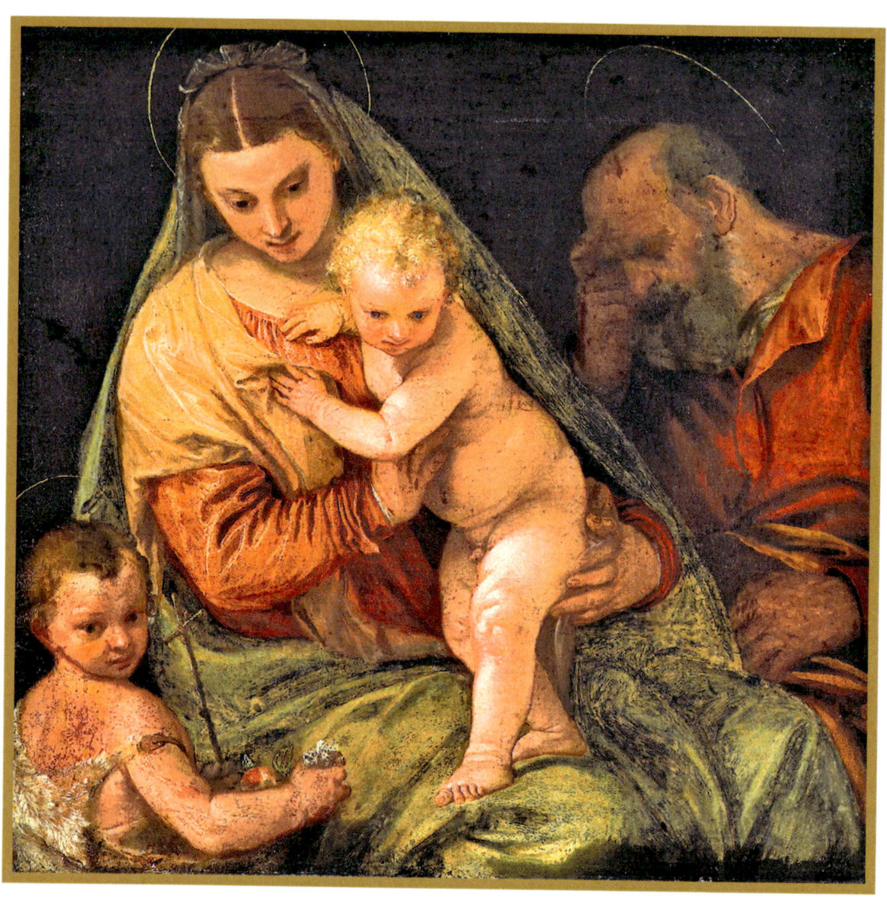

Holy Family with Young Saint John, c. 1550–75

May I say… that the media of this age provides new and beautiful avenues for the sensitive artist to externalize—whether in his life or upon canvas—products of new hope as charity to a waiting world, where the starry eyes of children beam in the promise of a future.

CHAPTER 22

THE DEVELOPMENT OF THE SPIRITUAL SENSES

Gracious Lovers of Beauty and Perfection,

The spectacle of art attracts relatively few people because the soul of the artist must enter into the beholder, and only the few are capable of making this attunement. Unless this occur, quite naturally man's interpretations often belie the universal message that true art is intended to portray, and the real meaning of the work is not appreciated. Consequently, it cannot hold the attention of the viewer.

Now the need arises for all who devote themselves to cosmic principle—who desire to see the salvation of the age rather than its destruction—to consider how they may best serve the Brotherhood. If we are to be honest, we will have to admit that the works of most artists in the fields of painting, sculpture, and music are clumsy and coarse by divine standards. Far too many of their creations are framed out of lower astral horror rather than in the joy of the Magnificat.[1]

We can understand the value of realism to depict the depths of degradation to which civilization has fallen in order to spur noble countermeasures, but we deem many of the outer forms in contemporary vogue to be nothing more than a surrealism of horror and distortion. Yet our critique is not destructive. We warn that we may teach.

The school of reality is the school of cosmic apprehension, where one seeks to define the Divine rather than merely to mold substance or to control sound. Harmony within the components of a work of art is as important as the harmony of the total work. Sculpture can be frozen harmony, and architecture a crescendo of the mind of God.

The Distortions of Past-Age Concepts

We seek through the cosmic impact of pure art forms to rupture mankind's regrettable resistance to spiritual things. The fact that Christianity has failed to exercise the fullness of its mission, and in its detours and circuitous routes presents the face of deviousness to mankind, is no reason for spurning it. Yet untutored minds and hearts—in the frenzy of rejection and the desire to replace their broken idols—turn unwittingly toward the sordid and the bizarre.

When mankind are unable to enthrone the Most High within themselves, they enthrone themselves within their concepts of the Most High. Making no pretense at hypocrisy, they surround themselves with it. Call the divine Creator by any other name than God, and he is still the same—the *summum bonum* of all good manifesting from the Beginning and shedding light upon his own purposes as well as upon the purposes of mankind. The consciousness of man was originally endowed with the plasticity of harmonic acceptance of each divine matrix or thoughtform. The response was the eclectic magnification of the peaks of joy.

When man lost hope in unseen glories and turned outwardly rather than within to affirm the Real, they felt the prick of foreign objects upon the matrix of consciousness. At first this distortion was uncomfortable, but as devious patterns became implanted in consciousness, the dutiful faculties of nature quickly molded themselves around them as easily as they had embraced the pristine elements of their divine origin.

Thus, through habit mankind found comfort in the familiar, albeit the imperfect world he had superimposed upon his true inheritance. The rebellion of the spirit, then, must be understood as the rejection of the distortions of past-age concepts, the heaving of the soul to shatter the clay mold that encases its identity.

A New Sense of the Beautiful

Man should reexamine the fabric of the eternal garment and mend the broken threads, weaving into the robe of life the energy of light wherever darkness doth appear. While the flaws of loomed textiles are not easily mended, men and women working with spiritual substance and cosmic ideas find the natural flow of light able to perfect the seamless garment and to heal all disturbances in the psyche of man.

Man must, of course, recover their faith and refine it in order to draw forth the omnipotent stream that will render their solar bodies[2] flawless under the scrutiny of the all-knowing Eye of God. But what magnificent potential exists in the consciousness of the individual who considers for the first time that the renovation of his person is a most practical possibility!

Unfortunately, orthodox religion has implanted in mankind's consciousness concepts of vileness and sin to replace the beauty of the lily of his immaculate conception in the mind of God. As "miserable sinners," mankind can only lament their lot, having scarcely any room in their hearts to let the Divine appear within.

We do not deny the gross errors that have been committed on a world scale or the personal errors that individuals have perpetrated in their own worlds, often ignorantly and many times with only half-knowledge of the consequences of their acts. But no continuing good can come to the advancing soul who seeks to hold the hand of Christ, of light, of creative energy by drawing in past participles of an old grammar. The ever-new Word must impart to man the hope that marches over the obstacles of the past to a new sense of the beautiful.

One of the problems of contemporary man is that they are seldom willing to consider the abandonment of their whole forte of knowledge. They have created a Leaning Tower of Pisa, and they cannot contemplate its ruin. It is far better to destruct all of man's wrong matrices at once and to rebuild from the ruins upward than to continue to deal with an unwieldy structure. We do not favor the destruction of individuals or of opportunities, but rather the destruction of that which was builded in error.[3] Thus we sound a note of warning.

The many benign qualities that were placed with good intention in the construction of the leaning tower can be kept intact and used in the new structure after their purification by cosmic light energy. Fear not, then, to seek to understand the ethereal, to develop a sense of the pastel colors,[4] of the gentle colors, of the swirling radiance of a swaddling garment of light. Know, however, that this light that is the light of God that never fails holds within its nature a crystal clarity and spiritual purity that is without alloy.

New Hope as Charity to a Waiting World

Aught that depresses, smothers, suppresses, or draws man downward into conflict may well be the psychic dominance of others. In this connection it should be understood that art wrongly used can become a key to Pandora's realm. The opening of that box—that rectangle (in this case "wreck tangle") of distorted consciousness—can never be enlivening toward good. The new sense of cosmic joy, like the sun's radiance upon sparkling waters, speaks of the nature of fluidity in motion, of flow, of regeneration, of vast-domed bubbles shimmering upon a splendid moment with all of the colors of the rainbow.

The age has been dark and heavy, the lives of the saints have been stilted and stultified with mortal concepts, and the shoddy facade of the social world that outwardly seeks to portray great class ever lacks the nature of true grace. As the chohans ponder what impetus could do more for each of our chelas, we seek to portray in this seven weeks of our cosmic effort[5] the thoughts that we feel will most marvelously advance man's consciousness and his adventure in living.

What tremendous import there is in the development of the spiritual senses. The old senses must pass away to give place to the new. Transmutation, transcendence, and transfer all speak of translucence, even of transparency. For the idea of seeing through a glass darkly but then face-to-face[6] is always the miracle of a moment when opacity yields to translucency, and translucency to transparency. The thinning of the veil and the clarification of nebulous concepts, together with their reduction to orderly simile, will provide mankind a golden rule by which he may measure his doings—his goings and his comings—and his progress in a universal sense.

May I say, then, in closing, that the media of this age provides new and beautiful avenues for the sensitive artist to externalize—whether in his life or upon canvas—products of new hope as charity to a waiting world, where the starry eyes of children beam in the promise of a future that in God's name we must make nobler than the past.

Raise the world to Christ's glory,
Enfold the world with Christ's story,
Reveal the hidden that is within,
Forget the sordid sense of sin,
Forsake the shadow and unreal,
By light's perfection mankind heal,
In cosmic beauty's rainbow seal
The children of good hope.

Lovingly in the beauty of creation, I AM

Paul the Venetian

January 21, 1968

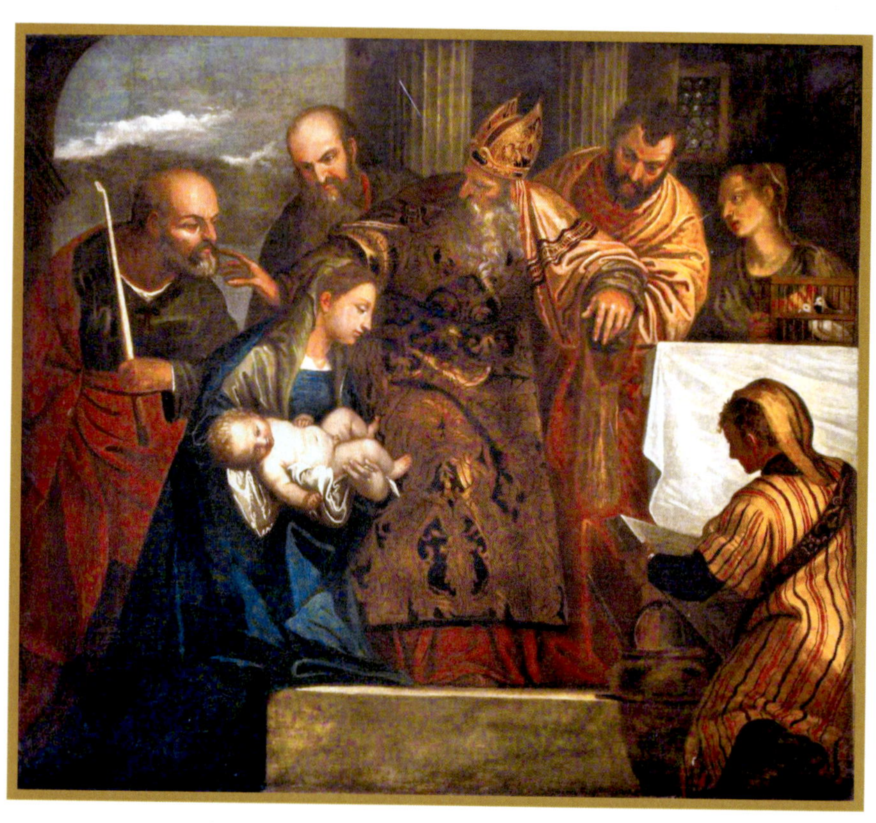

The Presentation in the Temple, unknown date

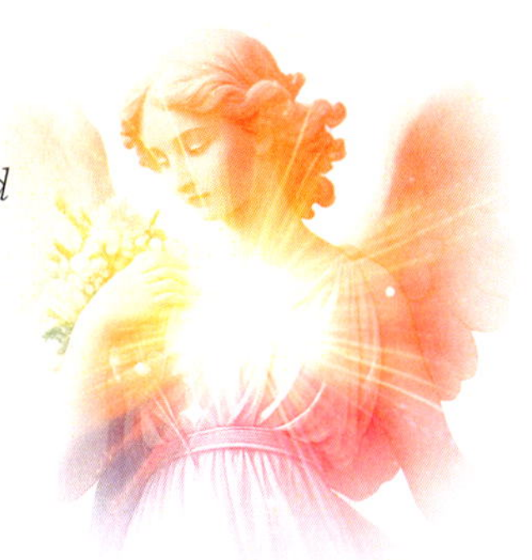

The soul is native to God and as pure as the flowers and more so. The soul is as pure as the newly driven snow, and all of its virtues are lovely where'er it does go.

CHAPTER 23

Beauty Is the Native Consciousness of God

Most gracious ladies and gentlemen who are lovers of beauty and of God, I come to you this morning to bring you our instruction in advancing the sense of beauty in your consciousness.

Beauty is the native consciousness of God. For the very idea of symmetry is elucidated by him in the soundless universe and in the universe of sound.

Whether beauty manifests in the soundless universe as form manifest to the eye, or the sound universe as the cascade of a falling waterfall, or the joyous bird notes manifest in the atmosphere, or in the tiny furry creatures, all is the native manifestation of the grace of Almighty God.

We call now to the angels of divine love to radiate into the atmosphere the precious sense of divine love that is as soft as a pink petal of a rose or as pleasant to the consciousness as the fragrance thereof.

We call to these precious angels of beauty and love to release from the bowers of heaven the very wondrous thoughtforms that exist at higher octaves of light to flood your beings and consciousness with the radiation of divine love, as divine love prepares for you a realm of such loveliness as to be beyond mortal conception.

Yet because there has been some misunderstanding in religious doctrine over the centuries concerning this, I would clarify for your consciousness the total subject by saying that God intends the consciousness of man to advance in its sense of beauty, not only by the direction of noble aspirations from within the being, the self of man, but also from the higher octaves and the realm of the ascended masters' consciousness. For the sense of beauty that a man has today can be enhanced by contact with the beauteous sense of the angels, the ascended beings, or his own Divine Presence.

God Is Truly within All Things

It is contact that makes the difference. And when contact occurs, there is a flow from the nature of the Higher Self into the realm of the lower that produces an elevation of the senses. This will of course, quite frankly, manifest in you as a sense of penetration into substance. For example, if I set before you a rose or a lily, you may feel a sense of your consciousness actually entering the substance itself and identifying with it.

In the case of the white lily, the consciousness may seem to be bathed in an ethereal radiance of cosmic light. This light will have a feeling of softness, of gentleness, yet of a swimming radiance. For you will note that where there is a penetration of the actual substance of the lily with the light of the sun, all of the fluids within the actual formation of the lily petals will be perceived to be swimming with light and liquid. This is *liquid* light. And the merging of the sun's rays within the soft folds of the lily will bathe the consciousness of man, as it does the consciousness of the elementals who care for the floral kingdom.

Some men may ask out of the crassness of their nature, "What benefit is this? It sounds like silly nonsense to me." But then these are they who have never had the soul of an artist, who have never understood how God is truly within all things. They did not reckon with or realize the meaning behind Jesus' statement, "If these should hold their peace, the stones would immediately cry out."[1]

Let us, then, ask that you shall not submit to the idea of bowing down your head in grief or feeling that life is but a falling of petals from the stalk until there is—in this commingling of the beauties of life with the dust of the earth—only annihilation. Nothing could be further from the truth! For the very power of the flame of the resurrection is the power that the little elementals utilize in forming the beauties of the floral kingdom, and every flowering tree is actually a manifestation of the angels' thoughts physically manifest to humankind.

Man influenced the rose long ago by his viciousness, his hatred, and his harshness, until accompanying the beauties of the angels there came forth the ugly and sharp thorn. From these they plaited the crown of thorns, which they pressed into the head of the Master Jesus.

The Soul Is Native to God and as Pure as the Flowers

We say to you today that there are many vicious experiences in human life that are thorn-like in their penetration of the aura and the consciousness of man. But none of these are God-willed or God-intended, and they are sustained solely by the consciousness of those who do not understand their unity with God. If they understood their unity with God, if they grasped the fragrance of the soul penetrating the pores of self and could feel the meaning of divine love, there would never be any need for criticism or condemnation or judgment of any part of life.

First of all, each part of life would give no occasion to life to criticize or to condemn. And secondly, wherever there was an embryonic child still learning to master his own energies, who would erstwhile, perhaps, make a display of those energies according to a human pattern, the thought of forgiveness would always flow forth into the consciousness of the divine devotee. And the divine devotee *would* never, *could* never cast even one pebble of aspersion against any soul.

For the soul is native to God and as pure as the flowers and more so. The soul is as pure as the newly driven snow, and all of its virtues are lovely where'er it does go. But the overlay of human personality seems to be the usurper, the abomination of desolation spoken of by Daniel the prophet, standing in the holy place where it ought not.[2] For there, where the beautiful soul that God saw was good—was very good—stands in its place the human person, with all of his fears so unnecessarily formed. For surely his image will be merged with God one day and will fade away completely. It is temporary. It falls.

And this is why the flowers in the world today fall—because they symbolize that even man's greatest beauty, his greatest achievements, are as nothing beside the power of the immortal God flame from whence he sprang.

The Adventure of the Spirit

When these ideas of beauty and immortality are wedded to the consciousness, when the consciousness offers itself in consecration without reserve to God, there is always the opportunity of adventure just ahead. This is the adventure of the Spirit, where all of the beauties of nature ordinarily hidden from the common mind are finally, one by one, revealed in such a pageantry as to resemble in part some of the fables of *The Arabian Nights.*[3]

Shining in jeweled loveliness, the very universe itself imparts its magnificent spiritual advantages to the soul. The diamonds of the Spirit sparkle radiantly as tiny suns with blue-fire center. The consecrated fruit of the Spirit hangs luscious and ripe before the gaze. The fragrances that are wafted to the nostrils by the beings of the air convey the sense of the sacred Presence to all of life that witnesses it.

And as man captures this, he perceives that the very sinews of cosmic progress and adventure are within himself. And there is a tightening of these sinews in that magnificent prestige of cosmic honor, the cosmic honor flame. He is a part of God; from God he came.

And as he breathes this air of freedom, the power to create does break before his gaze the precious bread of heaven. Each morsel that he takes is the bread unleavened, but leavened only with that oneness of the Spirit flowing, creating a new remolding of the soul that in its knowing fabricates cosmic destiny for all.

A Dramatic Presentation of Your Cosmic Destiny

Oh, if artists of the world and musicians would only understand the meaning of true love, the world would become all that God intended and a swiftening would occur of this magnificent adventure. All pain manifest in the rose's thorns would blunted be. And man himself—the highest destiny that God intends—would come unto his own inheritance to see at last what the meaning of true beauty is.

And so we call to souls—not to bodies, not to minds, not to beings, but unto souls—that as they approach the first day of creation they may imbibe the fruit of that day; that as they approach each day in succession, the fruit of that day may be rekindled as a flame within their consciousness.

For these days are but cycles of cosmic adventure, epigrams of eternity that fragrantly endow the being with a new sense of God's beauty and his love. And as they come forth, there is such a sense of progress that is born, as all the darkness of the world, receding from view at last, is seen but as the curtain of the night behind which the day does linger.

And then when the first day does end with the approach of eventide, it is always the sense of the sun of the Presence going to bed, only to rise again and produce the glow of the golden dawn of cosmic illumination and wonder.

Life is seen as an endless procession of conveyances, and the hands of God are the conveyances. The hands of God are the great benefactors of humanity. The mighty sinews of his faith by which he framed the worlds are seen in each finger and in each ligament underneath the flowing, rippling, radiant skin of the immortal purpose of it all.

God is everywhere! everywhere!
God is everywhere!
God is everywhere, becomes in me.

I feel thy fragrance round me now,
A mantle-flame that swirls,
A kindred tongue to utter words
Now lost from mind and view.
The written Word, the spoken Word—
All glow with cosmic hue,
With pink and blue and gold and swirling white,
As misty clouds of cosmic joy surround us all.

And when the gentle winds have blown it all away,
A fairyland of wonder and loveliness will stay.

Nevermore shall darkness seem to be a shroud,
But all the parent vision of the universe, so meek and mild,
Will flow into the brain and consciousness of man
To cast out from his being all that's din and sand,
Replacing all by fragrant gold
And glowing fires of sun from distant worlds,
And bringing to the eyes and vision of us all
A renewal of His love unfurled
As banner of the Mother of the World.

A plea goes out into the silent universe
And speaks to every man within his *own* heart:
"O live according to the beauteous sense of cosmic joy
And let the fragrance of His love impart without alloy
All that God is descending now to man,
The kingdom of His world, the universal plan
For the Great White Brotherhood,
For The Summit Lighthouse,
In its image of the Son of God."

We aspire to create the vision of cosmic symmetry
As universal *summitry,*
And then we know that men will walk
Upon the mountains tall,
And neath the fragrance of the towering pines
Will see it all
As yearning in the soul for more of God.

For when he comes,
As men are seated neath his chastening rod,
They say, "O Lord, not my will, but thine be done."
For by thy hand across the burning desert sands
The children of Israel did go,
And Moses carried them forward
Toward the Promised Land.
So the land of beauty will impart to all

That new sense by which they'll understand
That they should nevermore fall
Into the delusions of the senses
But keep the cosmic incense in their soul
That senses every thought of beauty
As an unfolding curtain, revealing the drama of the soul,
Universal, cosmic majesty that makes men whole
And shows to everyone
The fragrance of the Central Sun.
It permeates us, one and all.
It permeates us, one and all.
It permeates us, one and all.

Out of the heart of the archives of the Great White Brotherhood I have brought to you this dramatic presentation of your cosmic destiny. But my words will not do justice to that which the soul is witness to. And may you see it in its beauty—its infant beauty, its beauty mature. For then I think that vision will impart to you the power to endure whatever you must endure, until at last out of the sense of God's beauty you will find your freedom.

I thank you.

December 7, 1969

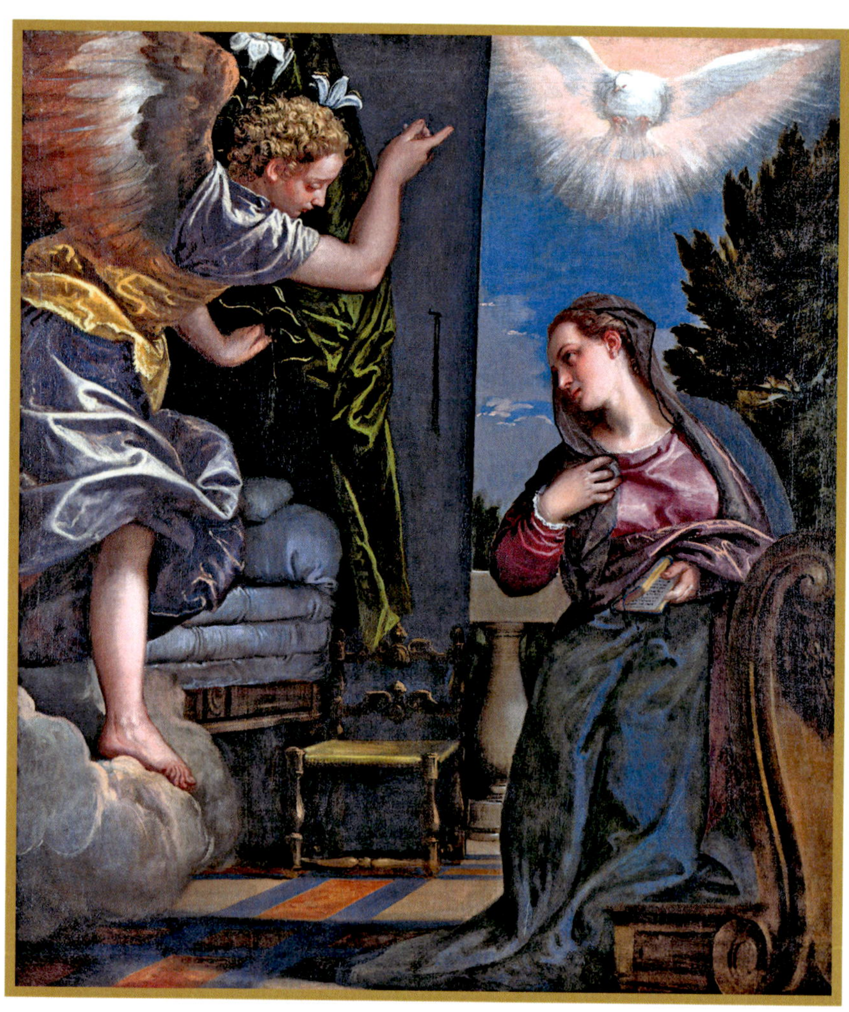

The Annunciation, c. 1580

The fire of movement and of the New Age dawns, the fire of a beauty whose supremacy will enable each heart to catch a glimpse of that which will one day be—because it already is.

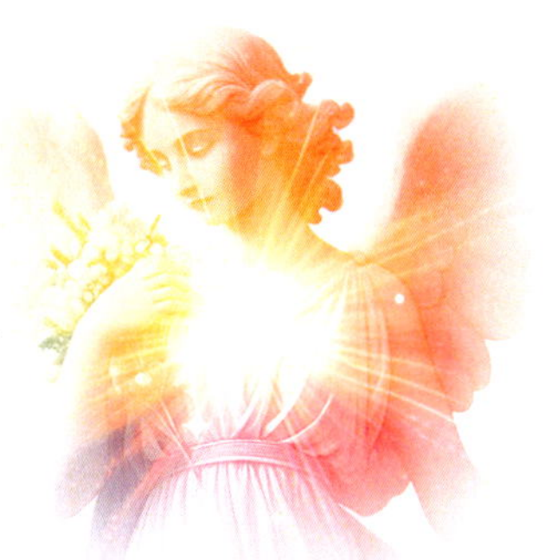

CHAPTER 24

The Chord of Cosmic Beauty

The tenderness of grace is before me now, a moment of serenity when all of the activity of the universe is stilled and the radiance of the universe, like a lustrous pearl, gleams through the orifices of consciousness and expands out, out, out beyond all that seems to be.

I am enamored by His grace. His grace is sufficient not only for myself but for every man. His grace abounds, and his grace is the essence of all beauty. He has formed the perfection of the lily and the rose, but above all he has formed the magnificence of the heart.

Hence, as I come this night, it is to cherish the ideals of the heart. For the heart is endowed with its own fire, and the majesty of that fire expands everywhere, to the farthest reaches of space, to the farthest reaches of consciousness, and is able to return home to the heart of the individual even as it is able to return the individual to the heart of Home, the heart of God.

You came forth from him, and all things came forth from him. All things were made by him. And the idea, in its sweet simplicity, is most enchanting when mankind are able to peer behind the mere cage of words into the heart of an idea. For out of great ideas are born great movements, and no movement is so utterly important to the world (now and always has been) as the movement of the being of man into the magnificent radiance of the love of God. The love of God encompasses all things, yet who can rule this power of infinite love?

The Beauty of God Is Displayed in the Beauty of the Heart

You have heard it said that the hand that rocks the cradle is the hand that rules the world. And so as a knight of God, I tonight honor the Mother of the World. In the concept of the Mother is born the idea of family unity—a family under God, where the beauty of interlocking harmony is manifest in the consonance of hearts, as hearts sing in harmony with that inward concept, "On Wings of Song"[1]—that inward concept that rights all wrong, that inward concept that makes man be an element of God-free radiance, of light outpouring over the threshold of the chalice and moving the world toward a state of regeneration.

The world throughout the centuries—and I cite it with gravity—has spewed out the same old dogmas of error. The concepts of mortal men welded in vanity are twisted in space. They stem from dimensions of darkness and error, and they create shame in the hearts of men. Let us shun, then, *all* that is negative, *all* that is destructive, *all* that creates a pallor upon the face of the world consciousness, and let us elevate the consciousness of man into the appreciation of God's beauty.

And where is beauty displayed more fervently than in the beauty of the heart? This is the "encanvassing"* of that supreme radiance from the mind of God, which by the Master Artist, with fingers of radiant light, is penciled within the darkness of the formative mind. For the mind and being of man are formative in immaturity. But standing forth now, man is hopefully learning the lessons upon this planet and thus ascending into that supernal radiance where the glow-ray of God is able to wipe from the consciousness and mind of man all tears of shame and those crocodile tears of self-pity and illusion, and reveal at last—to every heart-seeker for consciousness and bliss and freedom from fear—a realm of such magnificent faith as dispels doubt and gloom and casts aside forever the things of this earth that will never conquer the universe, and never can.

For man, in his frail house of clay endowed with the beauty of God,

---

*"encanvassing": a coined word that likely means to express or capture on canvas, whether on the physical or etheric plane

molders away even as he lives, not as Methuselah and the brave men of old endowed with the priesthood of Melchizedek,[2] but as a dying generation, a blight upon the branch of life. These, moved to stark nakedness and cold reality, stand, then, revealed "as wandering stars, to whom is reserved the blackness of darkness forever," as was spoken of old.[3]

The mass consciousness, as a charnel house of destruction and deceit, moves onward as a juggernaut caravan without purpose, empty and devoid, an abomination of desolation that God has vacated.

The Need for Diligence in Love

Now, then, we come to that radiant perfection of the living Christ, that supremacy of consciousness that is the virtue of Almighty God that strikes to light a flame within the heart of man.

This flame that is lit is a flame of radiant love! This flame that is lit is kindled from above! This flame that is lit and garnished by angelic radiance is surrounded, then, by that heavenly witness, a corollary to all truths spoken by all avatars of old and citing these words so faithfully rendered in the scriptures of old: "Beloved, a new commandment I give unto you, that ye love one another."[4]

Those who heard the Master utter those words understood it not as a fragile thing but as a power to move the millennia, to move through the manvantara* and the epochs of God-identification and historical movement, until the world plan could solemnly reveal itself to the world as a caravan of happiness, a bonanza of God's grace abundantly overflowing the chalice of each moment and rendering it beautiful, even when on the surface it might seem to be ugly.

The alchemy of change—so much now in the mind of the Brotherhood—is a holy activity intended to endow humanity with that love that would teach them the need for every aspect of love, which is also the *potential* of change, the *potential* of cleansing, the *potential* of realization, the education of the heart until the heart is able to perceive beauty and to portray it in the radiance of the life so lived.

*-*manvantara:* in Hinduism, the period or age of a Manu; one of the fourteen intervals that constitute a kalpa—the duration of time from the origination to the destruction of a world system (a cosmic cycle)

The life so lived is given to all, and all are touched by the outflow of the heavenly light of movement in their own lives, some misqualifying it to judgment and destruction and others creating beauty—beauty that endures, a lovely grace, a tranquil radiance, or a *bursting brilliance* that when it goes forth into the world is able to impress memory—cause, effect, record, and memory—with the need for diligence in love.

Without diligence in love, the corrosive elements of the world, my beloved, will create in the heart such irritation and resentment, such sympathy for those who are the harbingers of destruction, such confusion and chaos in consciousness as to opaque the beauty that God has placed everywhere. And nowhere do we see it more beautifully portrayed, as I said before, than in the heart. But until the heart speaks, we find that the floral tributes of the angelic hosts are the most vocal of all elements of beauty.

And I think also, as I see the stamp of beauty upon the face of a child, that next [in beauty] to a lovely flower is the face of a lovely child. And one day the children of the world, as their consciousness is more educated to the sublime ideas of the Most High God, will be as God intended—a hungry, budding flower seeking to lap up the identity of God and to absorb it wholly into consciousness. And when that moment occurs, I tell you, the golden age will be in full flower.

And of what value, I ask, would the creation of greater scientific achievement be to a world that cannot, in its understanding, understand the need to shun and shed violence everywhere, to stop it—to stop the action of violence? You have heard it said, "The kingdom of heaven suffereth violence, and the violent take it by force."[5]

The Reality of Beauty Is the Sustaining Momentum That God Foreknew in the Beginning

Now I come to you tonight to create in you the peace that is hidden in beauty.

Why do you go away from time to time from the busy, teeming marts of the world? Why do you seek to hide in mountain nooks and along quiet rivers? Why do you desire to listen to soft and gentle music?

It is because your heart yearns to muse, because your heart, filled with its long-remembered rivers of light, still has the radiant reflection of the cosmic mirror of Reality moving as a barge of holiness upon its surface, and it wants so much to reveal this beauty to each individual personally so that the individual may share in it because it is God's. And through that sharing in it, God may flow into it. And through that flowing into it, beauty may flow into that one's consciousness. And because it is there, the lineaments of beauty will be fashioned by that lifestream in all that that one does. For when the consciousness absorbs the beauty and perfection of God, it cannot help but shine forth and be mirrored in other ways.

I come to you, then, tonight, not as an outwardly perfected people but as a people who seek perfection, as people who understand and crave perfection, as those who have a need for it, like empty vessels who wait to be filled.

I come, together with others of the angelic hosts, and I am consumed and delirious in the consciousness of God's beauty. I have seen of old, in the days when I was known as Paolo Veronese, how humanity was able to create beautifully from the age-old memories of the soul in works of art, such as Titian[6] and others.

But now in this latter time when the possibility of great change comes to humanity, I would point out to you that when all the forces of darkness and the darkening of the age stand before mankind as an awesome specter, a bony skeleton pointing toward destruction, as it were, all of this ugliness can pass away in one moment, as the sunburst of heavenly light and color, music and perfume burst into the consciousness and shed forth the glory of God there.

When hope is kindled anew in consciousness, it is a sunburst of radiant light! And so tonight, as I come to you with the blessing of the Darjeeling Council, I, Paul the Venetian, am mindful of the need to kindle in those who are here at this *Class of the Resurrection Flame* a flame of the reality of beauty, because this was the sustaining momentum that God foreknew from the Beginning and by which he wrought age-old wonders of old.

Beauty Is in the Law

As your hearts are stirred, then, by the power of the Brotherhood playing upon you with the many fingers of mastery until the lutes of your heart are stirred to a cosmic, chordal response, I pray that Almighty God himself—from out the fires of the Great Central Sun, through the power of the angelic hosts—will kindle in the heart of each one of you that buoyant sense of God-reality that you knew before the world was, that stumbling no longer, *the world garment, the world garment, the world garment, the world garment* of Reality will be drawn together by the bonds of love until this love, generated in the fires of God's own heart, will kindle anew in you all a response that you will never forget. And thus you will determine to set the world aflame with that blaze that conquers all.

The harbingers of violence believe that in guns and destructivity they are able to rule the world. But they are most subtle in their machinations. They do not understand the need to protect freedom. They do not understand the need to protect humanity.

They sometimes feel that freedom is license to do whatever they will, and they do not understand that beauty is in the Law. This law to be loved, while it may be a chastening to humanity, is also the saviour of humanity. For those who do well will frame a world, as the carpenter of Nazareth long ago sought to do, where beauty and law are understood and welcomed. Then the children of mankind will look as the great sands fall from the hourglass of life. They will look as the great Karmic Lords hold up the scales of judgment. They will look and say, "Welcome, judgment! Welcome, reality! Welcome, beauty!"

For there is beauty in this, even as there is beauty in flowers and faces and hearts. There is beauty in the cleansing of the earth by the sacred fire. There is beauty in casting out hatred from the heart. There is beauty in beginning to relive. There is beauty in building a momentum in your life that will enable you to understand the great mysteries of the Law.

I Will Endow Each of You Who Will Receive It with a Cosmic Lamp upon Your Forehead

And so as I, Paul, come to you tonight, it is a coming as a gathering of humanity under the wings of God's beauty. We would create a culture not only for this age as a shadow that would stand before man, but we would create a long shadow of reality that is no shadow at all but a radiance that goes before man, blotting out his shadows and darkness and showing him that because God lives, he lives also. He lived with God before his flesh form knew the cellular life it presently enjoys.

Man will live in consciousness after the body is blown away by the gentle winds of the cosmic realm. He will live in God's light, a creator and not a man. He will live in God's light, the arbiter of a universal plan—all worlds then beneath his feet, his head aglow in the clouds. The fire of movement and of the New Age dawns, the fire of a beauty whose supremacy will enable each heart to catch a glimpse of that which will one day be—*because it already is.*

Only here in time and space dimensions do mankind assert limitations. In the sanctimony of cosmic reality, the virtue of true beauty shines forth. It is of words because it *is* the Word. It is beyond words because it was before the Word was. It is all things, and yet all things are commanded by it. It is light and it is the flow of the masses of humanity, as the great internal ripple of cosmic joy seeks to surge through humanity and they, in their blighted state of present consciousness, consider this as a fun game where they can each day seek to satisfy some base desire.

Now then, why is this so? It is because they have lost the fires of Reality. They have lost the glimpse of what God's mind is. They have become, as it were, shards, bitter and separated.

We then say to you all, cast it aside! As Aladdin of old cried out, "New lamps for old,"[7] so I cry out to you all: Cast aside the darkened consciousness of this age and see the beauty of the lamp of beauty, of the lamp of knowledge, of the lamp of the mind, because it is the lamp of God!

And so tonight I will endow each of you who will receive it with a cosmic lamp upon your forehead, a golden, cosmic lamp that the angelic hosts will fill with the oil of the Holy Spirit.

You may expect, upon the occasion of the coming of the Lord Maha Chohan, that your lamp will be filled with a more than ordinary radiance. For throughout this conference it is the intention of the ascended hosts to see that there is an interrelated activity of cosmic beauty and purpose whereby the student body will be permitted to absorb a larger measure of the largesse of the Great White Brotherhood, which would reach out with arms of the Spirit and cause humanity, *if we could,* to actually fall into a cocked hat, so large as the world itself, where they would find themselves literally bathed with the fires of love. And when this event would occur, I assure you that many today would find a renewed interest in living who have almost lost the zest thereof.

For living is giving. Living is loving. Living is being. But it is not living according to your own concepts. It is living according to the concepts of fiery beauty from the heart of God.

Yes, it is true, dear one. I have consulted with El Morya this day. And if you think that I sound a little bit like him, I am sure that you will reminisce in your heart and realize that it is I. For I am, by his grace, the embodiment of his beauty, and what I have I would bequeath to you all. The cosmic law does not permit me to give it to you for long. But tonight while your bodies sleep, if the Law permits, I would like to give you a nugget of cosmic beauty—cosmic-beauty concepts, cosmic-love concepts, cosmic-grace concepts.

The one thought occupying our entire consciousness is what beauty would do to the world. There are those who say, "Yes, but every man has his own idea of beauty." How true, beloved ones of the earth. But in the mind of God there is only one endowment of beauty, and that endowment of beauty, manifesting through the prism of each individualized consciousness, is always in consonance with all of the beauty and harmony flashing forth from the Universal, ever and anon.

The Chord of Cosmic Beauty Is Alive and Always Will Be

And so as I take my leave of you, I call to the angels that came with me to shower upon your hearts the roses of heaven, the immortal flowers that from our realm will perfume not only your lives but the lives of a distraught humanity. The *nation* needs binding up. The *nations* need binding up. The *world* needs binding up. For the wounds are many.

Let us then apply the unguents of the flowers of God to the hearts of mankind and to your own consciousness, that your consciousness may become each day more radiantly a reflection of the mind of God and of the abundant grace that he came to bestow through every avatar, through every mother's heart, through every soul's *start.* For in the Beginning God created man in his own image.[8] In the image of beauty created he him and endowed him with the power of love and peace. He gave unto humanity the power of industry and decision, the power of free will and creative love.

Will you then understand that that which is lost, that chord of cosmic beauty, is yet alive and always will be? It is but for you to reclaim it.

I thank you.

March 25, 1970

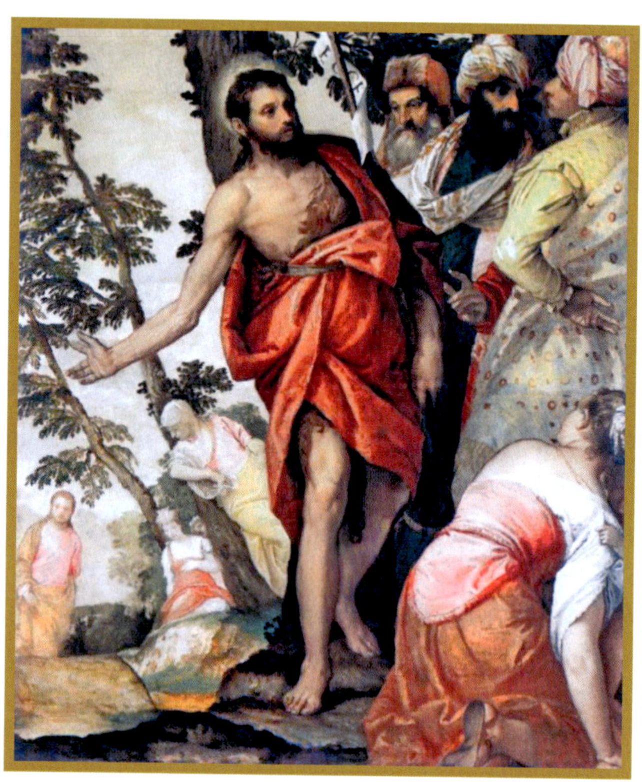

Saint John the Baptist Preaching, c. 1562

Truly, beauty is in the eye of the beholder,
but the transcendental nature of consciousness
is the highest gift.

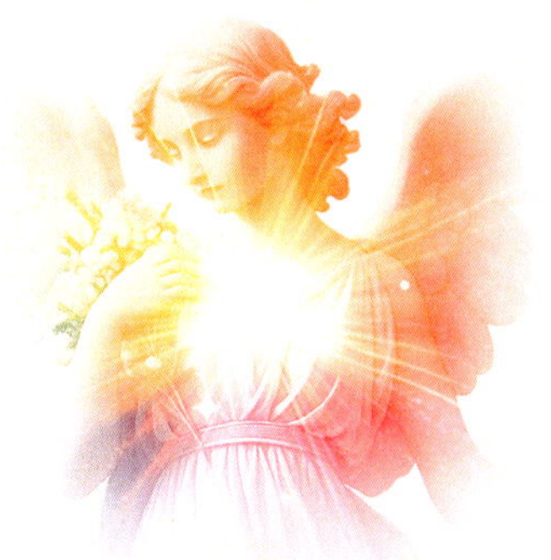

CHAPTER 25

Art Transcends an Era

Beloved Creators of Beauty,

The sternness of delight* is ours. The focalization of beauty brings to the devotee an awareness of the Christ that is produced by the bringing together of the divine energies at a point in space he may select.

Both concentration and diffusion are necessary in order to create at will, yet each requires its own perspective. Through diffusion, consciousness is able to expand in infinite degrees and to assimilate vast panoramas of the universe. Through concentration, consciousness magnifies a part of the whole in order to produce a true rendering in the microcosm of the eternal beauty of the Macrocosm. In the process of focalization, we learn to discern the myriad facets of creation. Then, taking in the wonder of it all, we expand (diffuse) our consciousness from one glory to another, until at last we are able to move in the direction God intended.

There are in the world today many trends that detract from the oneness of creativity—dangerous drugs that provide the youth with a temporal euphoria while consuming the delicate threads of consciousness that tether the soul to the reality of higher octaves; commercialized pornography that has replaced the classics in the bookstalls and flooded the mails, paving the way for moral decay; ragged forms of so-called music that drown out the heavenly oratorios and stupefy the sensibilities; the misuse of the sacred fire through the popularization

**delight:* Deity's light

of free love that drains the youth of the vital energies that would open the chakras and lead them into the way of Christian mysticism and the Eightfold Path of the Buddha.

The panaceas that have accompanied the age have had one purpose: to divert the consciousness of the sons and daughters of God from the track of spiritual discovery.

Man should understand that his consciousness is his point of contact with his Real Self. Therefore, those who interfere with the orderly unfoldment of the precious flower of identity and its innate beauty are literally defrauding man of his birthright and his noble inheritance—the mind of Christ. They and their methods should be exposed as the archenemies of righteousness and of every man's freedom.

The Beautiful Possibilities of Transcendence

We admire the wonder of autumn as it decorates the countryside and embellishes the consciousness with the vibrant qualities of the Spirit. We are reminded that fruit and flower have ascended only so high and that in the next cycle they will ascend still higher. Therefore, we wish to convey to the consciousness of humanity the beautiful possibilities of transcendence.

God is. And because he is, man is. Destined to become a co-creator with God, man can become all that God is—in time, in eternity. Thus, once eternity is attained, the infinite sense engulfs the finite and all things become one in the sense of the Infinite.

Beauty in a state of conception is wondrous indeed because it is untrammeled. But when carried into the arena of action, it is often superimposed with imperfect modes. Some of these have been so far removed from the original matrix that instead of providing man with the link to Reality, which true art is intended to do, they have brought him to the edge of the pit through psychedelic distortions.

Now, if we could, we would meet the children of God more than halfway. For even the masters recognize the advantage in stirring up the astral dust—the cleansing of the intuitive faculties of mind and heart for a greater receptivity to truth.

However, in the past when the Great Law has made an exception, allowing us to do just that, we have found that the sea of mankind's emotions was easily disturbed and that due to man's astral preconditioning, his sensitivities were such that even in the presence of the light he found the cosmic perception of beauty unacceptable. He resented being told the truth and would almost rather have entertained a masquerading entity than angels unawares.

We believe, whether or not our counsels are given heed, that we should place prime importance upon reaching our students and informing them of the truth of being through the *Pearls of Wisdom*[1]—one of the few media available to us—regardless of the consequences. And, if we create thereby the antipathy to truth that wells up in the natural man, then we shall send our angels to clean up the astral debris. And when the dust settles, we shall once more send the missive of truth. Needless to say, popularity should not be the objective when one seeks to communicate the truth.

The True Creativity of Higher Octaves

Man's first glimpse of true beauty conveys a fragile quality and an orderliness that appears as a stereotyping of the Law, which of course it is not. As a matter of fact, ugliness came about as the result of a contest between those who pitted their talents against the Creator to see who could create the most novel forms in contrast to what seemed to them to be the sterile environment of the Presence. Beloved ones, sterility never has been and never could be a part of reality. For the perfection of God, in all of its infinite wonder, is such that he literally dotes upon creativity.

When man determines to draw forth the true creativity of higher octaves, he encounters opposition to the "patterns made in the heavens."[2] He finds that only by an intense discipline and a sharpening of his faculties is he able to approach the realm of pure art to which he has tethered his devotions. He also finds that there is a pastel beauty that can be felt within the soul, even when it cannot be seen with mortal eye, and he knows that this contact is necessary if he is to create according to the cosmic plan.

The deep desire to execute faithfully the Creator's design has led countless devotees to copy the patterns of the angels as a point of discipline in order that they might master the basic techniques of cosmic art such as those taught in my retreat. Because the truly great artists have all sketched from the works of the ascended masters, there has been noted in their renderings a basic similarity of manifestation, a quality of balanced composition that comes only from those whose consciousness is imbued with the Christ and the threefold flame poised in the center thereof.

The ugly patterns of the purveyors of darkness seem to be of an almost infinite variety, for there appears to be a total freedom of expression in the astral sea of "Alice in Wonderland."[3] True freedom, however, is to be found only in the endless manifestations of Reality, albeit in their present limited consciousness, mankind are unable to tap the one Source of creative power.

The difference is primarily the contrast of life and vibrancy with death and decay. The former is always to be preferred, for death itself is a transfixion in matter, and by cosmic law the energies so qualified must be freed from their imperfect molds and returned to the heart of God for requalification.

It is enough, then, for the individual to understand that he has the choice either of creating according to the divine plan in the perfection and limitless beauty of God, or of creating according to the darkened concepts that lead from life unto death. It goes without saying that it is our desire to create in man a correct vision of the universe, for we know that in his vision lies the potential for metamorphosis by which he can be changed "from glory to glory, even by the Spirit of the Lord."[4] This, then, is the hierarchical intent. But the conveyance of the intent, the communication of the God-idea, is another matter.

The Art of the Spirit

We have long encouraged mankind to exercise their freedom of conscience, not as mere license to create whatever fancies the mind but to create the select gifts of the soul striving in living purpose to endow life with the graces of the Almighty. Through the centuries we have observed the results of man's wrong sowings. Where the sense of ugliness is amplified, it offers a divergence of difference but it can never insure the oneness of the effulgent life.

If in filling the chalice with beauty the individual may seem to be functioning within a limited sphere, then let him know that he is limited only by the chalice of his consciousness and not by beauty itself. If in filling the chalice with ugliness the individual may seem to be functioning within an unlimited sphere, then let him know that he is dipping into the bottomless pit to which there is no end save death. Regardless of the fact that over the centuries man has attempted to immortalize that in which he has excelled, his art and music have a vibratory quality that itself is transitory, evolving toward a more perfect matrix.

Man cannot with impunity fix the constancy of his being upon the qualities of imperfection. Therefore, when you turn your attention to the Presence and place your creative ability in the hands of God, you may at first seem limited, but in reality you will not be. When examining the beauty of true art, one must consider the subtlety of its expression. Comparing the Infinite with the finite expression, man may say, "These are as alike as two peas in a pod." But when examined by the faculties of the Higher Mind, their difference is apparent.

Man may seem to be making no significant progress in the art of self-mastery, but we who discern the subtleties of the Spirit understand that progress may be very great indeed, although not so apparent when we are working within microsegments of consciousness. In these levels great beauty is to be found, and that beauty is, in itself, unlimited. Viewed through the finite lens, change may not be significant. But through the divine lens, the finest aspects of change come into focus. Truly, beauty is in the eye of the beholder, but the transcendental nature of consciousness is the highest gift.

Our delight in speaking about the art of the Spirit is very much tied to our desire to bring in the higher culture. While some among humanity have unwittingly disrupted the phases of a higher spiritual existence by relating to the art forms of the present era, others have deliberately sought to destroy the soul's contact with Reality in order to keep it enslaved to the unreal.

Love Is the Key

When we were in embodiment, our consciousness was wedded to no particular school of art, for we sought to express the brilliance we perceived at inner levels in a color and in a form that would transcend the ages. Therefore, it cannot be said that our methods were entirely the product of the age in which we lived. For we recognized that in the purification of its forms, art transcends an era and that which is accomplished in time becomes a part of eternity. When one puts together all of the pieces of the puzzle of life, one finds that the true answers are to be found in the reality of the divine experience—

In the mystic light upon the water
In the sunlight
Weaving a tapestry through the air
In the cherished moment of the future
In the fabric of a holy prayer
In the weaving of the soul of man
Transcendent, never seen by finite eye
In transcendence never seeming
Mirage-like creature yet to fly.

I take my leave of you in that salutary faith that God is the answer, that the sublime moments he gives to the soul are well worth pursuing and recording. Such a man has no hang-ups, no unnecessary tensions, no delusions, but only the firm intention of his soul to fulfill its destiny and to be an unswerving arrow of hope in a glorious universe where love is the key.

Graciously, I AM

Paul the Venetian

October 25, 1970

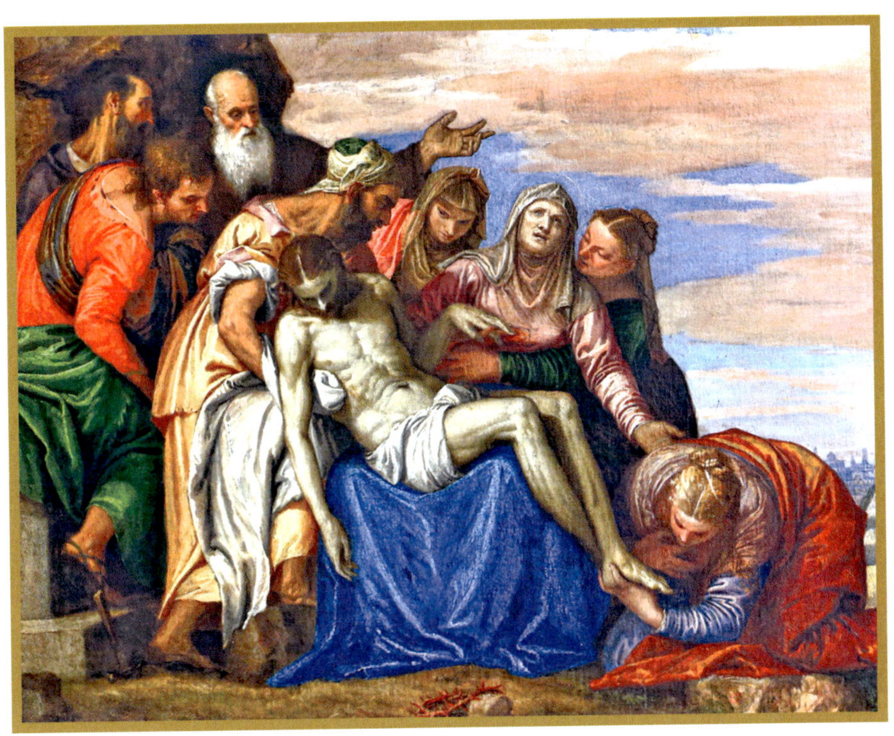

Lamentation over the Dead Christ (detail), c. 1547

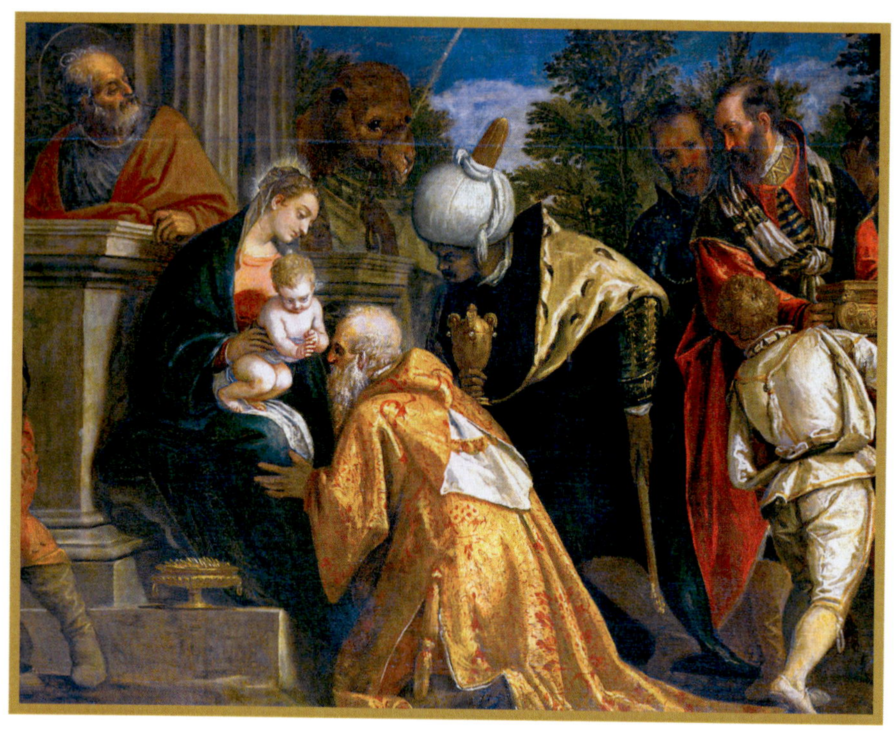

Adoration of the Magi (detail), c. 1580–88

Our thought for man today is first the thought of God—
a thought of blamelessness, sinlessness, and perfect beauty.

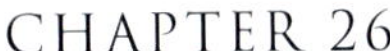

CHAPTER 26

In Christ "without Blemish and without Spot"

To All Who Love Truth and Beauty:

One of the magnificent feelings that God has ordained for every man is the sense of being in Christ "without blemish and without spot."[1] How marvelous is the soul stamped with the divine image, framed in the elements of universal truth foursquare, perfect in body, mind, and feelings, perfect in memory!

Unfortunately, feelings of personal guilt for wrongs real or imagined, for sins committed or contemplated, interfere with the beautiful and harmonious state of the soul fresh from God's own hand. In this frame of mind man becomes unduly uncomfortable; his emotions become unstable, his thoughts confused, until finally his whole being is guilt-ridden. In the name of the beauty that the LORD has placed in the souls of all men as well as the mercy he has extended to all, let me warn those who aspire to do his will that just as it is dangerous to be without conscience, so it is dangerous to be possessed with an unwieldy one.

The forward movement of a lifestream is best organized and directed by God through the threefold flame within the soul and through the Holy Christ Self, who is the divine Mediator poised just above the physical form, dispensing the energies and graces of the Presence into the human chalice. Thus has God provided the means, the link with himself, whereby man can receive the correct administration of cosmic justice and mercy in perfect balance—if he will invoke the legal aid of heaven and accept the hosts of light as the advocates of his Real Image.

Ah yes, there was a day when man was free from sin, when he walked in the paradise of perfection, which has been called the Garden of Eden. And all can walk there again when, through the divine Mediator of the Holy Christ Self, the Lamb "without blemish and without spot," they are able to absorb the cardinal principles of universal beauty and loveliness, to cleanse and free themselves by the electronic shower of the mercy of God of all energies stigmatizing the human soul and creating individual and national guilt.

The Perfect Law of Love between God and Man

How the manipulators of the world love to create segmental guilt, the guilt that arises when one segment of society is pitted against another. How they love to do the diabolical work of castigating and then fragmenting the peaceful nature of man, making him into a hunted animal that can no longer hold high his head and exhibit his true divine nature.

Our thought for man today is first the thought of God—a thought of blamelessness, sinlessness, and perfect beauty. The despoiling of the pristine state came about as the result of man's violations of the unwritten law—for the perfect law of love between God and man does not require recording without; it was already recorded within the soul of man from the founding moment when his Creator gave him individualized existence.

"The strength of sin," as Saint Paul says, "is the law."[2] Therefore, once man had broken the law inscribed in the heart and made his sin the law of his world, the Great Law was enforced as the ordinance of God, as a wall of light that would keep man within the bounds of order and decency. If it can be said that the strength of sin is in the restrictive covenants invoked by a wayward generation, it cannot be said that the strength of sin is in the universal law of cosmic love which first framed the worlds. For it is the letter of the Law which killeth,[3] when man is driven into a state of harassment wherein the Law itself becomes a barrier to his progress, repressing the design of his nature and replacing the Spirit of the inward law which giveth life and which was intended to be an expression of his buoyant, God-ordained freedom.

Stimulating the Divine Sense of Beauty That Is Within

Let men perceive the various methods of stimulating the divine sense of beauty that is within. Through the ritual of forgiveness of sins, through the balancing of man's individual debts to life, through the desire to do well wherever he finds himself, man is able to rise above his environment into the arms of his universal purpose which, when projected upon the screen of man's vision, becomes almost apocalyptic. It speaks of a New Jerusalem, of a Holy City,[4] of a holy Brotherhood, of a magnificent domain of consciousness in which man can forever happily dwell—if he elects to follow the high calling of the sons and daughters of God and the law that is written in their inward parts.[5]

So long as man is content to feed upon the husks of life, to hold vision of lesser dream, so long will he remain in bondage unto himself, a victim of his own desires. When the people of the world illustrate their faith in the divine design through an active sense of commitment to the principles of the Great Law, they will begin to invoke the protection and the direction necessary to find their way out of the maze of problems that beset the race. For faith begets love, and love obedience, which reaches up to a state of consciousness wherein man takes dominion over the earth.[6] Then his concern will be not so much with outer conditions as it will be with inner causes. Then, from the heights of communion with Reality, he will begin to untangle the skeins of the world web of deceit which, originating with the few, has gnarled the lives of billions of earth's evolutions.

But today such freedom is not the common lot of the race. Human greed, lurking in the hearts of the many, blinds them to the deceitful purposes of their overlords and closes the gateway to the realm of spiritual truth and perfection; thus they go their separate ways as neighbor is set against neighbor, race against race, and men demand economic equality in defiance of the law of their own karma.

Long ago the Master Jesus reminded Peter of this law when he sought to take justice into his own hands: "Put up again thy sword into his place: for all they that take the sword shall perish with the sword."[7] Thus man should not seek by intellectual or religious doctrine to cheat life or experience, which, in returning to him that which he has sent out, would teach him those momentous laws that alone can give him his individual freedom.

The Living Law of Cosmic Love

If the economic standard of the whole world is to be reduced to a common denominator, as some would have it—mostly those who have nothing to lose—the law of karma could not function. Albeit all men are created equal, they have not always acted as good stewards, allowing their lives to be used as vehicles through which the living law of cosmic love could function. Therefore, the law of love decrees that they cannot reap that which they have not sown.[8]

In state-dominated countries, where the central government has become a millstone around the neck of the people, the enforcement of an economic determinism, inconsistent with the divine economy which of necessity is determined by cosmic law, is wreaking havoc with the natural distribution of labor, talent, and supply planned by God. Here the course of human life is no longer divinely directed, but instead the strength of sin is in those laws which have not been sanctioned from on high, which bind the people to a system that utterly frustrates the soul's harmony with nature, until there is nothing left but a form of life devoid of meaning, empty and futile.

Those who understand the meaning of true love understand that this love is the result of God's infinite compassion and concern for the world as well as for the individual. When in the course of human events men inject into the stream of civilization those factors of deviation from natural law that abort their opportunities and prevent the onward movement of their progressive enlightenment or those of the race, they become the victims of their own misuse of free will. Then, when the law of their own sin has removed them from his Presence, they speculate that if there is a Deity, he must be very far away, when in reality God is very much involved with the evolution of the creatures of his own heart and has placed man above all upon this earth to take dominion over the stream of life in manifestation.

The current trend to demoralize the youth and to pit one segment of society against another through the misuse of those wondrous media and electronic facilities of the age is a sin against the Almighty, reminiscent of the violations of cosmic law which preceded the destruction of the planet Maldek. The hierarchy never threatens, but it does warn humanity. This is not a situation where the Lords of Karma say, "If mankind will not do what is right, they will be punished"; but it is simply the inevitability of the outworking of cosmic law.

Divine Love Will One Day Reveal unto All a More Perfect Structuring of Universal Purpose

Because the mandates of individual as well as collective karma prevent the light of true beauty from shining through in its total spectrum, we are concerned that the beautiful evolutionary pattern be sought in its entirety by men and nations. Those dark threads that are appearing on the surface of civilization may be cut away and removed from the garment; and in their place the motif of divine love, embroidered by millions of devoted hearts, will one day reveal unto all a more perfect structuring of universal purpose. Until the tapestry of life is thus completed, men must in patience possess their souls, putting on the whole armour of God, being "strong in the Lord, and in the power of his might."[9]

In closing, may I remind you of the words of the apostle who admonished the early Christians as the Brotherhood would also admonish you: "Stand therefore, having your loins girt about with truth, and having on the breastplate of righteousness; and your feet shod with the preparation of the gospel of peace; above all, taking the shield of faith, wherewith ye shall be able to quench all the fiery darts of the wicked. And take the helmet of salvation, and the sword of the Spirit, which is the Word of God: praying always with all prayer and supplication in the Spirit, and watching thereunto with all perseverance and supplication for all saints."[10]

Let men be about their Father's business, that the kingdom become a harvested reality.

For the increase of virtue and beauty, I AM

Paul the Venetian

April 25, 1971

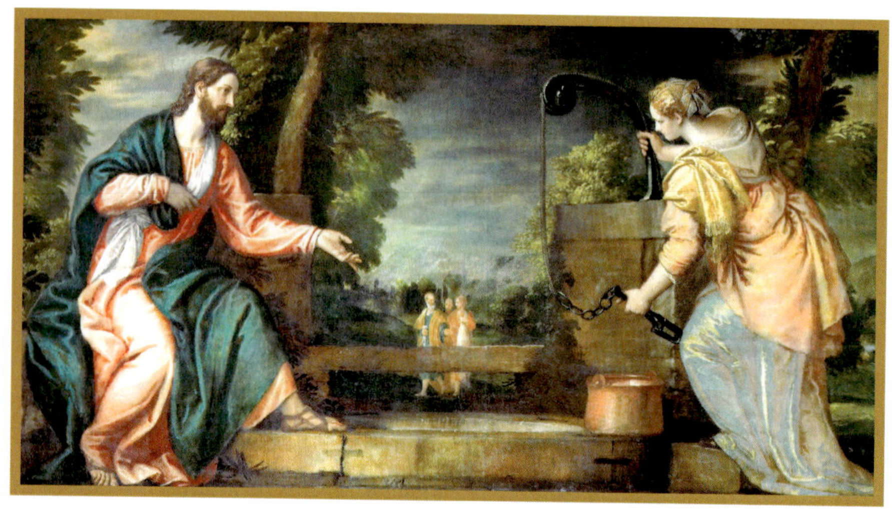

Christ and the Woman of Samaria, c. 1585

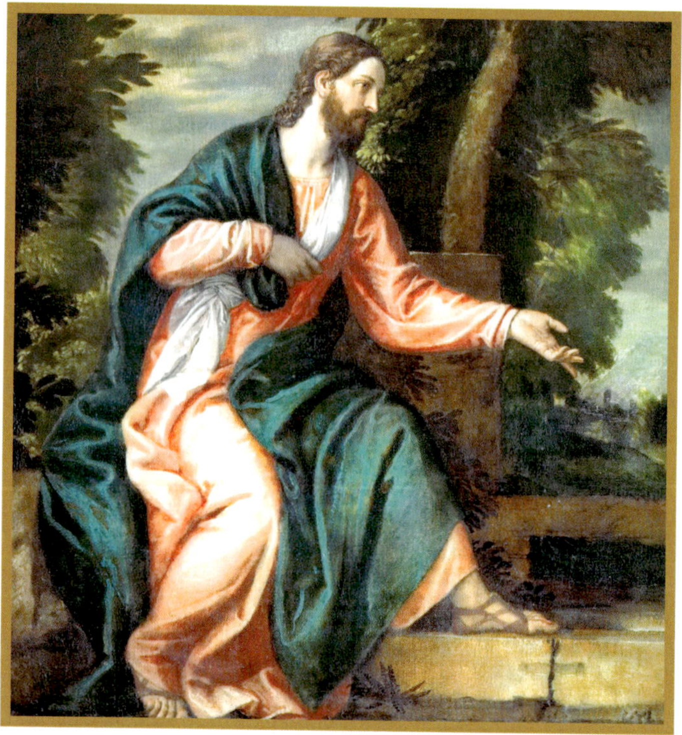

You are God's instruments, beloved ones.
And by the flow of your energy into the world,
you do outpicture upon the moving canvas of life's
experiences your portion of the eternal drama.

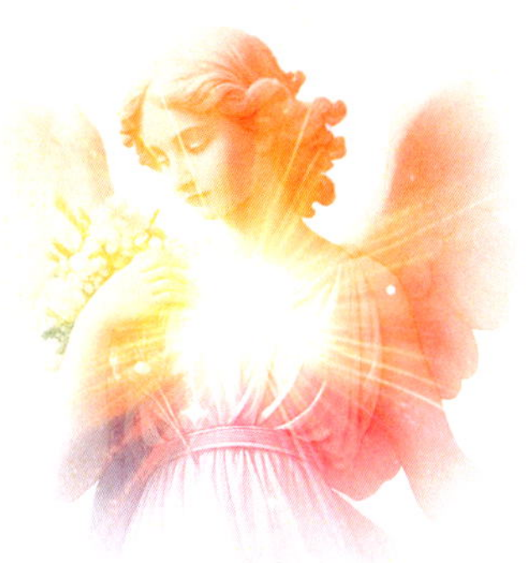

CHAPTER 27

BEAUTY IS AS BEAUTY DOES

The way of order and beauty continues to be sought. The anomalies of thought and feeling that plague mankind, denying to them the beauty of actual contact with the Great White Brotherhood, with the order eternal, must be smoothened by action as well as by intent. Although there are those who say that action without intent will draw the substance of benign intent into manifestation (which is a fallacy in itself), it is true that intent without action may wither away upon the vine.

There are so many beautiful concepts that come to mind with the advent of the Christ consciousness—the emergence of the brilliance of the star of the East flooding the heaven-world with such a soft expanse of light-beauty as to attract the shepherds in the fields, to draw the presence of the Magi, and to stir the hearts of all generations unto the present hour. The sacred mysteries surrounding the birth of the Christ, the legends of the holly and the mistletoe, the Christmas stories that are told not only to children, can be known and enjoyed by all.

We condemn not those who do not yet understand the mystery of the Divine, who hide behind the façade of agnosticism, who say, "To be or not to be," thus questioning their own identity and all reality in their unfirm worlds and questing consciousness.

We condemn not the atheists who, in denying the existence of God, deny their own existence. We spread abroad the raiment of his garment. We expand the mantle of light upon the planet in song, in legend, and in intangible feelings that flow forth from light sources through every ascended master and angelic being.

We seek to penetrate the veil of illusion, the sophistry of faint, worldly wit and the mockings of self-condemnation, which create feelings of inferiority in myriad individuals. We seek to draw aside the veil from every eye, from every consciousness, and to let each mind receive the floodlighting of divine beauty. For in reality, O mankind, all beauty is divine, and "the Beautiful" is another name for the Divine, whose symmetry and form are a matrix to draw man's thoughts upward.

The Moving Canvas of Life's Experiences

And what of art forms created not out of reverence for the Creator but in competition, whose ugliness would distort the divine design and draw mankind by the lure of worldly prize into a competitive cult?

What of those art forms and what of the individuals influenced by them? Do not the Karmic Lords keep the record of each man's defection from justice and truth, of each man's sale of his soul for the sake of mortal opinion?

Would it not be well, then, for all the world to seek to be constructors of the higher spirals, gathering as workmen in the divine temple to make each stairstep safe for the feet of succeeding generations to tread ever upward on the Path that leads to God?

The babe of Bethlehem is the carpenter of Nazareth, the Cosmic Christ who frames the world order while he shapes the destinies of individual souls. There are not many upon the planet whom the hands of the Masterbuilder may serve, for they are not ready to receive him. However, he is able to divide and to subdivide infinitely in order to touch the fingers of a groping humanity and to charge them with his victorious hope. While the world remains at its cups of violence, filled to the brim and overflowing with the works it has wrought in the darkness of blind struggle, the ascended ones and the legions of light move onward into the arena of action through every son of heaven who will lend his hands and feet to the Divine.

You are God's instruments, beloved ones. And by the flow of your energy into the world, you do outpicture upon the moving canvas of life's experiences your portion of the eternal drama. We doubt not the outcome, but when frustrating delays ensue and new lows of chaos and violence fill the world with the message of destroyed hopes, we can but admonish that if you had done your part, perhaps the light would be shining more brilliantly, the curtain of opacity drawn back, and the openings into the higher realms widened.

What Raises One, Raises All

Those among mankind who are under the inspiration of higher law can see the hand of God in all of nature and in themselves. But when they are caught in the net of personal delusion, they fail—because of the involvement of mind and feeling in dire confusion—to recognize and see that life is one. What harms one, harms all. What raises one, raises all. And thus by a sense of life mission, drawn around the flame of Self, coalescing as higher purpose, mankind do manifest a greater measure of adroitness in the execution of manifest beauty to the world.

The world hungers and thirsts after righteousness.[1] It longs to be filled with the water of Life that "I shall give."[2] The wellspring of the invisible springing up within man is the manifestation of the Christ-law, the golden-rule tool that shapes the temple of my God, of thy God, of our God.

Call Him by any name,
He is the same flame
That you must keep;
He is the One
That you must seek.

And so the message God does write
Moves onward,
And it is a lesson
For each day.
And so the vision of the Christ

Shines outward—
It is the shining
Of the true and living Way.

I AM is Being,
God has given,
Flowing from the wounds
That man has made.
In the soul of cosmic purpose
They have muttered
Shadow, blight, and tears;
They are afraid.

Perfect love as star of brilliant wonder
Shines within the star of being bright.
Perfect love casts out all fear and blunder;
Perfect love makes all things right.

The Christ was born in Bethlehem of eld
And Magi, angels, men did come to him.
The light of Cosmic Christ shines ever outward,
Seeking of the many to make one by cosmic meld.

"Beauty is as beauty does,"[3]
The law of gold proclaims.
Sweet frankincense of adoration reigns
While myrrh of untransmuted substance
Shows to all the need to overcome.

The banner of the Christ moves onward;
In the darkened purpose of mankind, it all is lost.
We must raise the light on high, move onward.
Open eyes of blind mankind at any cost.

There's no need to fear the dark if souls remember
I AM the light of all the earth;
I AM God's own Son.
My hopes for all the world the course of man reverse;

The lightning of my love forever sunders,
Gives to all mankind a new and cosmic birth.

Let the passions of thy souls, O men of goodwill,
Pursue the beauty of the divine goal, pursue it still
Until all can say together, "I AM made whole."

Paul the Venetian

November 19, 1967

Prayers, Mantras, and Decrees

We invite you to give the following prayers, mantras, and decrees, which are for the expansion of your threefold flame—the flame of life that is sealed in the eight-petaled chakra, called the secret chamber of the heart. The threefold flame within that chamber is your soul's point of contact with the supreme Source of all life. It is your potential to become the fullness of all that your Real Self is.

Spoken prayer is at the heart of the world's religions East and West. Decrees are a step-up of these forms of prayer in order to effectively produce personal and world change, all in accordance with God's will. A decree is a carefully worded spiritual formula whereby the consciousness of God enters into our world, unlocking the energies of our Higher Self for the purposes to be fulfilled through the spoken Word.

I AM the Light of the Heart

by Saint Germain

I AM the Light of the Heart
Shining in the darkness of being
And changing all into the golden treasury
Of the Mind of Christ.

I AM projecting my Love
Out into the world
To erase all errors
And to break down all barriers.

I AM the power of infinite Love,
Amplifying itself
Until it is victorious,
World without end!

The Way of Love

by Saint Germain

From Love I came, to Love I go;
And all this swing both to and fro
Alters not any jot
Of Cosmic Purpose I forgot.

I reach out now, to Truth I vow;
To Love in all I ever bow.
The universe is one alone—
No clash of multifacet tone.

The chime I hear is ever near;
'Tis Love that casts out every fear.
Where'er I AM Thy Love lives, too,
To free the many and the few.

Command Perfection, Love's great Law!
Command Perfection, Love's great Light!
Thy glowing beauty through the night
As star eternal, Light supernal,
Woos us all by present might.

For Love I AM and Love I live;
This is the allness that I give.
To each manchild the spark is given—
'Twill rend the veil and bring to heaven.

And in full Faith I consciously accept this manifest, manifest, manifest! (3x) right here and now with full Power, eternally sustained, all-powerfully active, ever expanding, and world enfolding until all are wholly ascended in the Light and free!

Beloved I AM! Beloved I AM! Beloved I AM!

Behold Love!

by the Ascended Master K-17

In the name of the beloved mighty victorious Presence of God, I AM in me, my very own beloved Holy Christ Self and through the magnetic power of the sacred fire vested within the threefold flame of love, wisdom, and power burning within my heart, I decree:

I AM content with Thy great plan,
The Wisdom-Love I really am.
O Secret Love Star, amplify
The Flame above me in God's eye.
Let me Perfection see and be,
For only Love can set me free.

O Love, invoke the Word He spoke!
O now be free! The Path to see
Is one of living just to be
All Love in action now!

Love-Wisdom flame I AM!
Love-Wisdom now command!
Love-Wisdom does demand
The Power to express
True beauty's happiness—
My world enfold right now!

(Repeat decree between each ending:)

By Christ-command (3x)
By God's own hand (3x)
By Love's great Power (3x)
Every hour, every hour, every hour

And in full Faith...

Love Me

In the name of the beloved mighty victorious Presence of God, I AM in me, my very own beloved Holy Christ Self and through the magnetic power of the sacred fire vested within the threefold flame of love, wisdom, and power burning within my heart, I decree:

1. I AM so willing to be filled
 With the Love of God;
I AM calling to be thrilled
 With the Love of God;
I AM longing so for Grace
 From the heart of God;
Yearning just to see his face
 By the Love of God.

Refrain: As a rose unfolding fair
Wafts her fragrance on the air,
I pour forth to God devotion,
One now with the Cosmic Ocean.

2. I AM hoping so to be,
 Made by Love Divine.
I AM longing Christ to be,
 Wholly only thine.
I AM so peaceful in thy Love,
 Feel at home with God above.
I AM at one with all mankind—
 The cords of Love God's children bind.
I AM fore'er one living Soul
 With angels, man, and God as goal.

3 I AM locked in God's great Love,
 His mighty arms of Power;
Cradled now by heaven above,
 Protected every hour.

I AM alight with Happiness,
    Wholly filled with God Success,
For I AM love of Righteousness.
    I love Thee, love Thee, love Thee,
My own God Presence bright;
    Love me, love me, love me,
Protect me by thy might.
    Remain within and round me
Till I become thy Light!

And in full Faith…

O Mighty Threefold Flame of Life

by Zarathustra

O Mighty Threefold Flame of Life,
Thou gift of God so pure,
Take my thoughts and energy
And make them all secure.

Under bond of Brotherhood
And understanding fair,
Send thee forth unto my soul
The gift of holy prayer.

Communication's strands of love,
How they woo by heaven's law
A tender blessing for the good,
Releasing holy awe

That draws me near the throne of grace
To now behold thy sacred face
And without fear dispense aright
The passions of pure God-delight

Which set me free from all that's been
The sinful nature of all men.

Christ, raise me to self-mastery,
The living passion of the free.
Determination, now arise
And lift me ever to the skies!

I AM, I AM, I AM
Enfolding life and being all
With the God-command
"Amen!" that shatters human pall.

I AM, I AM, I AM
The free—no bondage holds me back;
I AM the fullness of Love's law
Supplying every lack,
And consecration in full measure
Is my will and God's own pleasure.

Saint Germain and Jesus dear,
Hold my hand with Morya's here
And let the love of Mary then
Be the wings to raise all men.

Until they all unite in Love
To serve that purpose from above
That comes to earth at any hour
Responding to the call of Power;
Send thy shining Wisdom then
That is God's love
Expanded for all men.

I thank thee and I accept this done right now with full power. I AM this done right now with full power. This is the full manifestation of the Law of Love that raises me to my eternal Victory, now and forever!

Count-to-Nine Decree

by Cuzco

In the name of the beloved mighty victorious Presence of God, I AM in me, my very own beloved Holy Christ Self, I decree:

Come now by Love divine,
Guard thou this soul of mine,
Make now my world all thine,
God's Light around me shine.

(Visualize the white light filling the ovoid of the aura)

I count one,
It is done.
O feeling world, Be still!
Two and three,
I AM free,
Peace, it is God's Will.

(Visualize a band of white fire around the solar plexus)

I count four,
I do adore
My Presence all divine.
Five and six,
O God, affix
My gaze on Thee sublime!

(Visualize a band of white fire around the neck and throat chakra)

I count seven,
Come, O Heaven,
My energies take hold!
Eight and nine,
Completely thine,
My mental world enfold!

(Visualize a band of white fire around the head and third eye)

The white-fire Light now encircles me,
All riptides are rejected!
With God's own might around me bright
I AM by Love protected!

(Visualize the white light encircling all of the chakras and the four lower bodies)

I accept this done right now with full Power! I AM this done right now with full Power! I AM, I AM, I AM God-Life expressing Perfection all ways at all times. This which I call forth for myself I call forth for every man, woman, and child on this planet!

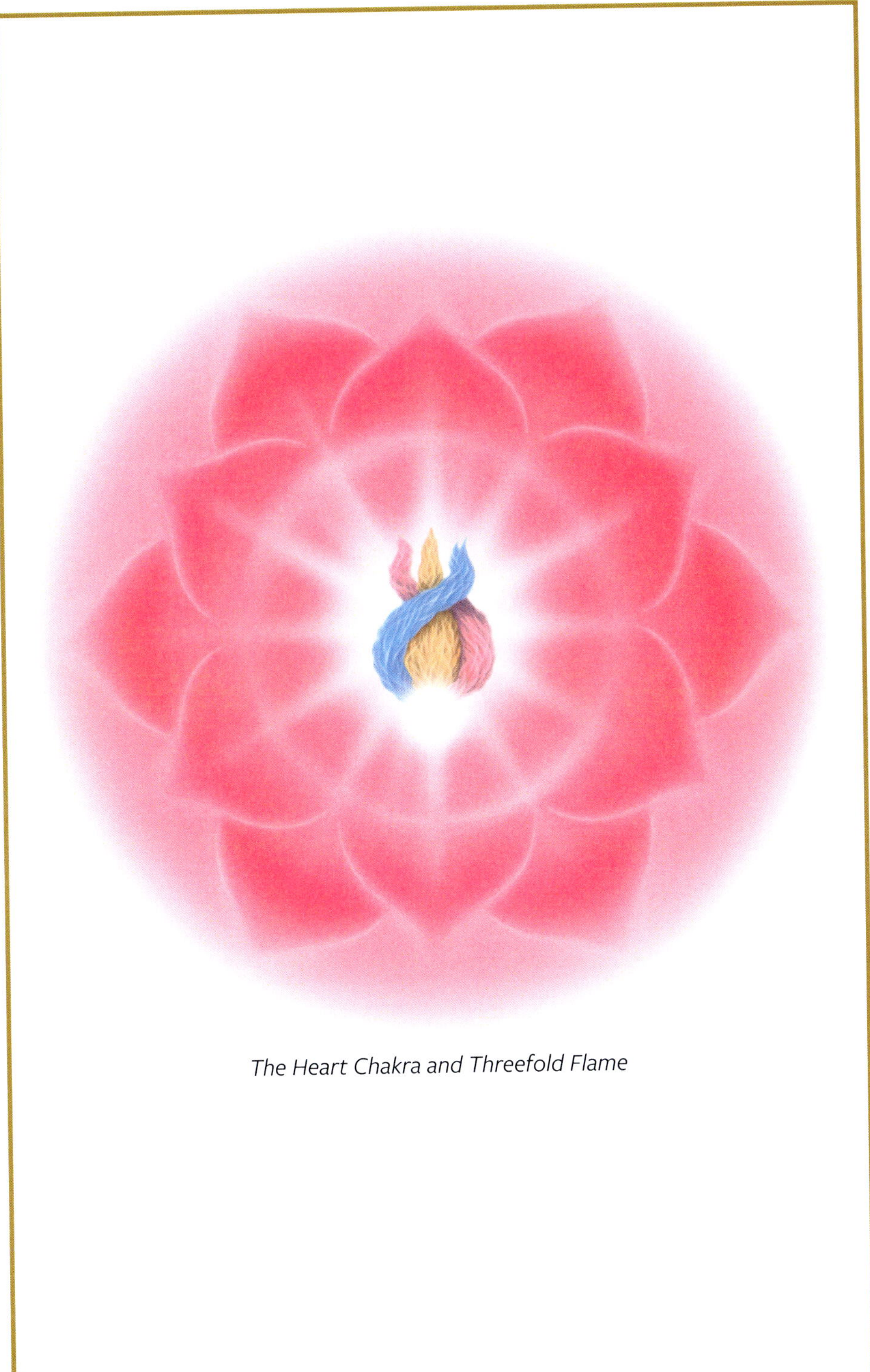

The Heart Chakra and Threefold Flame

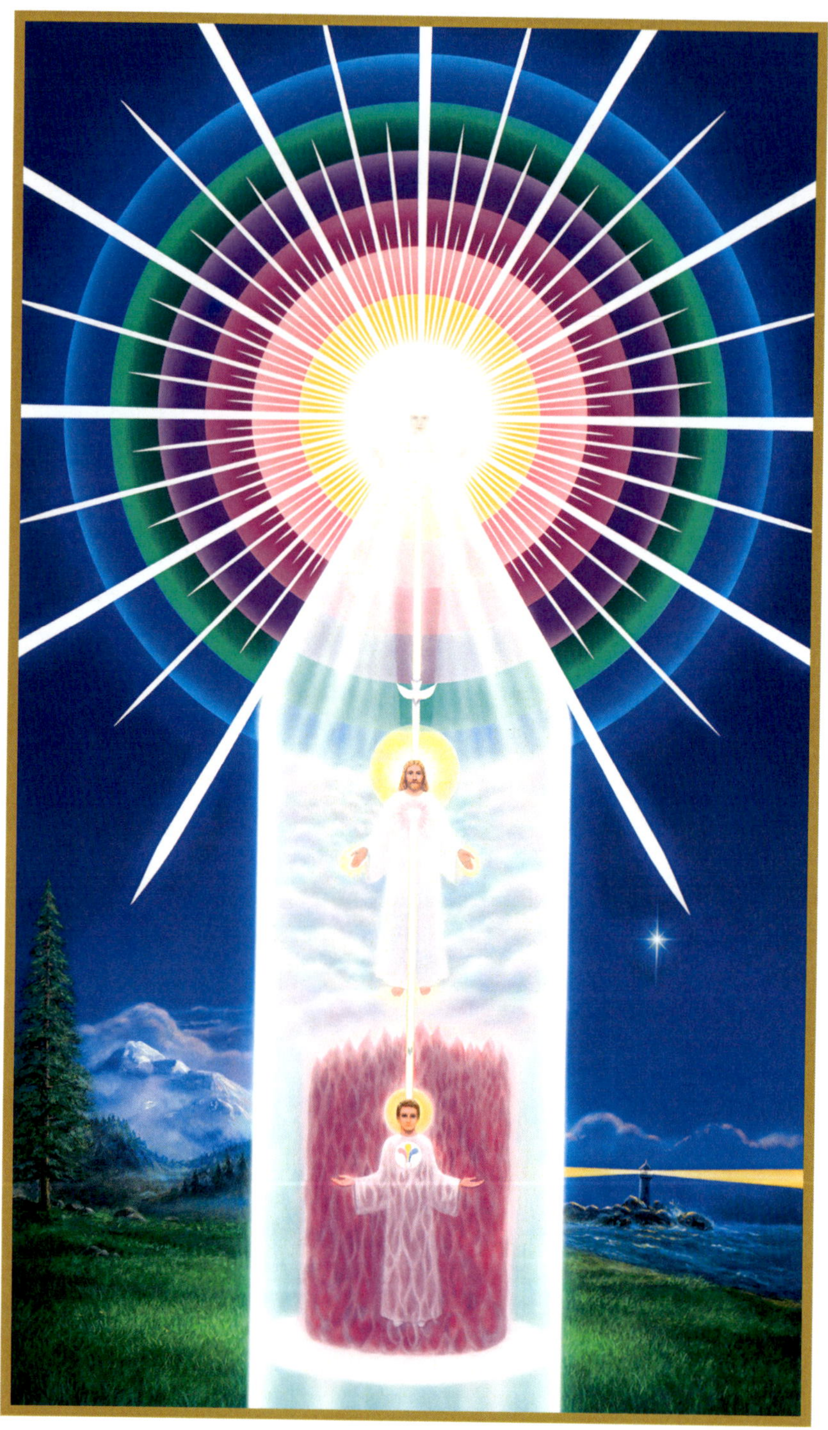

The Chart of Your Divine Self

The Chart of Your Divine Self

Is God really so far from us, as many people have come to believe?

In eternity and in the one flame of life, there is only one God. As we inhabit the dimensions of time and space, we can conceive of this God as very personal, very intimate, very close to us. The God to whom we speak, who answers our prayers, who speaks back to us, who comforts us in our aloneness—this is the individualization of God. That same one God can be speaking simultaneously to billions of lifewaves, but for the purpose of the organization of the energies of cosmos, that sphere, that identity of God, is individualized and focalized where we are.

If you take a drop of water from the ocean and put it on your finger, you will see that the drop is quite small. But all of the elements that make up the ocean can be found in that single drop of water. Your soul is a drop in the vast ocean of Being, a cell in the body of God. The profound truth is that out of his great love for us, God has placed his very essence within each one. This reality is demonstrated in the Chart of Your Divine Self.

This Chart is the unique outline of your inner identity, showing three levels of being, from the human to the divine. It explains how Spirit becomes Matter within you, how you can move from the midst of your everyday life to the heights of union with God. Many of the cosmic truths discovered by the great mystics and teachers of East and West throughout history are depicted in this Chart.

The Upper Figure

The upper figure in the Chart is the individualization of God's presence for every son and daughter of his heart, which we call your mighty I AM God Presence, or I AM Presence. It is your *personalized* I AM THAT I AM, the name that God revealed to Moses at Mount Sinai when God said, "This is my name forever and this is my memorial unto all generations."[1] To Hindus it is Brahma, Buddhists call it the Dharmakaya, while Christians think of it as God the Father. Whenever we say the words, "I AM," we are really saying "God in me is."

The I AM THAT I AM is the one God, and yet it is individualized for each of us. It is the drop in the ocean. It is really not separate, and yet it is separate. It is apart from God, and yet never apart from God. For the purposes of relating time and space to infinity, we talk about the I AM Presence. Yet it is not a symbol. It is a reality. It is more real than anything we have ever experienced. It is our true, Divine Selfhood.

The I AM Presence is surrounded by colored spheres of light that comprise the causal body, depicted in the Chart as colored rings. This is the body of First Cause, which contains within it man's "treasures laid up in heaven"[2]—words and works, thoughts and feelings of virtue, attainment, and light—pure energies that you have expressed in this and past lifetimes as the result of the judicious exercise of free will. It is like your cosmic bank account.

We might think that when we pass from this lifetime we lose all of the talents and qualities that we have gained, but this is not so. All of the good karma we have made since our soul's descent into Matter also rises to this body and multiplies our inherent talents, strengths, and gifts. When we tap into the energy in our causal body, it is released to us as blessing, bounty, wisdom, light, love, and direction.

The Middle Figure

The great avatars of all ages who have come to liberate us have been the full embodiment of the middle figure, and they have been greatly overshadowed by, and many times been bonded to, the upper figure in the Chart. Therefore they have walked the earth with the shining halo of their own causal body, such as the Buddhas who embody the Dharmakaya, the I AM Presence.

This middle figure in the Chart is the figure of the Inner Christ or the Inner Buddha. It is the body of your higher consciousness, your higher mind, your higher knowing, your higher intuition, your inner teacher. This teacher is called your Holy Christ Self or your Holy Buddha Self. Some Christian mystics have referred to it as the inner man of the heart. It is referred to here as the Christ Self, the inner Christ within our heart. We also refer to it as the Higher Self. Buddhists call this the Sambhogakaya.

The word *Christ* comes from the Greek word *Christos,* which means "anointed." This middle figure represents the office of the Christ, a certain level of God consciousness to which we can all attain. The Chart of Your Divine Self shows a picture of Jesus as an example of one who has attained this level of Christhood. At a spiritual level, the Christian concept of accepting Christ as one's Saviour or into one's life or heart is actually the accepting of this middle figure.

The Christ Self is sometimes called the Mediator because it is the go-between—the one mediating between your evolving soul consciousness (the lower figure in the Chart) and the God consciousness of the I AM THAT I AM. By following the path of initiation, you can gradually become one with that teacher and walk the earth in that level of consciousness, anointed with the light of your I AM Presence.

The Lower Figure

The lower figure in the Chart represents your soul clothed in a physical body as it evolves in time and space and learns the lessons of love and mastery. Buddhists call this the Nirmanakaya, the place where transformation and change take place.

The light of God descends from your I AM Presence to your Christ Self and then to your soul over what is called the crystal cord, or silver cord. This light of God, this spark of divinity, is anchored within the secret chamber of the heart, which is called the *Ananda-Kanda* in Sanskrit, "the root of joy."

This spark of divinity within you is called the threefold flame because it has three "plumes" that embody the three primary attributes of the love, wisdom, and power of God. It is the very point where God's energy in Spirit becomes God's energy in Matter within you. As the light of God descends according to your soul's desire, there is an increase in your holy love, wisdom, and power, or strength, to help you navigate through the entanglements of karmic existence and to rise to higher levels of awareness of the Christ within.

Therefore, right within your heart there is a point of contact with the Divine, a flame from God's own heart given to his sons and daughters of light! It is your soul's point of contact with the supreme Source of all life! This is great news!

The Tube of Light

In this lower figure in the Chart, the soul is standing in a pillar of light called the tube of light. The tube of light is an electronic forcefield that descends from the heart of your I AM Presence and surrounds your Christ Self and your soul, and it seals and protects you from all that is less than the Christ consciousness. This tube of light will be sustained for twenty-four hours as long as you guard it with harmony in your thoughts, feelings, words, and deeds.

You can visualize this tube of light as the dazzling white light of your I AM Presence, brighter than the sun shining on new-fallen snow, coalescing as a cylinder of light around you. You can visualize it as being about nine feet in diameter, extending from approximately nine feet above you to about three feet beneath your feet.

You can also visualize the violet flame surrounding you within the tube of light. As long as our soul has karma and is still working toward union with our Christ Self and I AM Presence, we have impurities and imperfections. So we need the violet flame within the tube of light to carry on the continuous process of transmutation.

You will see that just above the head of the Christ Self is the dove of the Holy Spirit descending from God. This signifies that the divine Comforter tends to each of us as we face the spiritual tests and trials that come our way. As the Holy Spirit comes into our life, there comes to us a great feeling of oneness with all life, of being at home in the universe. It is the energy of the currents of life, of the essence of God himself made personal for each of us.

The following is a prayer that you can give daily to anchor the light of your I AM Presence, your Holy Christ Self, the violet flame, and the tube of light into your world, right where you are!

Violet Fire and Tube of Light Decree

by the Ascended Master Saint Germain

O my constant, loving I AM Presence, thou Light of God above me whose radiance forms a circle of fire before me to light my way:

I AM faithfully calling to thee to place a great pillar of Light from my own mighty I AM God Presence all around me right now today! Keep it intact through every passing moment, manifesting as a shimmering shower of God's beautiful Light through which nothing human can ever pass. Into this beautiful electric circle of divinely charged energy direct a swift upsurge of the violet fire of Freedom's forgiving, transmuting flame!

Cause the ever expanding energy of this flame projected downward into the forcefield of my human energies to completely change every negative condition into the positive polarity of my own Great God Self! Let the magic of its mercy so purify my world with Light that all whom I contact shall always be blessed with the fragrance of violets from God's own heart in memory of the blessed dawning day when all discord—cause, effect, record, and memory—is forever changed into the Victory of Light and the peace of the ascended Jesus Christ.

I AM now constantly accepting the full power and manifestation of this fiat of Light and calling it into instantaneous action by my own God-given free will and the power to accelerate without limit this sacred release of assistance from God's own heart until all men are ascended and God-free in the Light that never, never, never fails!

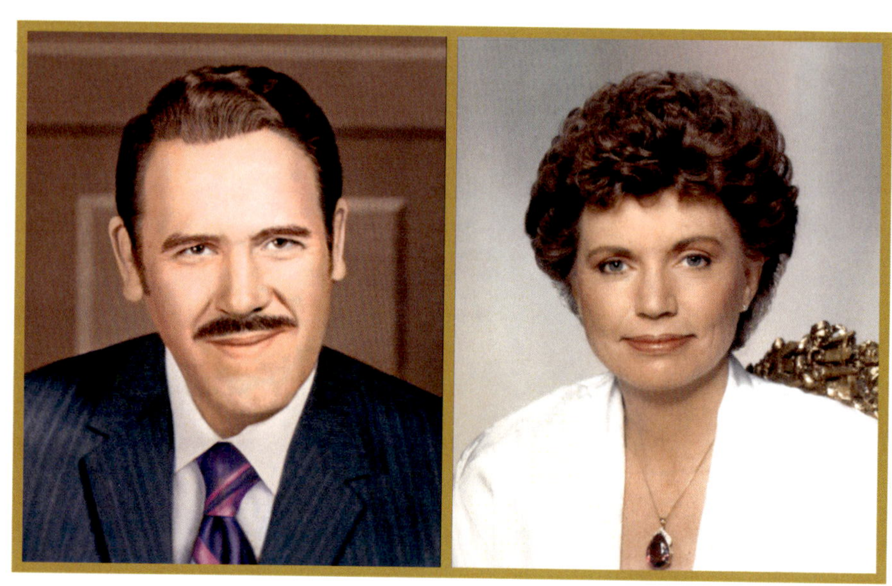

Who Are Mark L. Prophet and Elizabeth Clare Prophet?

For over fifty years, Mark L. Prophet and Elizabeth Clare Prophet served as authors, teachers, and messengers, whose calling was to be prophets of God—one who delivers the Word of God. In this role as messengers, Mark and Elizabeth communed with heavenly beings through the power of the Holy Spirit. Just as in the days of the prophets and apostles, one experiences an element of sacred fire in the messages they delivered to the world.

As you listen to or read the words of these messages, called "dictations," you may well experience a transfer of light that quickens and educates your soul.

Through these two messengers, profound teachings, messages, and prophecies have been released, which present a path and a teaching whereby every individual on earth can find his or her way back to God. As messengers, Mark and Elizabeth saw themselves only as the instruments of God and as the servants of the light to all students on the spiritual path and in all people.

During their mission and ministry, Mark and Elizabeth taught on a wide variety of spiritual subjects: karma and reincarnation, healing and wholeness, soul mates, twin flames and relationships, and practical spirituality, to name just a few. Their books and writings are intended to give everyone the opportunity to know the truth that can set them free. Their great desire has always been to share a path that will take true seekers, in the tradition of the masters of the Far East, as far as they can go and need to go in order to meet their true teachers—the ascended masters and their own Higher Self face-to-face.

As you read about the ascended master Paul the Venetian, you will understand that the purpose of these spiritual teachings and path are to lead the soul to the ascension—the reuniting of the soul into the Presence of the I AM THAT I AM, also called the I AM Presence. There are many souls who have reached this goal and who are therefore called ascended masters.

Mark L. Prophet and Elizabeth Clare Prophet fulfilled their mission as messengers and took their leave from this physical octave in the process of the ascension, leaving behind teachings such as those in this book. There is a banquet of teachings that have been published and are yet to be published, as the mission of the messengers carries on.

Notes

Paul the Venetian's Embodiment as the Sixteenth-Century Artist Paolo Veronese

1. Luke 5:30.
2. Matt. 9:12; Mark 2:17; Luke 5:31.
3. Matt. 25:21, 23.
4. The Château de Liberté is the retreat of Paul the Venetian located on the etheric plane over the South of France on the Rhône River. The retreat is congruent with and extends far beyond a privately owned physical castle. Much of the physical surroundings of this castle resemble its etheric counterpart. The Château de Liberté is a vast retreat containing galleries, museums, and archives of art and artifacts from many cultures and civilizations.

CHAPTER 1: • **The Light Within**

1. John 14:6. The ascended master ***Jesus Christ*** is the avatar of the age of Pisces and an incarnation of the universal Christ consciousness. He came during his Galilean embodiment to reveal the individual Christ Self to humanity and to show the works of the Father (the I AM Presence) that can be accomplished by his sons and daughters through the flame of the individual Christ Self. He currently serves with Kuthumi in the office of World Teacher.
2. See Paul the Venetian's embodiment as the sixteenth-century artist Paolo Veronese, pp. ix–xix.
3. The ***Goddess of Justice.*** The ascended lady master Portia is known as the Goddess of Justice and the Goddess of Opportunity. Beloved Portia keeps the flame of justice and opportunity on behalf of the evolutions of earth. She is the twin flame and divine consort of Saint Germain, the chohan of the seventh ray and hierarch of the Aquarian age.
4. John 1:14.
5. Ps. 139:7.

N.B. Books listed here are published by Summit University Press unless otherwise noted; available at Store.SummitLighthouse.org. For more information about *Pearls of Wisdom,* see SummitLighthouse.org/Pearls-of-Wisdom-Morya. For more information about the masters in these notes, see *The Masters and Their Retreats;* available at Store.SummitLighthouse.org.

6. ***Chamuel and Charity*** are archangels of the third ray of divine love, who serve to expand the flame of adoration and divine love within the hearts of mankind and elemental life.

CHAPTER 2: • **A Secret and High Calling of the Heart**

1. ***Micah, Angel of Unity,*** is the son of Archangel Michael. Micah and his legions serve to guard the unity for the Christ consciousness in all mankind. His task is to amplify the peace and harmony of unity throughout the world. Micah was the angel who overshadowed the children of Israel throughout their desert wanderings. He appeared to Moses and assisted him during the forty years of the Israelites' sojourn in the desert. During the long winter at Valley Forge, Micah appeared to George Washington in a vision of three great perils that would come upon the nation of America—the Revolutionary War, the War between the States, and a third world conflict. Micah guards the union of fifty States of America and the destiny of the nation.
2. The painting of *The Angelus* is an oil painting by Jean-François Millet, completed between 1857 and 1859. The Angelus is also known as a Roman Catholic devotional prayer, recited three times a day (6 a.m., noon, and 6 p.m.), announced by a bell. It is a responsive prayer commemorating the annunciation and conception of Jesus, interspersed with the Catholic Hail Mary. Describing the moment of prayer at the day's end, beloved Sanat Kumara, on July 4, 1970, spoke of the prayer, the Angelus, saying, "Oh, how thirsty the world is today for happiness! How people long to find peace at the end of a day of turmoil! How their souls cry out for the peace of the chimes of the Angelus. The day has ended. The heart is bowed in prayer. The harvest lies upon the ground. All mankind's fears and cares are found no longer; only love and peace abound—a cosmic prayer breathed out in space."
3. Luke 22:42; Matt. 26:39; Mark 14:36; John 5:30.
4. ***Sanat Kumara*** is known as the Ancient of Days. He is the Great Guru of the seed of Christ throughout cosmos, hierarch of Venus and one of the seven Holy Kumaras. He initiates us on the path of the ruby ray, which he sets forth in the book *The Opening of the Seventh Seal: Sanat Kumara on the Path of the Ruby Ray;* available at Store.SummitLighthouse.org. Sanat Kumara came to Earth, a voluntary exile from his planet Venus, to keep the flame until sufficient numbers among mankind would respond and begin once again to maintain the focus on behalf of their brothers and sisters. One hundred and forty-four thousand souls volunteered to assist Sanat Kumara in his mission and accompany him with legions of angels. His mission was completed on January 1, 1956, when his most capable disciple Gautama Buddha was awarded the position of Lord of the World.

Sanat Kumara then became Regent of the World, and in that capacity he continues to assist Earth's evolutions from his home on Venus.

5. I Cor. 15:52; I Thess. 4:17.

CHAPTER 3: • **Eternal Beauty Moves the Spirit of Man to Exclaim: "O God, You Are So Magnificent!"**

1. See Ps. 119:18.
2. ***Saint Germain*** is the chohan of the seventh ray (violet ray) and the hierarch of the Aquarian age. He is known as the God of Freedom to the earth, and sponsored the founding of the United States of America. He brought to us the knowledge of the violet flame in order to assist us in the balancing of personal and world karma. He is a most gracious and loving master who initiates souls in the ritual of transmutation through the use of the violet flame by the power of the spoken Word, meditation, and visualization.
3. Heb. 12:23.
4. Matt. 22:37–40; Mark 12:30, 31; Luke 10:27.
5. Ps. 23:1.
6. The ***Maha Chohan*** is the hierarch of the seven chohans of the rays. His name means "the Great Lord." He embodies the white light of the seven rays and teaches the balance and integration of these rays. He initiates our souls in preparation to receive the nine gifts of the Holy Spirit, spoken of in I Corinthians 12:4–11. He holds the office in hierarchy that represents the Holy Spirit of the Father-Mother God, of Alpha and Omega, to the evolutions of earth. Because of his pledge to all mankind to keep the flame of life until they are able, he is called the Keeper of the Flame.
7. Phil. 4:7.
8. ***El Morya*** is the chohan of the first ray, the blue ray of divine power. He tutors souls in gaining self-mastery in the throat chakra and in developing faith, goodwill, leadership, protection, perfection, and surrender to the divine will.
9. "This place" refers to the small sanctuary in Boston, located in an office building off Commonwealth Ave., presided over by Dr. Edward Whitney, who at that time was an early supporter of Mark Prophet.
10. The new civilization that shall be born in South America refers to the coming of the seventh root race, which is destined to incarnate in South America. In a dictation given through Mark Prophet on July 5, 1963, God Meru stated, "In days to come, when the seventh root race is ushered in to the fullest extent upon the continent of South America, the Brotherhood shall, once again, establish the wonderful civilization of old."
11. In a lecture given on October 5, 1969, Mark Prophet stated that "the seat of higher learning... is actually in the head of India. India is the head and America is the heart of the Brotherhood's focuses on the earth."
12. Devotees of Buddhism recite the mantram *Om Mani Padme Hum* (Sanskrit)

to invoke the merciful intercession of the one who holds the office of Bodhisattva of Compassion. This includes Kuan Yin (the feminine Chinese bodhisattva) and Avalokiteshvara (the masculine Indian bodhisattva). The mantram has been translated as "Hail to the jewel in the lotus!" It has also been interpreted as "Hail to Avalokiteshvara, who is the jewel in the lotus of the devotee's heart." For more information on Kuan Yin, see chapter 11, p. 261, n. 1.

13. Rev. 21:4; 7:17.

CHAPTER 4: • **"O God, Help Me!" The Call Compels the Answer**

1. Job 22:27, 28; Isa. 65:24; Matt. 21:21, 22; John 15:7.
2. James 1:17.
3. Matt. 7:7; Luke 11:9, 10.
4. "God tempers the wind to the shorn lamb" was originally a French proverb made popular in English by Laurence Sterne (1713–1768) from his novel *A Sentimental Journey through France and Italy* (1768).
5. The ***Karmic Board*** is a body of eight ascended masters who are assigned the responsibility to dispense justice to this system of worlds, adjudicating karma, mercy, and judgment on behalf of every lifestream. The Lords of Karma are divine intercessors who serve under the twenty-four elders as mediators between a people and their karma. All souls must pass before the Karmic Board before and after each incarnation on earth. The Karmic Board consists of the Great Divine Director (representing the first ray), the Goddess of Liberty (second ray), Ascended Lady Master Nada (third ray), Elohim Cyclopea (fourth ray), Pallas Athena, the Goddess of Truth (fifth ray), Portia, the Goddess of Justice (sixth ray), and Kuan Yin, the Goddess of Mercy (seventh ray). Recently Vairochana, one of the five Dhyani Buddhas, became the eighth member of the Karmic Board.
6. ***Mother Mary*** is the archeia of the fifth ray (green ray). The temple of Archangel Raphael and Mother Mary is in the etheric realm over Fátima, Portugal. Mother Mary also serves with Jesus in the Resurrection Temple in the etheric realm over the city of Jerusalem in the Holy Land.

CHAPTER 5: • **The Manifestation of Divine Perfection**

1. ***Elohim Arcturus*** is the Elohim of the seventh ray. With the Elohim Victoria, he focuses the energies of the seat-of-the-soul chakra of the planet from their retreat in the etheric realm near Luanda in Angola, Africa. This retreat is dedicated to the freedom and victory of the planet. The pulsations of the violet flame from the hearts of Arcturus and Victoria produce the rhythm and the ritual of application through service and reverence for life.
2. ***Cuzco,*** emissary of the God Star, Sirius, is a disciple of Surya and director of his retreat of God's will near Suva, the Sacred Retreat of the Blue Flame. This retreat is in an island northeast of Viti Levu, (the largest of the Fiji

Islands) and is both under the sea and within the mountains. Cuzco's retreat is dedicated to holding the balance of forces in the earth.

3. Paul the Venetian is referring to a dictation by Cuzco wherein he warns of the harmful effect of "riptides," which are "created by wrong thoughts and feelings that gain momentum in both a centripetal and centrifugal action." Cuzco teaches that "vibrations of discord seek out and unite with their kind" and become "huge astral pools" of immense size. Cuzco recommends that the students give the "Count-to-Nine Decree," which "imparts the power of the three-times-three and is the ritual for encircling your being with light's protection."

CHAPTER 6: • **A Chalice of Light**

1. Paintings by Paolo Veronese on display at the National Gallery of Art in Washington, D.C., include *The Annunciation, The Finding of Moses, The Martyrdom and Last Communion of Saint Lucy, Rebecca at the Well, Saint Jerome in the Wilderness,* and *Saint Lucy and a Donor.* Images of the paintings are available on the Gallery website: www.nga.gov.
2. The ***Great Silent Watcher*** is another name for the Elohim of the fifth ray, Cyclopea, the All-Seeing Eye of God.
3. John 5:6–9, 14.
4. We worship the one God and his light. We bow before that light in the heart of all of those whom he has sent forth, as they bow to the light in us. Wherever the light is, the light is God. Therefore, we have reverence for the ascended masters and worship God within them.
5. The Maha Chohan's retreat is the Temple of Comfort in the etheric realm with a focus in the physical at the island of Sri Lanka (formerly known as Ceylon).
6. The greatest comfort they shall ever have. On Christmas Day, 1986, Jesus gave a teaching about the chalice of Paul the Venetian: "Understand, beloved, that the chalice consists . . . of crystals containing, as in microchips, the complete inner blueprint of all those who must pass through the universities of the Spirit of the seven chohans unto the victory of the Holy Ghost. Thus, you will understand why the beloved Paul spent so many years working upon and perfecting that chalice. Thank God that your electronic blueprint is sealed in crystal in a chalice now present at the retreat of the Maha Chohan."
7. The ***Great Divine Director*** is the Manu of the seventh root race. A *manu* of a root race is the lawgiver who sets the divine plan for an entire evolution. He is a cosmic being. His causal body is a giant blue sphere that surrounds the entire planet. In addition to the Rakoczy Mansion in Transylvania, he maintains a focus in the Cave of Light in India. The Great Divine Director bears the appellation Master R—the "R" signifying Rakoczy. He is a member of the Darjeeling Council and also a member of the Karmic Board.

CHAPTER 7: • **Gratitude for All That Life Can Bring**

1. The ***Goddess of Liberty*** is the hierarch of the Temple of the Sun, the etheric retreat over the island of Manhattan, New York. She was embodied on Atlantis, where her momentum of dedication to the Spirit of Liberty was so great that after her ascension she was called upon to bear the title of Goddess of Liberty, denoting her office in hierarchy as the authority for the cosmic consciousness of liberty to the earth. The Goddess of Liberty is also the spiritual Mother of Paul the Venetian.

CHAPTER 8: • **Divine Gratitude**

1. James 1:17.
2. See Gen. 4:9.
3. Matt. 11:30.
4. Individual duality. On May 27, 1962, beloved Jesus explained the meaning of individual duality. He said, "I am come to speak to those who are the lonely hearts among mankind to tell you that when you entered into the realm of your own individualized God-identity and stepped forth from the altar of heaven to claim an individual duality-expression separate and apart—yet never separate from the heart of the Father—when you stepped forth to be vested with that individuality, you entered within the realm of separation, and yet a realm of never-separation. If you will only realize it, beloved ones, it was a realm of opportunity where you could acquire within the individualized duality all that the Father had within the immortal fire of his own cosmic being."
5. Matt. 7:6.
6. James 4:4.
7. Matt. 6:33.
8. ***Archangel Michael*** is the Prince of the Archangels and of the angelic hosts of light, the Defender of the Faith, the Angel of Deliverance. On Columbus Day, 1962, Archangel Michael saluted Saint Germain saying, "Heart friend of freedom to all mankind! How few know the story of thy devotion. How unsung to the mass consciousness is the saga of thy love. O Columbia, thou gem of the cosmic ocean, before whom the angels do bow, with what shaft of light shall we send down the remembrance of thy exploits? Thou mariner of love searching for a new land, country of the blessed; from Isabella's court to the land of Massasoit and Sachem; from the fabled dominion of the dons to the wigwams dotting the prairies: the light of thy searching heart did shine.... Let the bastions of freedom, like invincible towers of light, arise and protect the land of America, that the banner of faith may manifest and the words, 'In God we trust' become the watchword of the world!"
9. I Sam. 3:9, 10. The child Samuel was an embodiment of Saint Germain.
10. Christopher Columbus and Francis Bacon were previous embodiments of

Saint Germain. For more information, see Elizabeth Clare Prophet, *Lords of the Seven Rays;* available at Store.SummitLighthouse.org.

11. Matt. 14:15–21; Mark 6:32–44; Luke 9:10–17; John 6:1–14.
12. Isa. 11:6.
13. Released a year ago. In a dictation given through Mark L. Prophet on July 1, 1961, Lord Maitreya released a landmark dispensation on behalf of the students of the masters. He explained: "I, Maitreya, say to you today that the ascended masters, in the great deliberations and the councils of the Great White Brotherhood... have asked for a great petition whereby the student body today shall be given that which is known as the full power of the ten thousand times ten thousand. From this day henceforward, every decree that you utter shall be increased by the power of the ten thousand times ten thousand!"
14. The ancient prophecy refers to the prophecy of the defeat of Israel's enemies if Israel remains faithful to the Lord. Leviticus 26:8 reads, "And five of you shall chase an hundred, and an hundred of you shall put ten thousand to flight: and your enemies shall fall before you by the sword." The prophecy is repeated in Deuteronomy 32:30: "How should one chase a thousand, and two put ten thousand to flight, except their Rock had sold them, and the Lord had shut them up?" Joshua 23:10 reads, "One man of you shall chase a thousand: for the Lord your God, he it is that fighteth for you, as he hath promised you."
15. Ps. 8:5; Heb. 2:7–9.
16. John 8:32.
17. Luke 21:19.
18. Matt. 19:30; 20:16; Mark 9:35; 10:31; Luke 13:30.
19. Ps. 69:9; John 2:17.
20. Matt. 5:6.
21. See Gal. 2:20.
22. A sacrificial offering of grains made by the ancient Jewish priests that was raised up and moved (waved) to and fro before the altar. The offering was then given to the priestly families.

CHAPTER 9: • The Fragrance of Love and Liberty

1. In 1963, El Morya gave further teaching on the entering of the consciousness of another lifestream, including the following: "No one can enter another's consciousness without permission except in violation of cosmic law." Taking this concept of entering the consciousness of another lifestream to a higher level of understanding, beloved Lord Maitreya says, "Thus I commend you to the heart of the Buddha even as I stand before you. For I draw close to you, even to your very midst, and I accelerate the interchange whereby you now receive the sphere of light that contains the record of my own discipleship with Gautama under the Lord Sanat Kumara. For as I have pondered the sweet mystery of life, which is the chela in the heart

of the Guru and the Guru in the heart of the chela, I have desired that you should know truly what is the path of life whereby you put on concentric rings of the aura of the Buddha, of the aura of the Mother, and begin to experience in actuality that mighty figure-eight flow of being."

2. "The compound" is a forcefield on the astral plane where the darkest souls are confined and not allowed to come out until it is decreed by the Lords of Karma that they can reembody.
3. Matt. 5:8.
4. ***Helios and Vesta*** are the God and Goddess of this solar system. Helios abides in the very heart of the physical sun. With this twin flame, Vesta, he serves to represent the Godhead to those evolving on the planets orbiting the sun. It is their God consciousness that sustains our physical solar system. Helios serves on the golden ray and his twin flame, Vesta, on the pink ray.
5. ***Alpha and Omega.*** Alpha is the highest manifestation of God in the Great Central Sun. His complement is Omega, the personification of the God flame as Mother. John the Beloved spoke of them in Revelation as "The Beginning and the Ending." Together they focus the beginning and the ending of all cycles of life. They rule in the center of the Hub in the City Foursquare and preside directly over the twelve hierarchies of the Sun. Their flame is represented in the forget-me-not.
6. ***Hilarion*** is the chohan of the fifth ray (green ray) of healing and truth. He is the hierarch of the Temple of Truth on the etheric plane near Crete, Greece. Hilarion was high priest of the Temple of Truth on Atlantis, and he transported the flame of Truth together with the artifacts of the Temple to Greece a short time before the sinking of the continent. Hilarion was later embodied as Saul of Tarsus, who became the apostle Paul.
7. Phil. 4:8.
8. Rom. 8:22.
9. Luke 19:40.
10. Gen. 2:7.
11. Gen. 1:27.
12. Ps. 37:11; Matt. 5:5.
13. II Cor. 3:18.
14. II Cor. 3:17.
15. John 14:12.

CHAPTER 10: • The Constant Presence of Life within You

1. Rev. 3:11.
2. The Angelus is a Roman Catholic devotional prayer recited three times a day (6 a.m., noon, and 6 p.m.), announced by a bell. It is a responsive prayer commemorating the annunciation and conception of Jesus, interspersed with the Catholic Hail Mary. See chapter 2, p. 254, n. 2.

3. Matt. 26:27; I Cor. 11:25.
4. The chalice that I created for the Lord the Maha Chohan. See chapter 6, pp. 55–56.
5. Lev. 19:18; Matt. 22:37–40; Mark 12:30, 31; Luke 10:27; Rom. 13:9; James 2:8.
6. See Heb. 11:4.
7. See Gen. 4:6, 7.

CHAPTER 11: • **A Tribute to Spiritual Motherhood**

1. ***Kuan Yin.*** The bodhisattva Kuan Yin is known as the Goddess of Mercy because she ensouls the God-qualities of mercy, compassion and forgiveness. She serves on the Karmic Board as the representative of the seventh ray (violet ray). From her etheric retreat, the Temple of Mercy, over Peking (Beijing), China, she ministers to the souls of humanity, teaching them to balance their karma and fulfill their divine plan through loving service to life and application of the violet flame. Devotees invoke the bodhisattva's power and merciful intercession with the mantra *Om Mani Padme Hum*—"Hail to the jewel in the lotus!"
2. Luke 7:36–50; 8:1–3.
3. I John 4:18.
4. Matt. 16:25; Luke 9:24; 17:33.

CHAPTER 12: • **The Wonders of Soul-Artistry**

1. "Man, know thyself." Mark and Elizabeth Clare Prophet have explained that the inscription on the ancient temples of the East, "Man know thyself," was intended to say, "Man, know thyself as God." For when we know ourselves as God, we will have overcome our human state.
2. Luke 23:46.
3. Rev. 3:8.
4. Gen. 32:24.
5. See James 4:4.
6. Matt. 27:51.
7. Judg. 7:16–21.
8. Exod. 16:4, 12–15.
9. I Cor. 11:24.
10. Mark 14:22–24.
11. See John 6:53.

CHAPTER 13: • **The Fabric of Eternity**

1. Rev. 3:17.
2. Luke 13:27.

3. Matt. 25:29.
4. Mark 13:25.
5. Heb. 12:6.
6. ***Kuthumi*** is an ascended master who now serves with Jesus in the office of World Teacher. He and Jesus train students in the art of meditation and the science of the Word so that they may become master psychologists of their own psyche, or soul.
7. I Cor. 15:41.
8. On November 15, 1968, Elizabeth Clare Prophet gave an explanation of the great golden eagle from Venus. She said, "If you'll look at the top of the [American] flag, you will see a golden eagle. That is the symbol of Victory from Venus. It is not actually an animal, but it is a formation, a formation of the angelic hosts of [Mighty] Victory." Mighty Victory is a cosmic being from Venus, known as the "tall master from Venus." His love of the victory of the Christ and the potential victory of those evolving upon earth was the keynote of his response to Saint Germain's call for cosmic assistance to the earth in the 1930s. Mighty Victory came forth to stand behind Saint Germain and to lend his momentum of victory to Saint Germain's many projects to bring freedom to the earth.

CHAPTER 14: • The Great Abiding Presence of Beauty within the Human Soul

1. The ***Goddess of Purity.*** The Goddess of Purity focuses the flame of Cosmic Christ purity in her service to the evolutions of the earth. The Goddess of Light, the Queen of Light, and the Goddess of Purity form a trinity of three cosmic beings who have majored in the one-pointed goal of focusing the intense light of the Christ consciousness of God.
2. John 10:10.
3. Magog. The "land of Gog." Gog is an apocalyptic figure who marches from the north (Magog) and ravages Israel before being destroyed by God. See Ezek. 38–39. In Revelation 20:7–9, Gog and the destructive forces of Magog are devoured by fire from God out of heaven.

CHAPTER 15: • The Beauty of Creation

1. Matt. 5–7.
2. Matt. 5:3, 8.
3. Matt. 12:1–8; Luke 6:1–5.
4. On April 16, 1965, the Goddess of Liberty gave a dictation through Mark L. Prophet in which she admonished: "Let there be an emptying of the trash of human nonsense from the containers of the mind, and let mankind renew the patterns of God-ideation which will summon from the four corners of the universe that precious substance of the sacred fire that is a living, breathing flame-substance which I hold high in the torch, which I hold high in my arm,

yea, even in my right arm and right hand, holding up to enfold you for the elect of the world to see the great blessing of cosmic destiny.... The question which ought to be seriously pondered by you, blessed ones, is just what are you putting your attention upon? Just what are you interested in becoming? Are you interested in becoming more manlike or more Godlike? It is up to you to decide and 'choose ye this day whom ye will serve.' (Josh. 24:15)... Therefore, stand fast this day in the mighty powers of the spiritual light from on high, the generative powers of God, the regenerative powers of God, and make all things new by light and by devotion."

5. John 17:12; 18:9.

CHAPTER 16: • **Beautiful Concepts of the Heart**

1. ***Gabriel,*** archangel of the fourth ray (white ray). Gabriel is the Angel of Annunciation who greeted Mary with the words, "Hail, thou that art highly favoured, the Lord is with thee: blessed art thou among women." (Luke 1:28) Gabriel salutes each mother-to-be with the glad tidings of the coming of the Christ for whom she is privileged to prepare the body temple.
2. I John 4:1.

CHAPTER 18: • **The Beautiful Pearl of Great Price That Is Holy Innocence**

1. Isa. 9:2; Matt. 4:16.
2. Acts 9:18.
3. Acts 9:1–22.
4. Acts 9:5.

CHAPTER 19: • **The Hidden Beauty of the Soul**

1. Pss. 98:4; 100:1.
2. Acts 22:16.
3. Matt. 8:12.
4. On July 2, 1966, during the Freedom conference, the portrait of Paul the Venetian was presented by the messengers to those in attendance. The portrait was painted by artist and twin flame of Paul the Venetian, Ruth Hawkins, under the guidance of Paul the Venetian.
5. Mark 4:39.

CHAPTER 20: • **The Divine Ideals That Produce the Fruit of Immortality**

1. Gen. 4:9.
2. Luke 8:46.
3. Luke 8:48.
4. Each New Year's Eve the thoughtform of the year is released from the Silent Watcher of this solar system to the Lord of the World, Gautama Buddha,

who in turn releases it to earth's unascended evolutions from the Royal Teton Retreat. The thoughtform contains the keys to the outpicturing of the will of God for the planet in the coming twelve-month cycle. In a dictation given on December 31, 1966, Gautama Buddha described the thoughtform for the year 1967 as "a beautiful golden replica of the planetary body of Earth. And through the axis thereof and actually manifesting on the outer periphery of that Earth is the stalk of a beautiful golden calla lily—the calla lily rising up to what is known as the North Pole and extending its influences not only over the Earth and its people but over the immediate area of outer space surrounding your world.... Above the lily are the golden Old English letters entitled 'God-Purity.' The precious calla lily has within it the amrita, the nectar of the holy ones who have attained their victory upon every planet in this system of worlds and are, spiritually speaking, appointed by divine decree to be lords of the individual worlds of the planetary bodies of this system. And therefore, the radiance and momentum of each such a one is within this calla-lily cup, this golden vessel of the temple from on high. And purity, even God-purity, is the salvation of the Earth throughout the twelve-month cycle to come." For more information about the Silent Watcher, see *The Masters and the Spiritual Path,* pp. 246–49; available at Store.SummitLighthouse.org.

5. Matt. 19:6; Mark 10:9.

CHAPTER 21: • The Supremacy of Infinite Purpose

1. James 4:8.
2. See Exod. 3.
3. Matt. 5:8.
4. ***God Meru*** and ***Goddess Meru*** are Manus of the sixth root race. These masters are the sponsors of education, advanced learning, the acceleration of the mind, the heart, the soul, and the full development of the potential of the unborn child and all children as they mature. Their vast retreat, the Temple of Illumination, is located over Lake Titicaca, high in the Andes mountains on the Peru-Bolivia border. At their retreat, the God and Goddess Meru focus the feminine ray of the Godhead for the planet.

CHAPTER 22: • The Development of the Spiritual Senses

1. Luke 1:46–55.
2. The deathless solar body is the wedding garment that the soul must wear if she is to enter into the alchemical marriage (the soul's permanent bonding to the Holy Christ Self) and the ritual of the ascension (the Christed one's permanent fusing to the I AM Presence). See Matt. 22:1–14.
3. Matt. 5:29, 30.
4. The ascended masters teach that the use of pastel colors—blue, yellow, pink,

white, green, violet, purple and gold (the colors of the seven rays)—not only in works of art but also in clothing, home furnishings, and interior decorating are a most effective means of drawing the spiritual radiation and blessings of the angelic hosts to manifest as an actual focus of the higher realms in one's immediate environment.

5. On November 18, 1967, El Morya gave a dictation in which he said that the seven chohans, including himself, are going to dictate during the first seven weeks of the year 1968, the year of this dictation.
6. I Cor. 13:12.

CHAPTER 23: • **Beauty Is the Native Consciousness of God**

1. Luke 19:40.
2. Matt. 24:15; Mark 13:14; Dan. 9:27; 11:31.
3. Fables of *The Arabian Nights* is a collection of Arabic folktales originally titled *The Thousand and One Nights* (c. 1150), expressive of the length of time it took for the main character, Scheherazade, to relate the tales to her husband, the king. The collection contains tales of adventure, romance, history, tragedy, comedy, and fantasy, written in a descriptive, visual style. The first known English version of the tales was published as *The Arabian Nights* in the early eighteenth century.

CHAPTER 24: • **The Chord of Cosmic Beauty**

1. "On Wings of Song" is a poem written by German Romantic poet Heinrich Heine in 1827 and set to music by Felix Mendelssohn for voice and piano in 1834.
2. See Gen. 14:18–20; Heb. 7:1–3, 15–17. ***Melchizedek,*** Priest of the Most High God, is an ancient member of the sacred-fire priesthood that we know as the Order of Melchizedek. The Melchizedekian priesthood is very ancient, going back all the way to other star systems. It is the priesthood of the seventh ray, combining the perfect religion and the perfect science. Melchizedek is first seen in the Bible as the priest of the Most High God who met and blessed Abraham returning from the slaughter of the kings and to whom Abraham gave a tenth part of the spoils. He was the greatest initiate and adept of the Old Testament and ascended at the conclusion of that embodiment.
3. Jude 13.
4. John 13:34.
5. Matt. 11:12.
6. Tiziano Vecellio (c. 1488/90–1576), known as Titian, was a Venetian painter of the sixteenth-century Italian Renaissance. The versatile Titian painted portraits, landscapes, and religious and mythological subjects.
7. "New lamps for old" is a phrase taken from the Middle Eastern folktale

"Aladdin and His Wonderful Lamp," later added to *One Thousand and One Nights.*

8. Gen. 1:27.

CHAPTER 25: • Art Transcends an Era

1. *Pearls of Wisdom* are letters of instruction dictated by the ascended masters to their messengers Mark L. Prophet and Elizabeth Clare Prophet. These are a direct transfer of light and wisdom and contain both fundamental and advanced teaching on cosmic law, with a practical application of spiritual truths to personal and planetary problems. *Pearls of Wisdom* have been published by The Summit Lighthouse continuously since 1958.
2. Heb. 8:5; 9:23.
3. Lewis Carroll's *Alice in Wonderland* was among the first to puncture the astral envelope. "Through the looking glass" came a panoply of astral personalities that have since been followed by a host of others, perverting the true image of the Christ in the innocent consciousness of children.
4. II Cor. 3:18.

CHAPTER 26: • In Christ "without Blemish and without Spot"

1. I Pet. 1:19.
2. I Cor. 15:56.
3. II Cor. 3:6.
4. Rev. 3:12; 21:2.
5. Jer. 31:33; Heb. 10:16.
6. Gen. 1:26.
7. Matt. 26:52.
8. Luke 16:1–12; Gal. 6:7.
9. Luke 21:19; Eph. 6:10, 11.
10. Eph. 6:14–18.

CHAPTER 27: • Beauty Is as Beauty Does

1. Matt. 5:6.
2. John 4:14.
3. "Beauty is as beauty does" is a proverb that was first recorded by Chaucer in "The Wife of Bath's Tale" (c. 1387). It means that while one may be physically unattractive, a delightful personality makes one beautiful; good deeds are more important than good looks.

Chart of Your Divine Self

1. Exod. 3:14, 15.
2. Matt. 6:19–21.

Glossary

Art of Divinity

Akashic records. All that transpires in an individual's world is recorded in a substance and dimension known as *akasha.* These records can be read by adepts or those whose soul faculties are developed. An ascended master or an unascended adept can look at a record just the way an archaeologist would look through layers of the earth. They can look through layers of records and pinpoint any age or time since the earth was created and read the record of what happened at that particular point in time and space, both personal and planetary.

Ascension. The ascension is the culmination of the soul's God-victorious sojourn in time and space, often through many lifetimes, and is the ritual whereby the soul reunites with the Spirit of the living God, the I AM Presence. The path of the ascension is a spiritual acceleration of consciousness and a process that follows the natural course of spiritual evolution. All of the thoughts, feelings, and deeds from the present and past lives count toward or against the ascension. In taking progressive steps on the spiritual path, the Christed one ultimately finds his way back to the heart of God and enters eternal life.

Astral plane. The astral plane, or astral realm, is the frequency of time and space immediately above physical matter, yet below the mental plane and corresponding to the emotional body of man and the collective unconscious of the race. It is the repository of mankind's thoughts and feelings, conscious and unconscious. Because the astral plane has been muddied by impure thought and feeling, the term *astral* is often used in a negative context to refer to that which is impure or psychic.

Atlantis. The island continent that existed where the Atlantic Ocean now is and that sank in cataclysm (the Flood of Noah) approximately 11,600 years ago, as calculated by James Churchward. Atlantis has been vividly depicted by Plato, "seen" and described by Edgar Cayce in his readings, recalled in scenes from Taylor Caldwell's *Romance of Atlantis,* and scientifically explored and authenticated by the late German scientist Otto Muck. The history of Atlantis is also told by W. Scott-Elliot in *The Story of Atlantis and the Lost Lemuria,* based on clairvoyant readings by students of Theosophy who were trained by the adepts Morya and Kuthumi, and anthropological discoveries.

Bodhisattva. A Sanskrit term meaning literally a being of *bodhi* (or enlightenment), a being destined for enlightenment, or one whose energy and power is directed toward enlightenment. A bodhisattva is one who is destined to become a Buddha but has foregone the bliss of nirvana with a vow to save all sentient beings on earth. In the Mahayana school of Buddhism, becoming a bodhisattva is the goal of the Path. The path of the bodhisattva is generally divided into ten stages, called *bhumis.* The bodhisattva strives to progress from one stage to the next until he obtains enlightenment.

Causal body. The causal body of man surrounds the I AM Presence as the chalice for all good that the individual has elected to qualify in word, thought, and deed since the moment of creation, when the blueprint of the soul's identity was sealed in the fiery core of the God Self. (For more information, see the Chart of Your Divine Self, volume 1, p. 245.)

Chakra. Sanskrit for "wheel," "disc," "circle"; a term used to denote the centers of light anchored in the etheric body and governing the flow of energy to the four lower bodies of man. There are seven major chakras corresponding to the seven rays, five minor chakras corresponding to the five secret rays, and a total of 144 light centers in the body of man.

Chohan. The Tibetan word *chohan* means "lord, master, chief." Each of the seven rays has a chohan who focuses the Christ consciousness of the ray, which is the law of the ray governing its righteous use in man. The seven rays are light emanations of the Godhead, i.e., the seven rays of the white light that emerge through the prism of the Christ consciousness. Each ray focuses a frequency, or color, and has specific qualities. The first ray (blue) focuses faith, will, power, perfection, protection. The second ray (yellow) focuses wisdom, understanding, enlightenment, illumination. The third ray (pink) focuses compassion, kindness, charity, love, beauty. The fourth ray (white) focuses purity, discipline, order, joy. The fifth ray (green) focuses truth, science, healing, music, abundance, vision. The sixth ray (purple and gold) focuses ministration, service, peace, brotherhood. The seventh ray (violet) focuses freedom, mercy, justice, transmutation, forgiveness.

Cosmic Council. A court of appeal beyond the Lords of Karma. They function in grander spheres or dimensions and work with the Four and Twenty Elders. The Cosmic Council is known as the council of the one hundred and forty-four.

Cosmic clock. The science of the cosmic clock is a means for the charting of the cycles of our lives. It is not traditional astrology. It is an inner astrology whereby we can chart the cycles of our karma and be the master of our fate, our cycles, and our destiny. It also allows us to chart the cycles of our dharma and to fulfill our reason for being. As the wheel of the cosmic clock turns day by day and we experience the cycles of our tests and initiations in life, an awareness of this science can help us pass these tests. For more detailed teaching on how to chart your own personal cycles on the cosmic clock, see Elizabeth Clare Prophet, *Predict Your Future: Understand the Cycles of the Cosmic Clock;* available at Store.Summitlighthouse.org.

Darjeeling Council. A council of the Great White Brotherhood with El Morya as its chief and headquartered at his etheric retreat in Darjeeling, India, consists of ascended masters and unascended chelas. Members include Mother Mary, Kuan Yin, Archangel Michael, the Great Divine Director, Serapis Bey, Kuthumi, Djwal Kul, and numerous others whose objective is to train souls for world service in God-government and the economy, through international relations and the establishment of the inner Christ as the foundation for religion, education, and a return to golden-age culture in music and the arts.

Deathless solar body. Known as the wedding garment (Matt. 22:11, 12) that the soul must wear if she is to enter into the alchemical marriage—the soul's permanent bonding to the Holy Christ Self—and the ritual of the ascension.

Divine blueprint. That which is etched upon one's soul as one's own unique identity, one's own fiery destiny.

Divine Image. See Real Image.

Eightfold Path. Also called the Middle Way; the message Gautama Buddha taught in his first sermon and that is still the cornerstone of Buddhism today, which includes the Four Noble Truths and the Eightfold Path. The Four Noble Truths are:

(1) that life is *dukkha,* "suffering"
(2) that the cause of this suffering is *tanha,* "desire" or "craving"
(3) that suffering will cease when the craving that causes it is forsaken and overcome
(4) that the way to this liberation is through living the noble Eightfold Path, which consists of:

Right Understanding or Views
Right Thought or Aspiration
Right Speech

Right Action or Conduct
Right Livelihood
Right Effort
Right Mindfulness
Right Concentration or Absorption

Gautama explained that by avoiding the extremes of self-indulgence and self-mortification, one gains knowledge of the "middle path," which leads to insight, wisdom, calmness, knowledge, enlightenment, and nirvana. He advocated the Middle Way because he had learned from his own experience that the two extremes of sensual indulgence and harsh asceticism do not lead to liberation.

Etheric. Of or relating to the highest plane of the Matter cosmos, i.e., the heavenworld. The etheric frequency and its correspondent plane of consciousness is the repository of the fiery blueprint of the entire physical universe.

Etheric cities and retreats. See Universities of the Spirit.

Five secret rays. The five secret rays represent a going within for the mastery of God consciousness, whereas the seven outer rays represent the coming out and the mastery of the environment. These cycles are a pattern of the going within and the coming out—the Eastern teachings, going within; the Western teachings, coming out.

Four and Twenty Elders. The Four and Twenty Elders are described in the Book of Revelation: "And round about the throne were four and twenty seats: and upon the seats I saw four and twenty elders sitting, clothed in white raiment; and they had on their heads crowns of gold." (Rev. 4:4. See also Rev. 4:10, 11; 5:5–14; 7:11–17; 11:15–18; 14:1–3; 19:4.) They are twelve pairs of twin flames representing the twelve hierarchies of the Sun in the masculine and feminine power/wisdom/love of Elohim. This council of cosmic beings presides with Sanat Kumara at the Court of the Sacred Fire on the God Star, Sirius (the seat of God-government in this sector of our galaxy), as instruments of the judgment of Almighty God. In approximately 2000 B.C., we entered the age of Aries. Two thousand years ago we entered the age of Pisces, and we have now entered the age of Aquarius. Passing through each of the twelve signs of the zodiac, there is a dispensation from the Great Central Sun whereby the Four and Twenty Elders and the Four Cosmic Forces impart to the evolutions of the planet a new awareness of self in relationship to a new awareness of God.

Four Cosmic Forces. The Four Cosmic Forces sustain the vision of the LORD God Almighty as universal awareness of the Creator within the creation. Full of eyes before and behind, the Four Cosmic Forces are perpetually stepping down the light of Solar Logoi, cosmic messengers of Alpha and Omega positioned in the flaming yods of the galaxies. Thus by their six wings, the three and three, and the three-times-three, they render the light, the energy of the Word, intelligible to electrons small and great in man and beast, vegetable and mineral. (See Prophet, *The Opening of the Seventh Seal,* chapter 4.)

Fourfold consciousness of man. The four sheaths consisting of four distinct frequencies that surround the soul—the physical, emotional, mental, and etheric—providing vehicles for the soul in her journey through time and space. The etheric sheath, highest in vibration, is the gateway to the three higher bodies, which are the Christ Self, the I AM Presence, and the causal body.

Great Central Sun. Also called the Great Hub; the center of cosmos; the point of integration of the Spirit-Matter cosmos; the point of origin of all physical-spiritual creation; the nucleus, or white-fire core, of the Cosmic Egg.

Great Karmic Board. Eight ascended beings who are responsible for dispensing justice to this system of worlds are known as the Lords of Karma. They adjudicate karma, mercy, and judgment for the lifestreams of earth, who must pass before the Karmic Board before and after each embodiment. The Karmic Board includes seven ascended beings who serve on the seven rays, plus the Dhyani Buddha Vairochana. The members of the Karmic Board are the Great Divine Director, the Goddess of Liberty, Lady Master Nada, the Elohim Cyclopea, Pallas Athena, Lady Master Portia, Kuan Yin, and Vairochana.

Great White Brotherhood. A spiritual order of Western saints and Eastern adepts who have reunited with the Spirit of the living God through the ritual of the ascension and who comprise the heavenly hosts. They have transcended the cycles of karma and rebirth and ascended into that higher Reality, which is the eternal abode of the soul. The word "white" refers not to race but to the aura of white light surrounding their forms. The ascended masters of the Great White Brotherhood, united for the highest purposes of the brotherhood of man under the Fatherhood of God, have risen in every age from every culture and religion to inspire creative achievement in education, the arts and sciences, God-government, and the abundant life through the economies of the nations. The Brotherhood also includes in its ranks certain unascended chelas of the ascended masters. Jesus Christ revealed this heavenly order of saints "robed in white" to his servant John in Revelation. (Rev. 3:4, 5; 6:11; 7:9, 13, 14; 19:14)

Karmic Board. See Great Karmic Board.

Keepers of the Flame. Members of the Keepers of the Flame Fraternity, founded in 1961 by Saint Germain. This is a nondenominational spiritual order of men and women of goodwill who pledge to keep the flame of life on behalf of themselves and earth's evolutions. The fraternity warmly welcomes spiritual seekers from all religions, and members are encouraged to practice their religion or faith as they see fit. Keepers of the Flame receive graded lessons in cosmic law dictated by the ascended masters to their messengers Mark L. Prophet and Elizabeth Clare Prophet. (See KeepersOfTheFlame.org.)

Lemuria, or Mu. The lost continent of the Pacific, which, according to the findings of James Churchward, archaeologist and author of *The Lost Continent of Mu,* extended from north of Hawaii three thousand miles, south to Easter Island and the Fijis, and was made up of three areas of land stretching more than five thousand miles from east to west. Churchward's history of the ancient Motherland is based on records inscribed on sacred tablets he claims to have discovered in India. With the help of the high priest of an Indian temple, he deciphered the tablets. During fifty years of research, he confirmed their contents in further writings, inscriptions, and legends he came upon in Southeast Asia, in the Yucatan, Central America, the Pacific islands, Mexico, North America, ancient Egypt, and other civilizations. He estimates that Mu was destroyed approximately twelve thousand years ago by the collapse of the gas chambers that upheld the continent. The history of Lemuria is also told by W. Scott-Elliot in *The Story of Atlantis and the Lost Lemuria,* based on clairvoyant readings by students of Theosophy who were trained by the adepts El Morya and Kuthumi, and anthropological discoveries.

Logos. The universal consciousness of God that went forth as the Word, which God used to fire the pattern of his divine identity in his sons and daughters and to write his laws in their inward parts. The individual Christ is the fulfillment of this Word, this Logos, in the individed duality.

Lords of Karma. See Great Karmic Board.

Martian perversions. The ascended masters teach that Mars in its true state is the planet that represents the Divine Mother and the base-of-the-spine chakra. Long ago, the evolutions of Mars took that pure white light of the Mother and perverted it in war and misuses of the sacred fire. Through the misuse of free will and the base-of-the-spine chakra, they perverted the Mother light in what we call the "Martian misqualifications." These misqualifications can manifest through any of the chakras but specifically relate to the misuse of the Mother light in the base-of-the-spine chakra. They include aggression, anger, arrogance, argumentation, accusation, agitation, apathy, atheism, annihilation, aggravation, aggressive mental suggestion, criticism, condemnation and judgment, malicious, ignorant, sympathetic and delicious animal magnetism, anti-Americanism, anti-Father, anti-Mother, anti-Christ and anti-Holy Spirit manifestations in the four quadrants of Matter.

Mother of the World. The highest representative of the feminine ray on earth is she who attains to the Office of Mother of the World, or the World Mother. The one selected by the Lords of Karma and the Lord of the World as the representative of the World Mother to the earth wears the crown of the World Mother—a crown of twelve stars—and holds her scepter of authority, keeping the flame of the immaculate concept on behalf of all evolving upon the earth. "And there appeared a great wonder in heaven; a woman clothed with the sun, and the moon under her feet, and upon her head a crown of twelve stars." (Rev. 12:1)

Real Image. The true image of God after which man (male and female) was made in the Beginning. (Gen. 1:26, 27) The Real Image is the likeness of God, the Christ, or light emanation of God. It is the blueprint of the true identity of the sons and daughters of God.

Ruby ray. The ruby ray is an intense and holy love that is developed through the path of sacrifice, surrender, selflessness, and service to uplift all sentient life. The ruby ray activates the first secret ray and ultimately all five secret rays. It is the ruby fire of ultimate love that annihilates ignorance and evil.

Sangha. The spiritual family and community of the Buddha, traditionally composed of four groups: monks, nuns, laymen, and laywomen. In Buddhism the Sangha is one of the Three Jewels in which the disciple takes refuge and turns to for protection and aid. The Three Jewels are the Buddha, the Dharma, and the Sangha. The Buddha is the Enlightened One, the Dharma is the teaching of the Buddha, and the Sangha is the community of disciples.

Solar Logoi. Cosmic beings who transmit the light emanations of the Godhead flowing from Alpha and Omega in the Great Central Sun to the planetary systems. They are also called Solar Lords. The Solar Logoi maintain the tone and the sound of the Logos, or Word, that sustains the creation. We are all a part the vastness of the Solar Logoi, and they are a part of us.

Spoken Word. Also referred to as the science of the spoken Word. The release of the energies of the Word, or the Logos, through the throat chakra by the children of God in confirmation of that lost Word. It is written, "By thy words thou shalt be justified, and by thy words thou shalt be condemned." (Matt. 12:37) When man and woman reconsecrate the throat chakra in the affirmation of the Word of God, they become the instruments of God's own commandments that fulfill the law of their re-creation after the image of the Son. Forms of the spoken Word are:

Affirmation

Assertion that something exists or is true; confirmation or ratification of the truth; solemn declaration. A positive statement, usually beginning with the name of God, "I AM," that affirms and strengthens the qualities of God within oneself, helping to bring those qualities into physical manifestation. Affirmations are fiats that may be of greater length and more specific detail. They affirm the action of Truth in man—in his being, consciousness, and world. They are used alternately with denials of the reality of evil in all of its forms. Likewise, they affirm the power of Truth that challenges the activities of the fallen ones.

Call

A demand, a claim, a request or command to come or be present; an instance of asking for something; the act of summoning the LORD, or the LORD's summoning of his offspring. "And the LORD God called unto Adam, and said unto him, Where art thou?" (Gen. 3:9) "Out of Egypt have I called my son!" (Matt. 2:15) To call: *vb.* to speak in a loud or distinct voice so as to be heard at a distance; to recall from death or the astral plane, e.g., "Lazarus, come forth!"; to utter in a loud or distinct voice; to announce or read loudly or authoritatively. The call is the most direct means of communication between man and God, and God and man, frequently used in an emergency; e.g., O God, help me! Archangel Michael, take command! The byword of the initiate is "The call compels the answer." "He shall call upon me, and I will answer him." (Ps. 91:15) "They called upon the LORD, and he answered them." (Ps. 99:6)

Chant

A short, simple melody, especially one characterized by single notes to which an indefinite number of syllables are intoned, used in singing the psalms, canticles, etc., in a church service. In both East and West, the name of God is chanted over and over again in the ritual of atonement whereby the soul of man becomes one with the Spirit of God by intonation of the sound of his name. This is given in Sanskrit as AUM or AUM TAT SAT AUM and in English as I AM THAT I AM. By sounding the name of God or that of a member of the heavenly hosts, the vibration of the being is simulated and thereby Being itself is drawn to the one chanting. Therefore chants, when properly used, magnetize the Presence, whether universal or individualized, of the Divine Consciousness.

Decree

The decree is the most powerful of all applications to the Godhead. It is the command of the son or daughter of God made in the name of the I AM Presence and the Christ for the will of the Almighty to come into manifestation as Above, so below. It is the means whereby the kingdom of God becomes a reality here and now through the power of the spoken Word. It may be short or long and usually is marked by a formal preamble and a closing, or acceptance.

Fiat

An authoritative decree, sanction, order; a pronouncement; a short dynamic invocation or decree usually using the name of God, I AM, as the first word of the fiat, e.g., I AM the Way! I AM the Truth! I AM the Resurrection and the Life! Fiats are always exclamations of Christ-power, Christ-wisdom, and Christ-love consciously affirmed and accepted in the here and now.

Invocation

A form of prayer invoking God's presence; any petitioning or supplication for help or protection said especially at the beginning of a public ceremony; a call to God or to beings who have become one with God to release power, wisdom, and love to mankind or to intercede in their behalf; supplication for the flow of light, energy, peace, and harmony to come into manifestation on earth as it is in heaven.

Mantra

A mystical formula, often in Sanskrit, to be recited or sung for the purpose of intensifying the action of the Spirit of God in man. A form of prayer consisting of a word or a group of words that is chanted over and over again to magnetize a particular aspect of the Deity or of a being who has actualized that aspect of the Deity.

Prayer

A devout petition to God; a spiritual communion with God as in supplication, thanksgiving, adoration, or confession; a formula or sequence of words used in or appointed for praying: the Lord's Prayer, the Hail Mary.

Suicide entity. An "entity" is defined as "an independent, separate, or self-contained existence." "Discarnate entities" (or disembodied spirits, as they are commonly referred to) are made up of the personality consciousness as it expresses through the astral, mental, or etheric bodies of lifestreams who have passed through the change called death. The name of the suicide entity is Annihla, a she-devil luring her victims by her lust for death and for the light essence of her victims released in death. This entity projects feelings of depression, worthlessness, hopelessness, and utter frustration with life into the subconscious minds of those whose consciousness is open to this type of suggestion. When these feelings surface to the mental and feeling bodies, they influence the victim to accept a philosophy of nihilism, of his own nonexistence. Intense calls must be made to bind the suicide entity that may be preying upon an individual.

Sun behind the sun. The spiritual cause behind the physical effect we see as our own physical sun and all other stars and star systems, seen or unseen, including the Great Central Sun. The Sun behind the sun of cosmos is perceived as the Cosmic Christ—the Word by whom the formless was endowed with form and spiritual worlds were draped with physicality. Likewise, the Sun behind the sun is the Son of God in the Christ Self, shining in all his splendor behind the soul and its interpenetrating sheaths of consciousness called the four lower bodies. It is the Son of man—the "Sun" of every manifestation of God. The Sun behind the sun is referred to as the "Sun of righteousness" (Mal. 4:2), which does heal the mind, illumine the soul, and light all her house and as "the glory of God," the light of the City Foursquare.

Threefold flame. The flame of the Christ that is the spark of life anchored within the heart of the sons and daughters of God. It is the sacred trinity of love, wisdom, and power that is literally a spark of sacred fire from God's own heart. It is the soul's point of contact with the supreme Source of all life. It is also referred to as the flame of liberty.

Twin flames. The origin of your identity is in the white sphere that is Almighty God. Out of this white sphere, twin flames are born. The whirling action of the mighty sphere of life produces the polarity that becomes the plus and the minus of twin flames. These two souls, each making up half of the whole, have the same electronic pattern or blueprint, which is not duplicated anywhere in cosmos. Twin flames are intended to be the totality of the Father-Mother God in expression. Soul mates on the other hand are complementary souls who are working out a polarity of manifestation in one of the planes of consciousness. Their tie is for a particular mastery in time and space, whereas the ultimate union is with one's twin flame. The energies that twin flames share are the energies of God, and when these energies are consecrated to the glorification of the Real Self and of Reality, we find that joy and bliss and expansion of consciousness and creativity follow them wherever they go.

Universities of the Spirit. Spiritual classes are held in the etheric retreats where souls receive instruction and guidance from members of the cosmic hierarchy. At the universities of the Spirit, students can visit each one of the seven chohans of the rays for fourteen consecutive days and then go on to study with the Maha Chohan, who is the director of the seven chohans of the rays. In this way, students receive step-by-step instruction on the rays, which enables them to increase their self-mastery. While studying at the retreats, souls also prepare to more efficiently balance their personal karma in daily life.

Violet flame. The seventh ray aspect of the Holy Spirit. The violet flame is the sacred fire that transmutes the cause, effect, record, and memory of sin, or negative karma. It is also called the flame of transmutation, of freedom, and of forgiveness. The violet flame is more than violet light. It is an invisible spiritual energy that appears violet to those who have developed their spiritual vision. In previous centuries, knowledge of the violet flame was given only to a chosen few who had proven themselves worthy. Saints and adepts of East and West have long used the violet flame to accelerate their spiritual development, but this once-secret knowledge was not revealed to the masses until the twentieth century. The violet flame has many purposes. It revitalizes and invigorates us. It can heal emotional and even physical problems, improve relationships, and make life easier. More importantly, the violet flame changes negative energy into positive energy, which makes it an effective tool for healing. Today we are learning more than ever before about how disease can be rooted in our mental, emotional, and spiritual states. By transforming negative thoughts and feelings, the violet flame provides a platform for our healing.

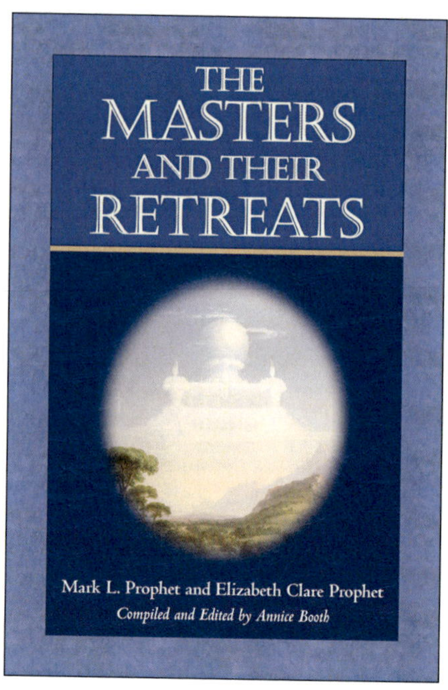

The Masters and Their Retreats

The great lights who have come out of all the world's spiritual traditions and graduated from earth's schoolroom have become widely known as Masters. They demonstrate to us that in the world of Spirit, there is no division of race, religion or philosophy—there is simply oneness, ineffable sweetness and love.

What is not so widely known is that these great Masters have retreats—temples and cities of light in the heaven world—where we can go in spiritual meditation and while our bodies sleep at night.

In this magnificent work, Mark and Elizabeth Prophet talk about these great Masters, the stories of their lives and their incredible spiritual retreats.

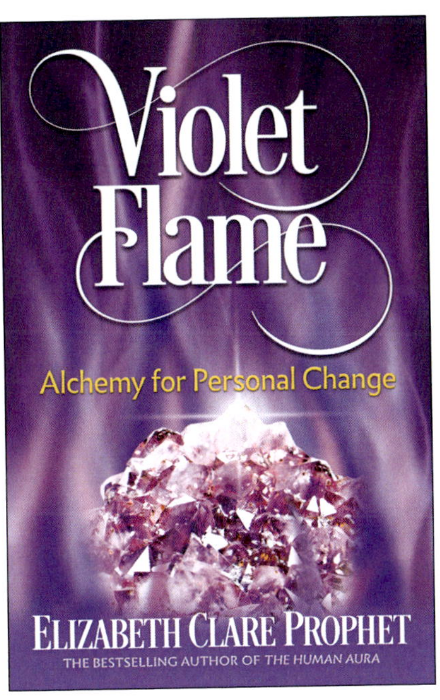

Violet Flame
Alchemy for Personal Change

For thousands of years the violet flame was a secret, experienced by mystics and known to spiritual teachers East and West who taught it only to their closest disciples. Now the violet flame is available to all!

The violet flame is a high-frequency light that you can use to change your life. It dissolves negative energy and restores it to positive energy. It is a missing key to vitality, health, and inner wholeness. This flame can transform and enrich your relationships. It can free the unlimited power that exists right within you.

World-renowned author Elizabeth Clare Prophet unlocks the mysteries of the violet flame. With penetrating insight and compassion, she explores how this flame works and gives practical techniques for using it to help resolve everyday problems. You can easily integrate the violet flame into any path you follow or simply try it by itself. The benefits and joy of the violet flame can change your life forever!

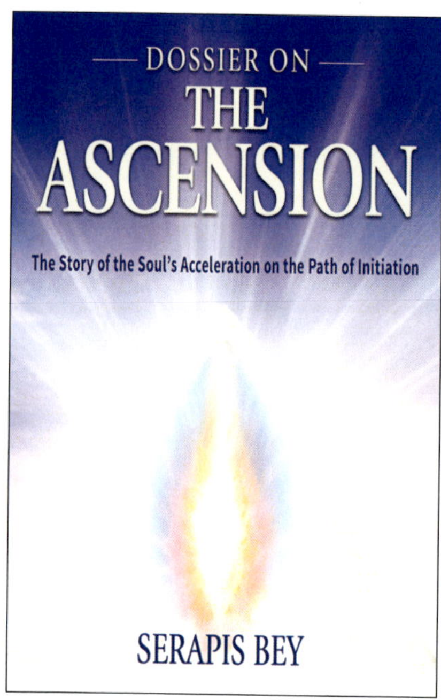

Dossier on the Ascension

The Story of the Soul's Acceleration on the Path of Initiation

Breaking the wheel of rebirth...
Union with God...
The ascension...

Throughout the ages, those of all faiths have sought to go beyond the limits of the mind, to attain immortality. History leaves the record of a few who reached that goal—Zarathustra, who ascended back to God in "the great flame"; Elijah, who was carried up into heaven in a "chariot of fire"; Jesus, who was taken up into a cloud from Bethany's hill.

Now, Serapis Bey and the Brotherhood of Luxor reveal inner secrets of the path to the ascension. They open the door to their mystery school, sharing keys to immortality. And they show how you can apply their spiritual techniques to find the answers to life's ultimate questions.

- Journey to the Central Sun through the meditations of the seraphim.
- Learn the meaning of the Deathless Solar Body as the vehicle of the soul beyond the veil.
- Find your ultimate freedom to be your Real Self.

The flame of the ascension is the key which unlocks the door to immortality for every man.

Serapis Bey

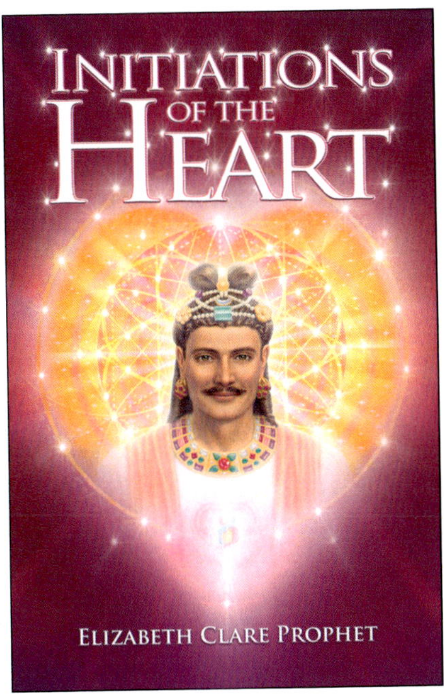

Initiations of the Heart

Teachings from the Mystery School

Did our hearts not *burn* within us . . .

The mystics have always known that the heart is the most important center of consciousness. We can gain visions through the third eye, enlightenment through the crown. But the true fount of cosmic consciousness is always the heart. How do we develop our heart—the chakra of Divine Love? How can we increase the fire of the heart? How can we expand the threefold flame, the very source of Life within us?

Within *Initiations of the Heart,* the ascended masters reveal the mysteries of the heart. Most importantly, as we enter into their Word, each one offers a transfer of light—a unique initiation of the heart.

The apostles felt the fire of the heart in their encounter with the risen Christ on the road to Emmaus. May you also experience that fire through your encounter with the masters in this age.

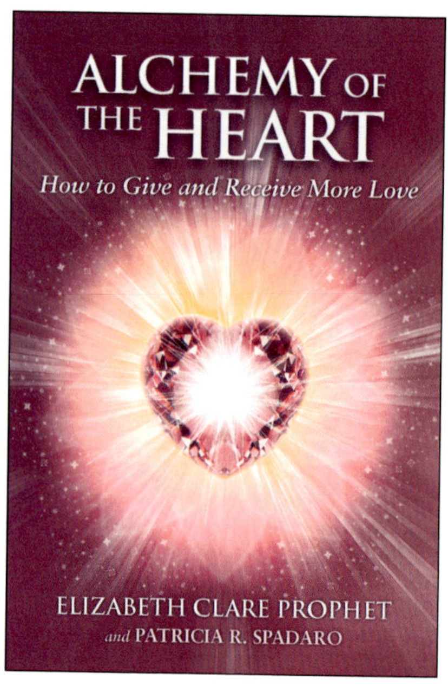

Alchemy of the Heart

How to Give and Receive More Love

Finding a higher love

These sensitive, profound and rare insights help us gain entrée into the most precious, and misunderstood, component of our being—the heart. They show us that while love can be compassionate and nurturing, it can also be powerful, dynamic and practical—a catalyst for spiritual growth.

You'll learn how the mature heart overcomes hidden blocks to giving and receiving more love. How you can soften and strengthen the heart to create more meaningful relationships in all areas of your life. And how even the most intense lessons of love, if we are willing to learn from them, can be the open door to a higher love—and a higher way of loving.

About The Summit Lighthouse

The Summit Lighthouse is an internationally recognized spiritual center for the advancement of inner awakening. Our international organization is a global family that is inspired, guided, and sponsored by those known as the ascended masters.

The ascended masters are the most beloved and trusted transcendent beings guiding our planet's material and spiritual evolution. Most of the world's religions are currently based on the revelations of one or more of these masters before their ascension. We openly embrace spiritual seekers from all paths of light including the mystical traditions of the world's religions.

The ascended masters and their messengers have given us over fifteen thousand hours of invaluable inner wisdom and insightful instruction, and they have provided the means for our direct initiation into higher consciousness.

For the ascended masters . . . no subject is off-limits! Their teachings contain amazing truths and awesome answers on spirituality, alchemy, astrology, sacred geometry, spiritual science, karma, reincarnation, ascension, archangels (and fallen angels), and even those issues that are considered taboo or "out of this world."

Primary Goals of the Teachings of the Ascended Masters

The ascended masters challenge us daily to be bold, to dare to be who we truly are, and to face adversity with courage, patience, perseverance, honesty, integrity, inner love, discipline, and discernment—all for a greater sense of inner peace, fearlessness, stillness and silence, harmony, self-mastery, compassion, and wisdom.

These teachings help our souls get back to the origin of their individualized inner source of True Self-Love—the Higher Self, or I AM Presence. Our point of contact with our Higher Self is the "Spark of Life" or "Sacred Fire of the Heart," the place where our consciousness expresses its true divine nature of unconditional love and happiness, universal oneness, and an authentic desire to serve others.

How Our Teachings Came into Being

Our teachings were all released through highly trained and trusted messengers, Mark L. Prophet and Elizabeth Clare Prophet. Mark was contacted by the ascended master El Morya at the age of eighteen and received training from him for many years before he was instructed to establish The Summit Lighthouse in 1958 in Washington, D.C.

With his ascension in 1973, Mark passed the torch for the mission to his gifted wife, Elizabeth Clare Prophet, who continued her service until her retirement in 1999.

The dictations of the ascended masters were regularly given in public. The ascended masters also inspired thousands of lectures delivered by the messengers. The content of the dictations are, by most human standards, beyond the mind's ability to construct in real time. They carry very powerful frequencies of light, awakening us to the highest truths we've ever experienced.

We leave it up to you to decide their value for yourself.

Moving toward Your Victory

No matter what path of light you are on, spiritual freedom is attained using tools that have been passed down in wisdom teachings through the millennia: meditation, selfless service, devotional music, prayer, mantra, and the science of the spoken Word. The masters bring an accelerated understanding of these principles, especially suited for the challenges of the modern world, including dynamic decree work and the use of the violet flame.

Next Steps

We are genuinely excited to meet you on the Path and hope you are too. We extend a warm welcome from everyone at The Summit Lighthouse, and we invite you to explore the teachings of the ascended masters at **SummitLighthouse.org.** Check out our free online lessons and hundreds of articles on a wide range of spiritual subjects. Browse through our online bookstore. And if you would rather talk to someone in person, please feel free to contact us today!

The Summit Lighthouse®
63 Summit Way, Gardiner, Montana 59030 USA

1-800-245-5445 / 406-848-9500
Se habla español.

info@SummitUniversityPress.com
SummitLighthouse.org